Canadian Centre for Management Development

SERIES ON GOVERNANCE AND
PUBLIC MANAGEMENT

This series will offer both practical and theoretical perspectives on governance and public management. It will marry the insights of practitioners and researchers, providing a window on practical developments and initiatives as well as leading-edge thinking throughout the world.

Topics to be covered in this series may include: measuring the achievements of public sector reform, the organization and structure of government, the legislative-executive-public service relationship, the role of central agencies, horizontal coordination for greater policy coherence, accountability, organizational effectiveness in the public sector, service standards and quality, leadership in the public sector, and the ethics and values of public service.

The Canadian Centre for Management Development is an agency of the Government of Canada established to provide executive development and to "study and conduct research into the theory and practice of public management," as well as to "encourage a greater awareness in Canada of issues related to public sector management and the role and functions of government." This new publication series is part of a wider research and publication program, including a range of activities such as case studies, fellowships, action research programs, a management resource centre, and the CCMD International Governance Network.

Governance in a Changing Environment

Edited by B. Guy Peters and
Donald J. Savoie

Canadian Centre for Management Development
Centre canadien de gestion
McGill-Queen's University Press
Montreal & Kingston • London • Buffalo

© Canadian Centre for Management Development/
Centre Canadien de gestion
ISBN 0-7735-1320-5 (cloth)
ISBN 0-7735-1321-3 (paper)
Legal deposit third quarter 1995
Bibliothèque nationale du Québec

Globalization, Nation States, and the Civil Service
by Donald J. Savoie which appears in this
volume is a revised version of a research
paper published in December 1993 by the
Canadian Centre for Management Development
under the title *Globalization and Governance*.
An earlier version of the chapter by B. Guy
Peters, *The Public Service, the Changing State,
and Governance,* was first published as a research
paper by CCMD in December 1993.

Printed in Canada on acid-free paper

Canadian Cataloguing in Publication Data
Main entry under title:
Governance in a changing environment
(Canadian Centre for Management
Development series on governance
and public management)
Includes bibliographical references.
ISBN 0-7735-1320-5 (bound)
ISBN 0-7735-1321-3 (pbk.)
1. Public administration.
I. Peters, B.Guy   II. Savoie, Donald J., 1947-
III. Series.
JFD1351.G68   1995   350   C95-900329-0

Contents

Preface
vii

Acknowledgments
xi

PART ONE · INTRODUCTION

Introducing the Topic
B. Guy Peters
3

PART TWO · THE CHANGING ENVIRONMENT

*The Civil Service Culture
and Administrative Reform*
Luc Rouban
23

*The Marketization of the State:
Citizens, Consumers, and the Emergence
of the Public Market*
Jon Pierre
55

*Globalization, Nation States,
and the Civil Service*
Donald J. Savoie
82

PART THREE · THE POLITICAL PROCESS
AND GOVERNANCE

*Politicians, Public Servants, and Public
Management: Getting Government Right*
Peter Aucoin
113

Policy Advice and the Public Service
John Halligan
138

Accountability and Administrative Reform:
Toward Convergence and Beyond
Phillip J. Cooper
173

PART FOUR · PUBLIC MANAGEMENT AND
THE REFORM OF GOVERNANCE

Management Techniques for the Public
Sector: Pulpit and Practice
Christopher Pollitt
203

Quality Management in Public Organizations:
Prospects and Dilemmas
Patricia W. Ingraham
239

Public Sector Innovation: The Implications
of New Forms of Organization and Work
Sandford F. Borins
260

The Public Service, the Changing
State, and Governance
B. Guy Peters
288

PART FIVE · CONCLUSION

Looking Ahead
Donald J. Savoie
323

Preface

The volume you are about to read is the result of a pathbreaking research program undertaken at the Canadian Centre for Management Development. It had its origin in two simple but fruitful ideas.

The first was that the world of public administration is shifting under the feet of Canadian public servants. It is therefore timely to begin to revisit certain fundamental issues in public management in order to establish, if possible, new points of reference, or to clarify and refurbish old ones.

The second idea was that such a process of reflection and investigation should not be undertaken in isolation but rather in a process of dialogue: dialogue among the researchers themselves, between the researchers and practitioners, and between practitioners also. Our intention from the start was to undertake not just a research program but an "action research" program, one in which senior public managers were involved from beginning to end, and which would help them to explore, debate, clarify, and advance their own thinking as practitioners of public administration.

In order to carry out the research process in this spirit of dialogue, we resolved on three essential steps. The first was to bring the research team together for extended exchange and debate at the beginning and near the end of the process. The second was to create an opportunity for dialogue between the researchers as a group and similar groups of senior public managers: this we accomplished by joint meetings between them at these same points in the process as above. The third step was to arrange encounters between the individual research contributors and focus groups of senior public managers. On a regular monthly basis, from early 1993 until the early spring of 1994, we welcomed individual contributors to Ottawa to meet with groups of senior public servants.

These evening discussions proved to be very rich occasions. They provided an opportunity, as we had hoped, for the researchers to absorb the perspective, experience, and insights of practitioners. They also created a unique forum in which thoughtful senior public servants were able to reflect together on some of the key issues facing their profession. Creating such a forum was by no means the least among the accomplishments of this pioneering research program.

In launching such a program, the Canadian Centre for Management Development was very fortunate to be able to call upon the advice and leadership of two of the leading international scholars of comparative public administration, B. Guy Peters and Donald J. Savoie, both Senior Fellows of CCMD. As leaders of the research team and co-editors of this volume, they helped to refine the research agenda, to identify and recruit an outstanding international team of collaborators, and to guide their work to completion in the form published in this volume. I am deeply grateful to both of them for their support, guidance, and leadership throughout this unique experiment.

I am also grateful to the large group of senior public servants who participated in this research program in various ways and at various stages in its evolution. Their support and interest were vital to its success, and confirmed for me that it is possible to conduct research not just *for* public executives but *with* them. At CCMD we are now building on this insight in a variety of ways.

Finally I am very grateful to each of the research contributors to CCMD's "Governance in a Changing Environment" research program. Their willingness to participate in this experimental program and the high calibre of their contributions were vital to its success. Through this program, the Canadian Centre for Management Development was fortunate to be able to establish links with some of the leading students of public administration across the developed world. This too is something we are continuing to build on, in several ways. "Governance in a Changing Environment" is not the end of something; it is just the beginning. It is the beginning of our investigation into the ways in which governance and public administration are being reshaped and rethought. A second collaborative research program, for example, will attempt to assess public sector reform initiatives over the past fifteen years. We have also established a permanent CCMD International Governance Network, linking leading scholars of public administration in some fourteen countries. This initiative will provide the foundation for a variety of future research activities on governance and public management.

I should like to note in conclusion that several people not represented in this volume were nevertheless associated with this research program in various ways. Henry Mintzberg, for example, one of the leading contemporary scholars of management, was a valuable contributor to our discussions, whose insights into private and public sector management were stimulating for practitioners and researchers alike.

Aaron Wildavsky, one of the most distinguished modern students of public administration, also agreed to participate in this research program. It was a matter of great personal and professional sadness to the participants in the program that Professor Wildavsky fell ill and passed away while it was still in progress. Although he was not able to contribute as planned, his spirit hovered over the project and was present to the minds of all contributors. In recognition of this, and in respect and gratitude for his enormous contribution to the study of public administration in our time, the contributors to this volume wish to dedicate it to him, and to his distinguished memory.

RALPH HEINTZMAN
Vice-Principal, Research
Canadian Centre for
Management Development

Acknowledgments

Organizing international research activities and editing collections of papers require the involvement and cooperation of numerous persons with many different skills. Our innovative "action-research" approach was no exception, and I would like to extend my warm thanks to all those who toiled behind the scenes to make the publication of this volume possible.

First I would like to thank Ginette Turcot-Ladouceur who managed the logistical side of this research program, including scheduling and making all the arrangements for the meetings of researchers and practitioners. I am also grateful to Maurice Demers for serving as liaison with the publisher and the authors and to our publications coordinator, Heather Steele, for her role in the revision and proofing process. Finally, let me mention the valuable support from our partners at McGill-Queen's University Press who, under the direction of Philip Cercone, have amply demonstrated their professional skills in the production and promotion of this inaugural volume in our new series of publications on governance and public management.

RALPH HEINTZMAN

PART ONE

INTRODUCTION

Introducing the Topic

B. GUY PETERS

Governance is a fundamental problem for any society. The root word for governance, and also for government, refers to steering and thus we are concerned in this volume with the ability of human institutions to control their societies and their economies. Regardless of the nature of the society, there must be some means of responding to the inevitable host of demands for collective action and to the host of collective and individual human needs. The political system, or the "State," is the mechanism usually selected to provide this collective direction to society. By employing its right to issue laws, its capacity to tax and spend, and its ultimate power to use coercion legitimately, the political system can attempt to shape the society in the ways desired. Therefore, as in the French aphorism, "gouverner, c'est choisir," anyone who would govern through the political system must be prepared to make difficult choices. The most basic choice is which social problems will become public and which will be left to individual decisions, or to the decisions of other institutions – most importantly the market.

Governance would be difficult enough if governments were homogeneous and had a unified, streamlined process through which they could make decisions that would then be applied readily to the entire society. Those ideal conditions are almost never attained in the case of real governments. Academic analysts tend to talk about THE state, but that political entity is almost always divided in a number of ways. First, the state is divided into a number of

3

levels; even in nominally unitary states local and regional governments do have some powers, and those powers tend to be increasing even in countries such as France that historically have been highly centralized (Costa and Jeguozo 1988). Further, at each level of government there are several policy-making institutions; even in nominally parliamentary regimes there is some separation of powers and some competition for institutional power (Pierce 1991). These divisions also appear to be increasing in importance in many parliamentary regimes. Finally, government is divided into a number of policy areas, and there is always competition among those sectors over financial resources and over the attention of policy makers (Muller 1985). This separation of policy areas is the basis of most bureaucratic politics and "turf battles." Further, these different policy areas confer upon their participants very different views of priorities and even of the nature of government itself.

The existence of all these internal divisions means that making decisions within any government is complex and involves developing coalitions across a range of interests. Making coherent decisions when faced with all these divisions becomes extremely difficult. All governments possess some unifying and coordinating elements, such as central budgetary, financial, and personnel organizations. The civil service itself also can serve as a unifying and coordinating institution. Still, the centrifugal forces tend to overwhelm the forces of unity and coherence.

We are discussing governance primarily in democratic regimes, and that form of government presents several distinctive problems. Almost by definition, policy making in democracies is more difficult than in more authoritarian regimes (Buchanan and Tullock 1962). Making decisions in a democratic regime involves balancing a number of competing views and a number of forms of participation: political parties and elections, interest groups and their lobbyists, individual citizen's letters and representations to their representatives, etc. All these forms of participation have some legitimacy, but the demands, claims, and ideas being pressed on government only rarely will be the same from all those sources. Again, governing requires making choices, in this case choices among a number of legitimate political pressures. Further, democracy increasingly requires that these decisions be made openly so that the actions of political or administrative actors are clearly visible to the public and the affected interests.

Governing may be equally difficult, if different, in other settings. For example, attempting to govern less developed countries involves coping with a range of socio-economic needs and demands that far exceed the capacity of the government to respond. That lack of capacity tends to be as true administratively as it is financially. Likewise, attempting to govern countries emerging from decades of one-party dominance presents the same problem of excessive demands combined with an absence of any real experience in living with the give-and-take of democracy as is found in more developed countries. Further, the state apparatus of these democratizing regimes may have been compromised by complicity with the former regimes and their governments may have only minimal administrative cadres with which to implement policies and attempt to build legitimacy (Hesse 1993; Peters 1994).

STRAINS ON GOVERNANCE: FAMILIAR BUT ENHANCED

The tasks of governance have been difficult ever since governments began to function, but the problems of the 1980s and 1990s were worse than those experienced during most of the postwar period. Most of the root causes of these difficulties are not entirely new, but they have been exacerbated and to some extent have become more visible than they were in the past. Further, these difficulties are occurring at the same time that the private economy is no longer generating the level of consumer satisfaction that had become familiar, and indeed expected, during most of the postwar period. There are, however, other emerging problems for government that have placed even greater strains on regimes.

Financial Problems

One of the most basic problems facing governments is that of funding their policy commitments. The continuing recession and economic uncertainty of the 1980s meant reduced incomes, more expenditures, and mounting deficits for governments in Europe and North America. This was true despite the control of many of these governments by right-of-centre political parties. For example, the federal budget deficit in both the United States and Canada increased dramatically – from 1 to 6 percent of GNP in the United States and from 3 to 11 percent in Canada, despite having politicians from right-of-centre parties in office. Even in those countries that did not run up large public sector deficits, the level of public spending did not decrease and often increased, again often in the context of political control by the political right. For example, in the United Kingdom public spending as a percentage of GNP was hardly changed during the eleven plus years of the Thatcher government, notwithstanding its rhetoric about reducing the size of government. Thus, for almost all governments public finance is the Damocles sword hanging over the heads of political leaders and threatening their capacity to govern in the way in which they might prefer.

That financial sword does not appear to be becoming any less threatening, and if anything the economic position of many industrialized democracies is becoming more perilous rather than less. To some extent this is a function of globalization (Savoie, this volume) and the economic pressures that this phenomenon imposes on national economies and their governments. For the industrialized world the economic certainties of the past are no longer certain, and with that uncertainty comes political discontent as well as "mere" economic difficulties. In the first place, the economic doctrines that guided decision making in the postwar world – Keynesianism and then monetarism and supply-side economics – all appear to have lost their ability to exercise the type of control citizens have come to expect from their governments (Hall 1989; Sahu and Tracy 1991). This loss of faith in economic orthodoxies by both the academic community and the public means that decision makers in the public sector are left to their own devices to muddle through with the problems.[1]

Perhaps the most important feature of economic change due to international pressures affecting governments is that employment has become less certain for a large number of workers, and when employment is available it is often less remunerative than in the past. For much of the postwar period it has been possible for an individual to leave school relatively early and to find an industrial job that would provide a middle-class income and that would last for a working lifetime. That is no longer the case, as manufacturing jobs are going to low wage countries and jobs in many wealthy countries have become divided into two classes: well-paying professional and managerial jobs and low-paying service sector jobs. Of course, some manufacturing jobs do remain in the wealthy Western countries but even when industrial employment remains, the number of employees is being decreased rapidly by automation and greater efficiency.

This economic change means that governments must either find ways to create new jobs for significant numbers of displaced workers, or they must generate the financial resources to support those citizens without an earned income. Both of these options appear to imply a more interventionist government than has become popular in most Western countries over the past decade. If the first option is adopted governments will have to become extremely active in education and training, labour market policy, and microeconomic policy. If the second option is adopted governments must be prepared to spend for welfare state programs, especially means-tested benefits, in much larger amounts than in the immediate past. Of course, governments could choose to accept neither option, but the price in terms of social peace and legitimacy might be too much to bear. The threats to legitimacy are increased when the displaced workers are concentrated geographically, for example, Newfoundland in Canada or the inner cities of the United States.

Legitimacy and Participation

The second major strain being imposed upon contemporary governments is a more strictly political one. It revolves around the fundamental question of the legitimacy of government as a problem-solving mechanism for society. The politics of the 1980s and 1990s has often focused on the question of which candidate would be the most against government. Bill Clinton, who appears to accept most of the social and economic programs associated with the Democratic Party, felt he had to run against government and to say that he was not an "old Democrat." Even the Scandinavian countries have had antistate politicians wage successful campaigns, e.g., Ny Demokrati in Sweden (Taggart 1993) and the Progress Party in Norway. Some of the loss of legitimacy of government is a function of the economic questions mentioned above – especially taxation – but some reflects a more basic scepticism about the ability of any government to do things properly and efficiently.

It is important, however, not to go overboard when describing popular discontent with government. As Rouban (this volume) shows for France and other analysts (Goodsell 1994) have demonstrated for other countries, the public tends to have a schizophrenic view about governments and their public officials. On the one hand citizens will report in surveys that government is remote, inefficient, and wasteful. When asked about specific services, however, and especially when asked about the services from which they benefit, the public is likely to give the public sector rather high marks. In general public services are rated as well as private services (Bodiguel and Rouban 1991, 25-36). Likewise, when questioned about politicians as a whole, the public is likely to describe them as "lower orders of life," but when asked about their own MP or Congressman they are again likely to award high marks. This makes it appear that, paradoxically, an evil system is composed of virtuous individuals and programs.

Associated with the popular discontent surrounding government is a populist demand for greater public participation as a means of solving problems and making the outcomes of the political process more equal (Wildavsky 1991). The sense here is that the leadership of government has lost touch with the people and has appropriated power and benefits for itself. In the United States Ross Perot's campaign was a clear example of the belief that if "ordinary people" with common sense were in charge, then many of the problems could be solved. A less benign sense of discontent is manifested by political parties on the extreme right and left that want to exercise control in the name of the people but without some of the procedures that help produce the "messiness" often observed in democratic governments. That apparent disorder in governing is actually essential to making government and its procedures more "transparent" to the public.

Beyond the demands for mass political participation there are also increasing demands for participation at lower levels of policy making. It appears that many citizens are not pleased with the representation their views are receiving through political parties, elections, and legislatures and want to have more direct influence over policies. In much of Western Europe these needs generally have been met through corporatist or corporate pluralist institutions, but these have been less developed in Anglo-American regimes. It is not surprising, therefore, that many of the greatest demands for involvement and participation have been found in those regimes. These demands range from NIMBY ("not in my back yard") and NOTE ("not over there either") movements against the siting of hazardous or undesirable facilities to demands for participation in administrative rule-making (Schoenbrod 1993).

These demands for popular participation present some paradoxical pressures on governments attempting to be more efficient and more responsive to the market. On the one hand, government officials are frequently being told to be decisive, entrepreneurial, and responsive to market signals. On the other hand, these same leaders are being told to be more sensitive to public demands and to the wishes of lower echelon workers. They are also told to institute a range of procedural devices that will slow down decisions and perhaps divert them from the "discipline of the market."

Difficult Problems

Contributing to the popular perception that governments are less effective than they have been in the past is the fact that the policy problems they now face appear less tractable than those of the past. Governments have already done the easy things and now are faced with a number of extremely difficult problems. For example, governments now must attempt to manage the economy without the benefit of a widely accepted theory about the way the economy works, and they must also manage it in a more competitive and contentious environment. Most elected politicians know that economic performance is one of the clearest predictors of their re-election, so they must attempt to deal with the economy, a task that is increasingly difficult if not impossible.

In addition, the social problems that governments face now appear more difficult than those "solved" in the past. The welfare state programs of the past decades were reasonably simple programs, largely based on giving people money. This could be done through well-established methods such as social insurance or means tested benefits, depending upon the type of social need addressed and the political values of the country in question (Esping-Andersen 1990). To be sure, these programs are now well-established, but governments now face some more formidable social policy tasks. These include coping with a younger generation for whom there are not enough good jobs, increasing social diversity and the need to manage social change peacefully. Add to those family breakdown, crime, drugs, and persistent poverty, all at a time that governments have serious fiscal problems. The list could be extended but the point would remain that there are few methods agreed upon for "solving" these problems and governments are left with the need to address the problems as best they can.

Finally, even foreign policy is more difficult now than it was in the past. During the Cold War it was usually clear who the enemy was and what the general strategy should be. In a world with an increasing number of small conflicts, often based on internal cultural and ethnic differences, the approach of industrialized democracies is much less clear. In many ways, the world has become a more dangerous place than even during the Cold War, but the dangers are more difficult to classify. Further, the tax-paying public appears less willing to fund the type of military establishment that may be necessary to cope with the new and emerging problems.[2] As well, the lessening of large-scale international tensions means that policy differences among former (and continuing) allies become easier to accept, and economic and other tensions are likely to become more important than military conflicts in international affairs.

If the policy problems of government taken individually are less tractable, then taken together the difficulties in governing are even greater. Policy areas have never been watertight compartments as they are sometimes portrayed, but the interactions across sectors appear to have increased significantly. Thus, governing effectively in one sector will depend to a greater degree upon decisions taken in other sectors. Policies such as welfare, education, and the labour market interact to an ever greater degree and present more significant challenges of policy definition and management (Rochefort and Cobb 1994).

GOVERNMENT REACTIONS TO STRESS

Faced with these threats to their capacity to govern effectively, governments have sought not only to become more efficient and effective but also to make policies that enable incumbent politicians to be re-elected. Indeed, we can interpret much of the spate of reform activity during the 1980s and early 1990s in this light. However, it should also be understood in the light of changes in the dominant ideology concerning government and the public sector. In a large number of countries, governments of the political right were successful electorally and sought to impose radically new forms of action on the public sector. Yet, in the cases where the political left remained in power, it tended to adopt many of the techniques used by the right and in the case of New Zealand seemingly surpassed all other governments in its devotion to privatization and devolution (Scott, Bushnell, and Sallee 1990).

The fundamental direction of change has been to make government function more like the private sector. This tendency is captured well in the phrase "the new public management" (Pollitt, this volume; 1990). Several other popular phrases such as "reinvention" and "re-engineering" also attempt to capture the changes that are occurring (Oswald and Gaebler 1992; Borins, this volume). The underlying assumption here is that if the public sector would only follow the lead of the private sector most problems of governance would be over. These reforms are all in pursuit of a format for governance that will be at once efficient, effective, and democratic (Peters, this volume). Different political leaders will assign differential importance to each of those three criteria, and might impose some additional ones of their own, but almost all would see a better government as being the product of the reform process.

One important aspect of response to challenges to governance has been to make the political system more "user friendly," as well as "employee friendly." On the one hand, governments are encouraging their civil servants and anyone else who interacts with the public to treat the public as a "customer," very much as it is assumed they would be treated when in contact with the private sector (Pierre, this volume; Behn 1993). The idea of being a customer also means that there should be some choice of services available to the public, so that the monopolies that traditionally characterized the provision of public services must be broken up. This goal can be achieved by the division of large departments into a number of more autonomous organizations, and through use of mechanisms such as vouchers to create greater choice for citizens. Also, quasi markets can be created within government organizations, e.g., the National Health Service in the United Kingdom (Burke and Goddard 1990), to attempt to create some greater choice.[3]

Government is also supposed to become more friendly to its own employees, especially employees at the bottom of the organizational hierarchies. Indeed, government organizations are being driven to become less hierarchical, with the lower echelons of public organizations being "empowered" to make more decisions on their own. This empowerment reflects in part the reality that most decisions important for average citizens (consumers?) are made at the lowest echelons of a bureaucracy (Lipsky 1980). It also reflects a management style intended to give a great deal of latitude and responsibility to lower level workers, within the context of a strong corporate culture that guides their actions. Finally, empowerment also reflects a way in which governments can save money. If lower level workers are empowered, then the supervisory work of many middle managers becomes less important and these more costly employees become superfluous. This is indeed part of the recommendations of the National Performance Review (Gore Report) in the United States.

Another part of the attempt to make government more userfriendly, and more friendly to its own employees, is to emphasize the importance of quality in public programs. Total quality management (TQM) has become common practice in much of the private sector and is becoming more common in the public sector (Ingraham, this volume). The concept of TQM is that just as public employees are being empowered to make more decisions, they should be involved in generating ideas about improving the services rendered the public. Further, rather than just being the responsibility of top management, quality becomes a shared concern for the entire organization. Again, as well as serving the customers better, this approach to management may also be a means of saving money for the cash-starved public sector.

Finally, another part of the reform effort has been to enhance participation in government. This is especially true for clients of public organizations, but consultation and control (or at least influence) over policies by the affected interests is an increasingly important feature of policy in a number of countries. On the one hand, this style of decision making may enhance the legitimacy of the decisions once they are made. On the other hand, it can make decisiveness on the part of policy makers all the more difficult. In some ways, this participatory approach to reform is antithetical to the thrust of managerialism described above. If a manager is to be an effective entrepreneur, as assumed by the managerial approach, then he or she must be able to position the organization strategically. That may be difficult to do if there is a strong program of consultation.

PREVIEW

We have assembled a collection of distinguished scholars to address these issues of changing patterns of governance. We all met together twice to discuss these issues and to refine our perspectives. This process has, we believe, resulted in an integrated set of papers that address the principal issues facing governments, citizens, and scholars.

Challenges to Governance

The first section of the volume discusses several of the important challenges facing contemporary governments. First, Luc Rouban discusses the importance of the cultural values of the civil service in defining the nature of government and strategies for influencing the society. Civil service culture is also crucial for defining the role of the civil servant in government and constraining the latitude of action of the technocrats. One of the most important facts about civil service culture is that it is not uniform but varies significantly according to the level and function of civil servants. Rouban illustrates these points in reference to French administration, but the points would almost certainly be true in other advanced democracies.

Another aspect of cultural change affecting the conduct of government is the altered definition of the relationship between government and the people whom it serves. There has been an increasing emphasis on the definition of the public as the "consumers" of the services provided by government. Jon Pierre examines this cultural change as well as the impact of the differences among characterizations such as "citizens," "clients," and "consumers" when referring to the public being served. In particular, he finds that the definition of the public as consumers may undermine important political and constitutional values associated with citizenship.

Donald Savoie discusses the impact of the globalization of economies and of governance questions on national governments. He points to the declining capacity of governments to control important aspects of policy within their own countries, with power flowing out to the international environment and down to subnational governments. With these changes come a consequent need for political leaders to think about new instruments for influencing society. The public service in most countries is ill-prepared to cope with these emerging patterns of governance, and therefore there is a need for governments to rethink their use of senior personnel.

Fundamental Political Processes

The second section of the book addresses itself to some fundamental political questions arising from changes in the public sector. First, Peter Aucoin discusses the changes occurring in the relationship between civil servants and their political masters within the changing patterns of governance. Usually described as "politicization," the

administrative reforms of the 1980s and 1990s have tended to reduce
the influence and policy-making activities of senior civil servants. The
one area in which the role of the civil service has been increased is
management. Much of the thinking contained in the reform efforts
stresses the role of political leaders as the source of policy ideas, with
civil servants being principally charged with implementation. Aucoin
discusses these changes and their implications for governance in
Anglo-American democratic systems. Again, many of the same
points would hold true in many other developed democracies.

John Halligan looks at the policy advice given to ministers and
how sources and methods of advice have changed over the past few
decades. The senior civil service has been the traditional source of
policy advice, but its role has been diminished by several changes.
As Aucoin discusses, there has been an increased politicization of
the public service, and with that there is a demand for more advice
from partisan sources rather than from more dispassionate permanent officials. Another change has been the development of alternative sources of policy advice, such as interest groups and think
tanks. In principle, the multiple sources of policy advice available
should improve the quality of decisions, but it is not clear that policy
makers actually use all the advice that they could.

Philip Cooper deals with the question of accountability in the
public sector in the era of the new public management. Although
accountability is an enduring problem of government, the recent
emphasis on managerialism has cast those enduring issues in a
very different light. In addition, it has forced some fundamental
rethinking of the mechanisms used for enforcing accountability.
The market now comprises a major portion of the apparatus for
defining accountability. With that change, market-based instruments such as contracts require a different approach to accountability questions than would be encountered in administratively
oriented management systems.

Managerialism and the Public Service

The third section of this book is concerned with the responses of
government to the challenges it faces. Although there are a variety

of changes, the concentration is on transformations of traditional public administration. Guy Peters discusses four alternative models of administration that appear to undergird the changes that have been occurring. The most obvious of these is the market model and its attempts to impose private sector models on the public sector. An alternative vision being implemented simultaneously depends upon participation by both employees and clients (customers?). Another manner of coping with the identified problems of governance is to create more temporary organizations and depend more on temporary employees. Finally, government can attempt to deregulate its activities and behave more entrepreneurially. What is most important is that these visions of reform are all being implemented at the same time, often without understanding their frequently contradictory implications.

Christopher Pollitt provides an excellent review of some of the issues associated with the "New Public Management." He focuses attention on the introduction of a number of specific techniques into the public service and their impact on the policy process. These techniques tend to have a private sector foundation and to focus attention on specific performance standards of organizations, rather than the more diffuse values of "public service" associated with traditional public sector management. Rather than only bewailing the many incursions made by private sector values into government, Pollitt provides a scheme that can be used to evaluate these techniques and relate them to specific public policy problems.

Patricia Ingraham addresses another of the methodologies associated with administrative transformations in the public sector. This is the increased emphasis on quality in public services, or "total quality management" (TQM). The private sector has been pursuing quality through a variety of techniques, and many of these are being copied by the public sector. Ingraham first describes the nature of the process of implementing TQM in government. She points to the difficulties in defining quality in government, and the extent to which this particular reform strategy embodies different values than those contained in other managerialist reforms. She also points out the extent to which this program may be a useful remedy for problems of certain types of organizations, and the extent to which its benefits may decline over time.

Although the public often thinks that the public sector is hopelessly inefficient and bound up in its own bureaucratic rules and procedures, Sandford Borins points to the numerous innovations that have been adopted successfully in the public sector in the United States and Canada. While most of these innovations have been at the subnational level, there are opportunities for analogous changes at the national government level. Even at the subnational level these innovations do demonstrate the creativity of managers in the public sector and their capacity to improve the efficiency and quality of their services.

CONCLUSION

Donald Savoie provides a conclusion for this book. He discusses a number of points learned as a consequence of this one research effort. He also points to the need for additional research on the reactions of governments to their numerous challenges. The challenges to government discussed above will persist and are likely to increase. This means that political and administrative leaders will have to continue their efforts to make government work better. Governments will have to be more effective, more efficient, and more willing to serve their clients in the manner in which those clients demand. Simple solutions such as "re-engineering" and "reinventing" are not likely to solve the problems. What will be required is a continuing search for ideas and values that can guide the continuing development of governments and governance.

NOTES

1 It does appear that there is an increasing interest in, and use of, microeconomic policy to manage economics. Even in the U.S. "industrial policy" is no longer a dirty phrase and there is some interest in more targeted interventions by the federal government.

2 It might be argued that, everything else being equal, the type of military force needed for the present situation is more costly than that required for the Cold War. Contemporary forces will have to be relatively personnel-intensive, while those of the Cold War were technology-intensive.

3 In internal markets the major choice makers are professionals rather than individual citizens ("consumers"), but there are still choices that can be made.

BIBLIOGRAPHY

Behn, R.D. 1993. Customer service: changing an agency's culture. *Governing* 12:76-8.

Bodiguel, J.-L., and L. Rouban. 1991. *Le fonctionnaire détroné?* Paris: Presses de la Fondation nationale des sciences politiques.

Buchanan, J., and G. Tullock. 1962. *The Calculus of Consent.* Ann Arbor: University of Michigan Press.

Burke, C., and A. Goddard. 1990. Internal markets – the road to inefficiency? *Public Administration* 68:389-96.

Costa, J.P., and Y. Jeguozo. 1988. *L'administration française face aux défis de la décentralisation.* Paris: Les Editions STH.

Esping-Anderson, G. 1990. *The Three Worlds of Welfare Capitalism.* Princeton: Princeton University Press.

Goodsell, C.T. 1994. *The Case for Bureaucracy.* 3d ed. Chatham, NJ: Chatham House.

Hall, P.A. 1989. *The Political Power of Economic Ideas: Keynesianism Across Nations.* Princeton: Princeton University Press.

Hesse, J.J. 1993. From transformation to modernization: administrative change in Central and Eastern Europe. *Public Administration* 71:219-57.

Lipsky, M. 1980. *Street Level Bureaucracy: Dilemmas of the Individual in Public Services.* New York: Russell Sage Foundation.

Muller, P. 1985. Un schéma d'analyse des politiques sectorielles. *Revue française de science politique* 35:165-89.

Osborne, D., and T. Gaebler. 1992. *Reinventing Government.* Reading, MA: Addison-Wesley.

Peters, B.G. 1994. The civil service in the consolidation of democracy. *International Social Science Journal.*

Pierce, R.C. 1991. The executive divided against itself: cohabitation in France, 1986-1988. *Governance* 4:270-93.

Pollitt, C. 1990. *Managerialism and the Public Service.* Oxford: Basil Blackwell.

Rochefort, D.A., amd R.W. Cobb. 1994. *The Politics of Problem Definition: Shaping the Policy Agenda.* Lawrence: University of Kansas Press.

Sahu, A.P., and R.L. Tracy. 1991. *The Economic Legacy of the Reagan Years.* New York: Praeger.

Schoenbrod, D. 1993. *Power Without Responsibility.* New Haven: Yale University Press.

Scott, G., Peter Bushnell, and N. Sallee. 1990. Reform of the core public sector: New Zealand experience. *Governance* 3:138-67.

Taggart, P.A. 1993. The new populism and the new politics: transformations of the Swedish party system. Ph.D. diss., University of Pittsburgh.

Wildavsky, A. 1991. *The Rise of Radical Egalitarianism.* Washington, DC: American University Press.

PART TWO

THE CHANGING

ENVIRONMENT

The Civil Service Culture and Administrative Reform

LUC ROUBAN

The fact that officials and other agents of the public service share a particular culture would seem to directly affect (or limit) any real opportunities to reform the governmental machine. When administrations seek to introduce management techniques or to transform the relationships they maintain with users, all governments of the industrialized Western world are confronted with the fact that the public service is organized around values that are not identified either with politicians' values or with cultural phenomena occurring across society. For historical, sociological, and functional reasons, the public service cannot be considered as an undifferentiated group of men and women engaged in routine work.

Public service culture is not only a set of values linked to the history of institutions or to the place that the administration occupies in each state; it corresponds also to strategic interests different from the collective interests promoted by politicians and by public or private pressure groups. The culture of the public service is not, therefore, the product simply of custom or the blind defence of the bureaucracy's professional interests. It results to a large extent from functional necessity, especially from the balance to be established at a given time between contradictory objectives: to ensure the same service to the greatest number while recognizing different user categories, to implement governmental policy while respecting legal rules or constitutional principles, to rationalize the use of public funds while respecting principles of equity. The culture of the public service, therefore, is linked to practices gained from experience, to the underlying rationality of the administrative activity that cannot be reduced to cost/benefit calculations or speculations.

The task of officials has become more difficult since the 1980s when the reduction of budgets and increased expectations and demands from citizens have forced governments to intervene more frequently, despite reduced staffs, salaries, and blocked careers. A general managerialist movement has fostered the search for alternative solutions to the traditional bureaucratic state, through institutional innovations (executive agencies) or through the introduction of a new governance style, that is to say the development of a new civil service culture. Behind this search for organizational solutions a need has emerged to define the normative framework of modern democracies and to secure a new and legitimate deal between the public and private sectors.

This future framework is still hypothetical because one can observe, in the early 1990s, that the changes that occurred in the 1980s in the name of neoliberalism and managerialism did not enhance citizens' opinions of governments' accomplishments. The displeasure with regard to the public sector's performance has not disappeared and governments have again lost a bit more of their legitimacy. As a matter of fact, Western governments are today more politically fragile than they were twenty years ago. Persistent rumours of bribery and misconduct have put politicians under public scrutiny, regardless of their efforts to reform the internal administrative machinery. Unfortunately for politicians, administrative reforms belong to those low-key issues that generally do not raise public passions. On the other hand, civil servants feel generally much more concerned with these reforms than with substantial changes occurring within the realm of public policies.

In order to assess the role of the civil service culture in this reforming trend, it seems necessary to ask three questions: Is there a civil service culture? Is this culture homogeneous? What margin of change does it allow for managerial reforms? Of course, it would be foolish to ignore the fact that the answers to such questions are related to each specific national set of values. Nevertheless, given that there is a Weberian dichotomy between politicians and civil servants in all Western countries, it seems legitimate to answer these questions on the basis of the lessons we can learn from specific examples, in order then to draw out broader avenues for reflection. As the French civil service was always regarded as a case study of a strong culture, and as it was recently engaged in a large managerialist "modernization" process, we shall use it as a test.

THE CIVIL SERVICE CULTURE: A TENTATIVE IDENTIFICATION

Many studies have been devoted to the question of administrative culture. Some have focused on the search for an irreducible identity, contrasting administrative culture with political culture. Others, from a critical perspective, have sought to focus on the bureaucratic culture, that is to say the culture of public sector organizations (Crozier 1963). One can try to define administrative culture negatively, from what it is not, then positively, by trying to identify some distinctive features.

While it is impossible to examine here the diversity of situations that prevail in Western countries, one can rightfully argue that the culture of the public service is not that of politicians. Legal norms have an overwhelming presence in their values. Civil servants are not dependent on short-term promises; on the contrary, they work within a long-term framework. According to Max Weber, they are guided more by rationality than by passions (Weber 1959). The public service has always appeared as the "cold" part of Western democracies and, at least in European countries, civil servants have served as a political support in times of serious crisis. They have provided a safeguard, at a minimum a rational power, in periods of war or revolution. The development and then the maintenance of a public service in Western countries means that the policy process cannot be totally irrational. In this regard, the development of the public service is linked to the will and the ability to study scientifically the rationales for and results of public action. During the 1960s and the 1970s, moving to the other extreme, attempts to rationalize the welfare state have led us to ignore the political interest factor, and ambitious top-down reforms have failed.

The culture of the public service is no longer the culture of private sector wage earners. Generally, public officials are likely to work outside the economic world. The main difference lies in the absence of a link between compensation and the economic value of the task accomplished. It is also related to the legalities which offer job protection. This means, in particular, that the public sector cannot be entirely governed by rational calculations but must also take into account ethical values.

A certain number of positive values seem to characterize civil servants. In the traditional Weberian dichotomy, bureaucrats respond to facts and politicians respond to interests on behalf of ideals. Traditional criteria of bureaucratic action include analytic problem solving, responsiveness to a narrow political and professional constituency, and, of course, the mastery of techniques (Aberbach, Putnam, and Rockman 1981). Today, such a clear-cut separation or strong cultural difference could hardly exist as bureaucrats have to produce some kind of political consensus within and outside public administration in order to make public policies succeed. Nevertheless, the common participation of both politicians and civil servants within the policy-making process does not allow them to fully bridge differences in strategic environments. Functional specialization is still a frontier between the two professional groups. Aberbach, Putnam and Rockman (1981) have clearly shown that there is a sharp contrast in role definitions between bureaucrats and politicians, especially regarding partisanship, policy advocacy, and technical skills. Of course, socialization processes and political institutions may strongly interfere in the orientation of professional roles. Where political authority is weak, as it is in the case of the United States, bureaucrats are encouraged to play a political role and politicians seek to be involved in details of administrative action in order to strengthen their own resources. However important the national differences in Western democracies, they cannot hide the fact that bureaucrats are still thoroughly trained, with legal and technical skills, and that politicians are still engaged in catch-all actions for electoral success. On the other hand, both bureaucrats and politicians participate in the policy-making process, but this does not tell us much about their real ability to do it with efficiency and responsiveness.

What does culture mean in a civil service context? Of course, there is room for many definitions: civil service culture may refer to the whole set of values shared by civil servants as members of public administrations, or to values determined through a specific legal framework. Unfortunately, these comprehensive definitions obscure the fact that organizational or legal criteria cannot determine the behaviour of civil servants under every circumstance of their professional (and perhaps private) lives. On the one hand, there are various kinds of public organizations within the same national administrative system. For instance, it is highly doubtful that a civil servant working in a business-like activity shares common professional prospects and behaviour patterns with a colleague bogged down in routine bureaucratic tasks. On the other hand, the legal criteria which govern public operations apply equally to clerical staff and senior executives. They are all civil servants having to pay due attention to common legal commitments, and they enjoy similar kinds of privileges. Nevertheless, everyone can easily observe that clerks and senior executives do not react in the same way when confronted with changes in their professional circumstances. Clerks and senior executives do not necessarily share common educational and social resources. As a general principle, the more social resources you derived from your overall education, as well as from your family background, the more likely you are to adapt to new collective challenges. When the French postal service and the Telecom public company were turned into more business-like entities, it was clearly observed that clerks reacted in a negative way and joined their professional unions to oppose the change, while senior executives had prepared themselves to handle this managerialist change, having worked previously in private or publicly owned companies.

In order to answer the introductory question, I think it is necessary to avoid two classical pitfalls. The first pitfall is the belief that there is just one "bureaucratic" culture within each national administrative apparatus, such as Crozier's famous bureaucratic reflex.

This is just a scientific packaging for common feelings, aimed at criticizing public administration as a naturally inefficient mechanism inducing auto-destructive or negative behaviours. The other pitfall is the suggestion that there are as many civil service cultures as there are public organizations. As cultures are made of stable, coherent, and normative values, it would be surprising if there were absolutely no common cultural ground between various civil servants. If this were so, how can we explain the fact that civil servants can work together or can improve their know-how and experience through their professional mobility?

In order to assess the role of civil service culture in the reform process, I suggest that we distinguish professional culture – the set of values attached to specific jobs (different skills are required to build a bridge and to fight criminality), from social culture – the set of values defining the ranking of social components (including the ranking of professional values and skills in the social hierarchy), a set of values which is generally but not totally inherited from the individual background. Organizational cultures are made of a specific combination of professional and social values. It is necessary to underline the fact that the respective weight of professional and social values is not the same at the various levels of the administrative hierarchy. Social considerations have much more impact in higher spheres of organizations, while the defence of professional values is generally the fall-back argument of street-level bureaucrats trying to avoid any change.

For instance, it was clearly observable, in most large-size French municipalities which have been engaged since 1983 in managerial changes, that local clerical staffs used their traditional and informal professional knowledge as arguments to oppose performance assessment reviews based upon formal criteria of productivity. This exemplifies the fact that change is all the more difficult when professional values are so connected with day-to-day life that administrative positions or responsibilities become the natural way of life. Change is easier when professional and social values are disconnected. This is a major difficulty to face when it is necessary to ask senior executives to make drastic changes, because their professional values are generally closely connected with their social values. For instance, the criteria of both their professional success and social success were generated during the acculturation process they were submitted to within the *Grandes Écoles* and further reinforced when they accepted their first position in a technical or administrative *grands corps*. Any major change in their professional set of values (for instance, when performance indicators are used regardless of their seniority) could jeopardize their own personal success story. This is not usually the case for street-level bureaucrats, as mentioned earlier, except when they identify strongly with their organizational life. In other words, change is much more difficult to manage within clerical ranks in professional organizations and, on the contrary, easier in line administrations, while change is much easier to implement within senior executive ranks in professional organizations, but more difficult in line administrations where the weight of social values is the determinant. This implies that there is no "best cultural approach" to the reform process. Reformers have to take into careful account the identity of each organization as well as the distribution of professional roles along the lines of each administrative hierarchy.

This study focuses on senior civil servants because they are at the heart of any global reform. Moreover, the weight of their culture is crucial to explaining major differences among national administrative settings. One may observe, then, that governmental functions are generally carried out more effectively when they are linked to the specific character of professional training. In countries such as Germany, where civil servants have been trained in legal matters, policy implementation through legal tools is likely to be of a very good quality. In countries such as France, where professional engineering schools, along with the *École nationale d'Administration*, are among the main sources of senior civil servants, the technical dimension of state intervention may be overdeveloped, even though the corporatist decision-making framework may sometimes hinder policy legitimacy. The major problem we face here is that these professional features are closely connected to the social position of these various senior civil servants and the emphasis they place on their social role. Their professional training has largely determined the other social resources from which they can benefit. For instance,

German public officials can easily be offered positions within the court system, while their French counterparts are well known for their cross-overs between public administration and the industrial sector. Each of these career advancements is differently ranked from one country to another, but they heavily determine the calculations civil servants can make in order to maximize their professional gains. So, the second question we face is, deductively: to what extent will these public officials invest in managerial values? Their acceptance of managerialism, whatever its practical effects on public action, will closely depend on (1) its place in the ranking of social values, and consequently, (2) its place in the ranking of professional administrative values.

FACTORS OF CHANGE: THE NEW DEAL BETWEEN POLITICAL CULTURE AND ADMINISTRATIVE CULTURE

The managerialist reform requires cultural changes that cannot be isolated from their context. Though attention has recently been given to productivity, cost/effectiveness, and quality as a new set of administrative principles at the micro level, there are other problems connected with global political variables. The very nature of the political culture may impede or encourage managerial values. Thus, the first question to be raised concerns the place of public administration in the political culture. The second question concerns global trends that can change the relationship between administration and policy.

Public Administration and Public Opinion

Most recent reforms have been launched in the belief that users are generally disappointed with the quality of public services. This contention can be looked at from two points of view: the first one, largely correlated through opinion polls in most Western countries during the 1980s, is that some government programs are viewed as costly, wasteful, and inefficient (Levine, Peters, and Thompson 1990). The second one, which cannot logically be deduced from the former, is that public administration is viewed as a wasteful business whatever the policy goals may be. This ideological stance needs to be confronted with systematic data. Public opinion seems generally satisfied with public officials' personal conduct but dissatisfied with public service procedures and constraints. In this regard, most opinion polls show that administrative services and officials get high scores when viewed in their totality. As far as France is concerned, a large consensus prevails:[1] 75% of persons questioned favour a large public service, with 15% against, regardless of their political preference. Similarly, a large majority considers that public services are low profitability businesses: 65% against 23%. Here again, socio-professional category or political opinion does not matter (72% of right-wing users give this answer as compared to 62% for users close to the Socialist party). Similarly, to the question "Who is accountable for the trouble you face with public administration?" one finds only 28% replying "the officials" but 84% replying "the complexity of procedures." The main preoccupation is now the quality of direct contacts with users. For 76% of the users questioned, officials are competent, for 49% (against 42%) services are not sufficiently well equipped, and for 69% (against 27%) public administration does not sufficiently take care of relations with users.

On the whole, public opinion is very stable and has not undergone a drastic evolution: the very principle of a public service is still supported. Users have adopted a pragmatic attitude: they just want to obtain more and better service, with tax-cuts. But public opinion polls do not reveal a clear connection between fiscal pressure and protests about public service quality. Nevertheless, there is today an increased sensitivity to indirect costs, especially loss of time due to poor information procedures (Who is in charge of this file? What documents must be provided? Is this procedure a correct one? Is there any opportunity to contest the decision? and so on). Responsiveness has become a crucial factor in the perception of quality in the public service. One can observe that public opinion is particularly satisfied with public services within the community such as:

- firemen (96% against 1%)
- municipal services (90% against 7%)
- electricity and gas supply (85% against 14%)

- the postal service (82% against 17%)
- hospitals (79% against 18%).

There is, on the contrary, general dissatisfaction with public services regarded as anonymous bureaucratic machines, such as:

- fiscal services (62% against 35%)
- social security (58% against 37%)
- education (57% against 28%)
- justice (53% against 32%).

The main point to be addressed here is that the evolving culture of public opinion does not allow much room for legal reforms. Traditional changes in the "administrative public relations system," such as users' committees or rules concerning the freedom of access to administrative information, have not, in the end, had much impact. The more preoccupied public opinion becomes with the economic dimension of public administration, the less advisable do legal measures prove to be. The crucial question to be answered through the managerialist reform is, "Beyond what point does privatization become more reasonable and effective than any other administrative reform?" Privatization of public services is not always easy to manage, however, because strong ideological and historical commitments work against it. For instance, a September 1986 survey demonstrated that 50% of persons surveyed would encourage their children to look for a career within the public sector, while 28% would prefer them to seek a career within the private sector (22% did not express an opinion on this subject). Moreover, during this neoliberal period, at a time when the French government tried systematically to privatize public enterprises, one could observe that public opinion was divided as to whether or not such reforms could do much to improve service quality. When asked: "Do you think that privatization could improve the functioning of these services?" public opinion appeared to be perplexed, if not sceptical, as shown in Table 1.

In the same way, most people think that quantitative reforms, for example, increases in personnel in some sectors, such as employment and human services, would not result in better service. One can thus

TABLE 1

Privatization Would Allow a Better Performance (%)

	Yes	No	Without much effect	No opinion
Health insurance	25	30	27	18
Postal service	27	27	32	14
Education	29	32	24	15
Prisons	20	23	20	37
Hospitals	30	29	24	17

notice the development of a common administrative viewpoint across the political spectrum, leaving aside the right-wing or communist extremists. Of course, there is a slight difference between those close to the Gaullist Rassemblement pour la République (RPR) (55% support the idea that more staff and resources would allow for a real improvement in the quality of the public service) and those close to the Socialist party (63% support this proposal). These figures are considerably less than the number supporting this proposal within the ranks of persons close to the Communist party (76%) and, on the other end of the political spectrum, within the ranks of the National Front partisans (76%). At these two extremes of the French political spectrum two typical attitudes can be found: when a problem occurs during contact with the public administration, persons close to the National Front are the first to blame the officials' personal misconduct (43%), while persons close to the Communist party are more likely to denounce the fact that public administration was not given sufficient resources to act efficiently (69%). In general, the two most radical and simple solutions (to control more closely civil servants' behaviour or to give more resources to public institutions) are invoked only by political extremists, while partisans of the RPR and the PS seem to be ideologically very close in their analysis of the administrative predicament.

The Evolving Rationale of Political Action

I shall put forward the hypothesis, therefore, that the cultural dimension of public administration has changed because political values themselves have changed. Since the Second World War, the various Western states have all subscribed, with national variations, to the ideology of intelligent choice (Brown and Wildavsky 1987) and to what I would like to call "reasonable scientificity." This social and ideological basis was itself composed of two elements: on the one hand, rationalistic prospects for public action in the foreseeable future and, on the other hand, a relatively strong social control over individual behaviour. These two elements have disappeared since the late 1970s. New values have developed, based on an implicit refusal of any rational construction of the world and the defence of the status quo, and perhaps the rediscovery of community values, as can be seen through the development of new social movements for the protection of the environment or the defence of minorities' social identities (Dalton and Kuechler 1990). In the same way, world economic instability and the destruction of the industrial economy by irresponsible financial speculations have severely limited the intellectual and practical possibilities for systematic social progress (Perrineau 1994). As a main consequence of this dual change, one can observe that politics is no longer regarded by most citizens as a legitimate tool for the rational organization of the world. One has to look, therefore, for administrative ways to compensate for this sense of political deficiency. This desperate search for administrative rationality, in the absence of any global political rationality, has changed the balance that prevailed previously between the two components of "governance." Today, a "scientific" administrative process is not supposed to extend or to complete a "scientific" or "quasi-scientific" political process, but to serve as a substitute for it. Such an evolution means that public administration is not only expected to act efficiently and rationally, as usual, but also that it is called upon more than ever to build social support and legitimacy for political action. This evolution is summarized in Table 2.

Table 2 shows the four solutions stemming from the theoretical relationship between administration and politics, according to whether or not they follow the path of this "reasonable scientificity." The disappearance of the rationalistic politics of the 1960s leads toward two theoretical solutions, examples of which

TABLE 2

	Rationalistic Politics	Unrationalistic Politics
Rationalistic Public Administration	Welfare dreams	Managerialism
Unrationalistic Public Administration	Political development theories	Archaic society

can already be found. Managerialism is the first one, as a solution to compensate for poor political legitimacy in modern societies; the upheaval of archaic societies is the second one, wherein Western political institutions are disregarded in favour of community social integration. Recent political troubles in Africa have demonstrated such a movement, especially through the upheaval of Islamic protests. Surprisingly, the two types of reform occur at the same time. For the Western societies, the failure of the welfare state means that social integration cannot be attained through growing public expenditures. As for developing countries, the failure of social modernization means that development theories are no longer worthwhile. Even though the starting point was different in each case (as public administration was supposed to obey Weberian principles in Western democracies), the same move toward unrationalistic politics can be observed. Welfare state or proto-welfare state rationalistic politics are disappearing in both cases, making administrative reform all the more crucial. Similarly, the political status of administrative reform has changed. For Western countries, the administrative reform movement is a hypothetical attempt to rationalize society with managerial tools, that is, with cultural tools coming from the business world. For the time being, it is hard to tell if this managerialist trend is not further destroying the political basis on which our societies are run. For developing countries, the administrative reform appears to be the only way to stabilize governments whose long-term policies have been jeopardized by economic failure. However, in this latter case, the weakness of bureaucratic traditions could make people even more reluctant to accept administrative reforms, generally pursued in an authoritative manner.

A second element of change in the evolving policy/politics equilibrium is the fact that government action has lost its identity. Public administration, whatever its Weberian or managerialist flavour, always implies that the policy maker is clearly identified. The notion of accountability, at the heart of the democratic architecture, has suffered serious challenges. The globalization of the international economy plays a crucial role here because it has allowed a growing number of actors to intervene in the political game. The basic idea of a political life organized around a centre has given way to interrelated policy networks (Mazey and Richardson 1993). Public officials are no longer the spokespersons of a well-identified power. Bargaining then becomes more important than regulatory activity. Normative functions of administrative life seem today less politically determinant than functions of intermediation, even in those professional sectors such as the police, where bureaucratic traditions are still strong. Civil servants are not as likely to be a mouthpiece for or an interpreter of the Prince as to organize the civil peace between private or public pressure groups that have increasing technological expertise. The legal culture becomes, therefore, less important than the economic culture and the political know-how. Today, a wise civil servant has to know which rules are not likely to be applied. This evolving role of the public service is dangerous because it accelerates the degradation of democracy. What Western political systems have gained recently in administrative productivity, they have lost in political credibility. What is the reason for increasing public policy efficiency, if government global action is no longer a matter of concern for citizens? Why conduct expertise and policy evaluations if hardly 30 percent of citizens are likely to vote? We are still unable to imagine a new set of political values for managerialism (Rouban 1994b). For the time being, is seems clear that the administrative reform process is working on the basis of a two-fold assumption: (a) it is possible to drive politics through bureaucracy; and (b) it is possible to run the bureaucracy using business concepts. Finally, this simplistic equation means that it is possible to reduce politics to business values. Most Western governments suffer from this contradiction, caught between a growing demand for political accountability and a fragmented bureaucracy, whose managers cannot be held politically accountable.

TABLE 3
Perception of Daily Work (several answers possible) (%)

	Grands Corps	Managers in central ministries	Managers in field offices
Decision	50.0	45.3	80.0
Expertise	54.8	57.6	57.3
Project management	32.3	47.5	72.7
Contacts with professional groups	24.2	28.8	60.7
Internal management	24.2	38.1	69.3
Control	74.2	37.4	18.0
Bargaining	29.0	33.8	40.3
Work on files	22.6	33.8	44.7

ONE OR MANY BUREAUCRATIC CULTURES?

In order to assess the effectiveness of the administrative reform of management, it is necessary to study the nature of civil service culture. As there is no systematic comparative study of civil service culture in Western democracies, we will use data collected from a systematic survey of a sample of 500 French public sector executives (Rouban 1994a), representing approximately 10% of the senior civil service population. The French case is all the more interesting in that it is generally regarded as a case study for Weberian-Napoleonic bureaucracy, a closed and rigid world of elite members, whose lives are dedicated to the state and who systematically defeat any attempt at reform.

It appears clearly that senior officials share a common set of values. Nevertheless, one can see that these values are likely to change dramatically according to their various positions within the decision-making process. For instance, managers in field offices define their professional role principally in reference to decision making, project management, contacts with professional groups, and personnel management. Managers in central ministries (i.e. those who work in Paris) refer to tasks of expertise, and *grands corps* members (members of the State Council, of the Court of Accounts, regional and departmental *préfets*) refer to control functions, as shown in Table 3.

The professional culture of civil servants depends obviously upon the conditions of development of the public service within each political system. Important national differences exist depending on several variables, notably on the institutional distribution of power inside as well as outside public administration settings. The nature of the professional role can also be reflected in the degree of fluidity that one finds in the professional community. One can, indeed, oppose two models: that of the American manager working on the basis of multi-year programs with individualistic career values (job description system), and that of the French official where the corporatist emphasis on careers leaves only a narrow margin for managerial values to be implemented. The institutional pressure is still very strong. When asked: "In your daily activity, do you think that decisions are always taken within the same group of officials?", 42.1% of officials answer "Yes, entirely," 35.3% answer "Yes, most of the time," and only 12% answer "No" (6% of them did not answer). The existence of a stable internal decision-making process is noticed especially by field office managers, 85% of whom answer "Yes, entirely" or "Yes, most of the time." The same answer is given by 67.8% of the members of the *grands corps*, and by 65.4% of the managers in ministries. There is no specific statistical variation according to professional sector. What are the variables which determine the composition of these internal decision-making networks? When asked, the civil servants answered: personal characteristics (31.1%), professional experience (56.3%), and the official position (68.3%). Support from political circles appears far behind (10.8%), as is the case for the personal relationship network (9%).

Though the answer "the official position" had the highest score, whatever the institutional membership, one notices that professional experience, i.e. the skill to function competently day-to-day, is especially mentioned by managers in field offices (62.3%), followed by ministries' managers (53.2%) and *grands corps* members (33.9%). Generally, answers given by *grands corps* members are appreciably less varied. One can notice, furthermore, the fact that in the three groups, personal characteristics rank in third position behind the official function and professional experience. While the question included an open item in order to collect spontaneous answers, it appears that technical expertise is hardly mentioned, and then only by field office managers (4.3%). The comparison that can

TABLE 4
Factors Influencing Membership in the Decision-making Groups
(several answers possible) (%)

	Grands Corps	Ministries	Field Offices	U.S. federal managers[1]
Official position	69.4	63.3	70.3	68/63
Professional experience	33.9	53.2	62.3	41/18
Political support	12.9	19.4	6.3	51/52
Personal characteristics	16.1	34.5	32.7	5/3
External relationship	3.2	7.2	11.0	5/15
Technical know-how	1.6	2.9	4.3	*

[1] The first figure refers to answers given by U.S. federal managers during the Carter administration while the second refers to answers given during the Reagan administration. The data is drawn from Colin Campbell 1986: 218-19.
* Statistics not available.

be made with federal managers in the United States shows, consequently, two characteristics defining the French administrative culture: the influence of politics is rejected in favour of the institutionalist conceptions; but this institutionalist perspective is always associated with personal characteristics. By way of comparison, in the United States personal characteristics are practically ignored, while political support is systematically mentioned. As shown in Table 4, professional experience is more often mentioned by Democrat administrations, while the external relationship system is more often mentioned by Republican administrations.

Within each system, variations of historical significance often play a crucial role in the transformation of a civil service culture, according to whether the political power is strong or weak. But one has to keep in mind that this professional culture is largely the consequence of a specific acculturation process. Civil servants become civil servants not just because they have successfully passed professional competitions. Their professional culture is the result of a long-term process, during which they discovered the best possible strategic behaviours in their own professional world. It is necessary to stress the fact that this professional culture is not inherited but acquired. Second, training is a major factor of change and most Western governments have made systematic efforts to modify this professional culture. For example, the creation in 1945 of the famous *École nationale d'Administration* in France was inspired by the idea that it was necessary to train public officials in a new way intended to foster professional and functional mobility, so as to make them able to confront all the challenges of postwar modernist society. Professional specialization was then regarded as a handicap, because it was likely not only to make civil servants unaware of their external environment but also to ignore demands coming from other administrative sectors. The reform of the public service has always placed considerable emphasis on training as a means of radically changing the functioning of services. The administrative school question has been debated at length in France since a national training school for civil servants was first projected in 1846! After the Second World War, the idea that civil servants needed professional training was largely accepted.

The main point to be debated today relates to the fact that this professional culture is likely to be modified only on the periphery of the social culture. Training in public management is successful only if the new set of values does not jeopardize those social values which define the social hierarchy within public administration. Field experiments in France have demonstrated that ENA students were relatively reluctant to take managerial training as soon as they had the feeling that this training could result in technical careers in field offices outside the golden road of the *grands corps*. In many respects, managerialism reforms have clearly put an end to the mythical unity of the administrative world. A second point to stress, then, is the fact that the professional culture itself is very fragmented. This raises another question: to what extent is it possible to change only a few professional values without changing the whole cultural framework?

Some questions were intended to assess the extent to which the civil service culture is fragmented. When asked: "What are the factors that favour the most success in a civil servant's career?" the civil servants gave various answers, depending on their professional position. On the whole, the most often quoted factors of success were (percentages are cumulative): intellectual capacities (65.1%), administrative and technical knowledge (64.1%), and the membership in a prestigious administrative corps (47.3%). A second group of factors concerns variables related to individual characteristics: individual relationship network (29.7%), the support of a superior

TABLE 5
Factors of Success in a Civil Servant's Career by Administrative Spheres
(several answers possible) (%)

	Grands Corps	Ministries	Field Offices
Knowledge	59.7	47.5	72.7
Prestigious corps	38.7	61.2	42.7
"Godfather"	17.7	31.7	27.0
Political support	30.6	36.0	19.7
Intellectual capacities	71.0	59.7	66.3
Patience	12.9	12.2	22.7
Personal relationship network	30.6	24.5	32.0
Chance	25.8	28.1	23.7
Work	6.5	5.8	5.3

or a "godfather" (27.1%), and political support (25.5%). One can observe, therefore, that only a few senior civil servants spontaneously underline values associated with public management. These answers, however, are not randomly scattered but depend on each specific administrative world. Criteria for success in a career reveal important cultural differences between the various groups, indicating that all senior civil servants do not share a common work pattern. Members of the *grands corps* gave highest ranking to intellectual capacities, individual relationships, and political supports; managers working in line ministries favoured the prestige of their corps, the endorsement of a personal "godfather," and political supports. Managers in field offices put the emphasis on their professional knowledge and their ability to manage public relations at the local level. As shown in Table 5, the social hierarchy of the various administrations is here largely confirmed: on the top, members of the *grands corps*, who mention more than others an individual success linked to personal factors; then the managers in central ministries, whose professional world is obviously politicized; and finally the field office managers confronted with daily management and proud of their technical merit.

Are social origins determining factors? As managers coming from the upper classes are more numerous within the *grands corps* and as managers coming from the middle and lower classes are more numerous within field offices, it would appear logical to observe, for example,

TABLE 6
Factors of Success in a Civil Servant's Career by Social Origins
(several answers possible) (%)

	Upper classes	Middle classes	Lower classes
Knowledge	58.9	69.1	64.8
Prestigious corps	53.7	40.6	44.3
"Godfather"	25.5	28.6	28.4
Political support	24.7	26.9	25.0
Intellectual capacities	66.2	62.9	67.0
Patience	18.2	18.9	18.2
Personal relationship network	33.8	26.3	26.1
Chance	22.5	25.1	30.7
Work	5.6	4.6	18.2

that intellectual capacities are especially mentioned by managers coming from the upper classes or that patience is especially mentioned by managers coming from the middle and lower classes. Data distribution shows, on the contrary, that these two factors are mentioned equally by managers, whatever their social origin. Different answers are not connected with social origins but rather with specific sets of professional values, as shown in Table 6.

One can argue, therefore, that there is a French administrative culture, as demonstrated through the ranking of these various items. This administrative culture is built around the following basic values, listed in order of decreasing importance and regardless of the managers' social origin:

• intellectual capacities
• knowledge
• membership in a prestigious administrative corps
• personal relationship networks
• the existence of a personal "godfather"
• chance
• political supports.

This cultural scale is then modified by the institutional membership. Answers largely depend on the professional sector and the practical requirements of each job. Political supports are more particularly mentioned in ministries such as Interior (37.9%), Welfare

(35.6%), Culture (33.3%), and National Education (32.7%), where politicization has been sensitive in recent years, due to policy changes. Personal relationship networks are mentioned at the Culture Ministry (41.7%), at the National Education Ministry (34.5%) but also at the Infrastructures Ministry (33.3%) and at the Veterans Ministry (40%), where contacts with interest groups, local and professional, are of crucial importance. Membership in a prestigious administrative corps is mentioned especially at the Industry Ministry (77.3%), at the Transportation Ministry (71.4%), where major positions are occupied by managers coming from *Polytechnique*, and at the National Education Ministry (56.4%). Intellectual capacities are quoted in technical sectors such as the Labour Ministry (79.3%), the Postal Service (73.3%), and the Culture Ministry (75%). Knowledge is quoted equally at the Veterans Ministry (80%), at the Infrastructures Ministry (75.8%), at the Finance Ministry (75%), at the Welfare Ministry (73.3%), and at the Industry Ministry (72.7%). Significantly, managerial values such as professional success are mentioned in technical or business-like administrations such as the Telecom Administration (12%), the Postal Service (3.3%), and the Infrastructures Ministry (3%), while patience is mentioned in the most bureaucratic sectors such as the Veterans Ministry (53.3%) and the Agriculture Ministry (27.8%). There is no value dissension across generational lines, apart from the fact that older managers tend to stress individual merits while younger managers put the emphasis on individual relationships.

The fact that there is no common professional pattern implies that catch-all managerial tools cannot be very successful. Beyond the fact that managerialist reforms are viewed as "soft cultural revolutions," the various Western governments have to deal with a fragmented implementation of administrative reform.

THE CONNECTION BETWEEN THE CIVIL SERVICE CULTURE AND THE REFORM PROCESS

Managerialism as a Cultural Challenge

The modernization process is supposed to be based upon a cultural change within the civil service ranks and within society at large. The Thatcher and Reagan governments founded their reform efforts on the fact that it was necessary to reconcile administrative values with social ones. It was felt that business values were becoming very intense within society while public administration remained unresponsive to users' demands (Pollitt 1990), though these suppositions were far from being supported by strong scientific evidence. Nevertheless, most recent reform efforts have assumed that it is possible to change the civil service culture. This is only partially true, as there are many bureaucratic professional cultures. Interestingly enough, not all Western governments have managed the managerialist reform in the same way. In Britain, the Thatcher government tried to implement business values through the Financial Management Initiative, without paying much attention to the specific needs of the public administration (Metcalfe 1993). In Sweden, the contradiction between the overall legal legitimacy of the bureaucratic apparatus and the requirements of a new culture of organizational efficiency gave a strong impetus to privatization in order to "export" services which could not meet market competition (Pierre 1993). In France, the reform movement initiated in 1989 tried, on the contrary, to engage civil servants in a kind of pure cultural reform without changing legal or organizational rules. In all of these various cases, administrative reform was supposed to enhance professional values and to soften boundaries between the public and private sectors. The main hypothesis was, therefore, that there were no longer huge differences between civil service culture and market culture. This assumption remains to be verified, as managerial reforms cannot be implemented without the active support of the various categories of civil servants.

Cultural Changes within the Civil Service

Has civil service culture changed in recent years? The answer is partially affirmative. Surveys have indicated that civil servants and private wage earners share a common organizational culture (Bodiguel and Rouban 1991). This relative social proximity of the two sectors has fed social tensions within the public service because it affects two dimensions at the same time. While, in response to the users' needs, civil servants have to obey implicit social rules largely followed in the private sector (for example, to avoid going on strike at any moment for any purpose), civil servants have also tried to get an explicit recognition of their skills as professionals, whose activity could be negotiated with the employer (for example, through quasi-contractual arrangements within the ministries between budget offices and line offices). Such a social change does not mean that social stratification has disappeared. It means, rather, that the cultural frontier lies not between public officials and private sector wage earners but between managers and employees.

Data gathered in a national survey (Observatoire interrégional du Politique 1989) allows us to differentiate the attitudes and behaviours of these two groups. One of the major results of this study is that there is no ideological opposition between private sector wage earners and public officials as regards the respective roles of public administration and business firms. Both civil servants and private sector wage earners trust business firms (68.6% against 68.5%), and both think in equal proportions (46% against 47.7%) that these firms are in a better position than the public industrial sector to lead economic development. Of course, these results have to be modulated according to socio-professional category. The higher they are in the social hierarchy, the more people trust business firms: 44% for private sector blue-collar workers as compared to 64.6% for senior managers. But one can find the same data distribution in the public sector: 37.6% for employees as compared to 61.5% for higher civil servants.

Labour unions and political institutions are similarly criticized by both private sector and public sector workers. On average, only 16.2% of private sector wage earners trust political parties as compared to 16.9% in the public sector. In the public sector, this distrust may be seen particularly within the ranks of technicians (85.6%) and middle-level managers (79.9%). Unions also get low scores: 38.6% of public officials trust them as compared to 33.8% in the private sector. In the public sector, this distrust may be seen within the ranks of higher civil servants (59.6%), and, here again, among technicians (58.7%) and middle-level managers (56.8%).

Employees in the public sector can be distinguished from those in the private sector according to their politicization rate, their union membership, and the "global" obedience to social norms. Although figures measuring union or political membership are globally very low, one can observe slight differences. Up to 5.7% of private sector wage earners are members of a labour union as compared to 13.8% in the public sector. The contrast is particularly significant for middle and upper level categories (9% for private sector middle-level managers as compared to 19.1% in the public sector; 11.6% for private sector engineers as compared to 34.3% in the public sector; 10.1% as compared to 21.7% for senior managers). Similarly, participation in a political party is more frequent in the public sector than in the private sector: 3.9% as compared to 2.5%. There is a regular increase in political participation depending on socio-professional status. In the public sector, 11.4% of wage earners say they have a lot of interest in politics as compared to 5.9% in the private sector.

Generally, public officials seem to have more respect for social norms and institutions than do private sector wage earners. They trust the judiciary (49.6% as compared to 45.1%) and the police (71% as compared to 67.6%). But the recognition of social constraints varies appreciably according to socio-professional category, although in the opposite way: the lower the socio-professional level, the more social norms seem to be respected. The status of laws and public regulations is defended by 59.1% of public sector blue-collar workers (as compared to 57% in the private sector), against 50.3% within the ranks of senior managers (as compared to 48.5% in the private sector).

A general conclusion can easily be drawn from this survey. Public officials have a more active commitment in public life and they still have some belief in public institutions. But they share with private sector wage earners the same values concerning business firms and public administration, and they do not trust political parties or labour unions. Obviously, this cultural evolution does not indicate that public officials have converted themselves to the managerialist ideology. It only highlights the weakening of traditional normative structures (unions, the symbolism of the machinery of state) and reveals a new sensitivity to economic values at a time when high unemployment rates undermine the legitimacy of the privileged social status enjoyed by civil servants.

A second point to be made is that day-to-day work has changed. For a long time, legal knowledge and general culture constituted the basic civil service training. Paradoxically, the "technocratic" side of French society disguised social disdain for pure technical knowledge, a notable difference from the German situation. The French senior civil servant was not a pure British-style "amateur," nor an American-style "professional." By the late 1970s a clear separation had occurred between *grands corps* members, whose culture remained unchanged, and middle-level managers systematically confronted with technical predicaments in central departments as well as in field agencies. Purely technical jobs appeared in those sectors where personal contacts with users were crucial for global efficiency (e.g., hospitals, transport, telecommunications). Emphasis on technical values fostered a new quest for personal accountability but stressed also compensation inequalities between public administration and business firms as well as between various kinds of organizations within the public sector.

Our study of French public managers shows that there is a growing dissatisfaction with the career prospects and the level of compensation, since 28.5% of them say that they are ready to leave the public service. This proportion varies according to the age of the respondents. The younger they are, the more frequently they plan a future departure: 38.3% are between 41 and 50, and 59.1% are between 25 and 40. The answers vary also by sector. The biggest proportion of respondents who say they are ready to quit can be found in technical or scientific sectors (Telecommunications, Infrastructures, Industry and Finance Ministries), where private sector salaries are currently 50% to 100% higher than those offered in the civil service. This trend is far from being as important within the *grands corps*, whose members have always enjoyed a privileged situation. When asked: "Do you think that your compensation is equal to your responsibilities?" only 10.6% answered "Yes, absolutely," 32.7% answered "Yes, partially," 32.5% answered "Not really," and 22.2% answered "Not at all." Only 2% did not answer the question. The same pessimism can be observed when civil servants were asked a question about their career prospects. Only 5.4% of them answered that these prospects are "very good" while 39.5% answered that they are "good," 24.4% that they are "poor" and 7.6% that they are "very poor." While 23.2% of the sample did not answer this question, other cross-tabulations reveal that this group shares the characteristics of those respondents who answered that their career prospects are poor.

As a whole, senior executives feel strongly that their social status has suffered a severe decline in recent years. Money is not the only value at stake. Most managers are convinced that recent trends in public administration spell the end of the traditional roles of civil servants and feed a new organizational arrangement within which the politicians could be more powerful.

The Demand for and the Supply of Administrative Reform.

In France, the modernization process was driven by cultural considerations. It was supposed that the main obstacles to renewal did not come from structural dimensions of public administration but from cultural ones. In particular, the absence of good communication channels between services and the lack of precise goals were regarded as major problems. The Prime Minister's decree of 1989 described the philosophy of this reform. A high priority was given to human resource management (through training sessions, professional and geographical mobility, career path renewal), personal accountability (through systematic "administrative statements" describing targets and resources in each service), policy evaluation (through the creation of new advisory and analytical institutions), improved services to users (through communication efforts and businesslike relationships). Within these broad guidelines, each agency and bureau was free to set up experiments or long-term innovative procedures.

As for demands for further reform, a large majority of public executives are asking for more autonomy in personnel management matters: 89.8% ask for more personnel performance appraisal, 84.4% for freedom to choose their closest colleagues, and 76.6% for the right to fire incompetent colleagues. Other indicators clearly show that these civil servants, who are currently the beneficiaries of administrative culture and tradition, are looking for more drastic change that could initiate a quite different administrative model.

For instance, 75% would agree to give up the traditional category and grade pay system for a pay-for-performance system. Moreover, 70.7% think that things could be better if general legal constraints were eliminated. It seems that there is room for further steps in the direction of private sector-style management. On the other hand, other questions reveal that these executives maintain traditional values as far as their social role is concerned. This is especially true for civil servants working in purely administrative sectors (such as members of *grands corps*, managers working within the Ministry of Interior or the Ministry of Education). Institutional memory relies heavily on personal contacts (83.2% of them know their predecessor, 26.3 worked with that person), personal accountability is largely ignored (72.3% of them answer that they are accountable to 3 people at the most, and 6% are accountable to no one), and tasks are not precisely defined (for 35.5% they are not defined at all). Modernist elites may be found in scientific or technical sectors (such as the Ministry of Infrastructures, the Telecom Administration, the Postal Service) where the proportion of private sector-style managers is noticeably larger. This is easily understandable because these sectors have conceptualized their environment in business terms and are likely to use the most interesting applications of management tools.

The Impact of Administrative Reform

Has the modernization policy changed the civil service culture? It is difficult to answer this question objectively. As we have seen, the reform involved long-term transformations affecting the civil servants' culture. Of course, managerial tools imperfectly met their demands for more professional autonomy. Nevertheless, one can observe significant changes at work. For instance, hierarchical relationships have been eased and communications have been dramatically intensified between services (through the channel of internal newspapers, meetings, and training sessions). Relationships between services have been improved and service to users was made the centrepiece of business-like activities. Through the modernization process, civil servants discovered that they could work together in a more cooperative manner without changing the legal rules.

All these positive aspects of recent reforms cannot hide the fact that a main contradiction lies at the heart of the managerialist effort at reform. As this reform movement is supposed to improve professional autonomy, management rules imply that the civil servants are regarded as tools in the hands of politicians. Managerialist culture implies that managers have to be accountable, which means they can no longer enjoy the traditional autonomy of the administrative sphere. Politics and administration have been separated but hierarchical lines between the two worlds have been reinforced. It is crystal clear that managerialist reforms in most Western countries have been backed by a strong politicization of the civil service.

We are now facing two main hypotheses. In one case, the reform movement would be simply a necessity in order to safeguard the traditional privileges of the core administrative power. In many respects, one could say that this is the case in France. Data clearly show that managerial values are shared especially at the periphery of the administrative system. Managers in field offices ask for more managerialism because they lack sufficient social power to get higher positions, while members of the *grands corps* seem to be largely sceptical. The enhancement of professional values is regarded as a reward to compensate for poor social status. As shown in Table 7, members of the *grands corps* got low marks on a scale of 7 variables with regard to acceptance of managerial values (such as individual performance assessment, contractual relationship between administrative units, and so on).

A first assessment of the British managerial reform draws exactly the same conclusion: as policy advisers, senior civil servants in ministries were not very concerned with the reform. As long as their social role remained untouched, they did not worry about the setting up of executive agencies whose managers came from business circles (Hood 1994).

A second hypothesis is that the managerialist reform process is an attempt to eliminate administrative specificity. Public administration would disappear in the long run. The ongoing reform would be a political reform aimed at a new style of governance. Public functions would still be performed, but they would no longer imply any political process. Political demands would be directly addressed to the politicians, and even normative action

TABLE 7
Attitudes towards the modernization process (%)

	Very favourable	Mixed feelings	Negative
Field offices' managers	47.9	35.8	16.3
Ministries' managers	34.5	37.4	28.1
Members of grands corps	10.0	43.3	46.7

would be delegated to private business entities. But if these private services really have to observe the same set of rules that confront civil servants daily, the economic success of this formula would certainly be difficult to assess.

CONCLUSION

Civil service culture is not independent from national organizational structures. Professional values depend closely on the nature of the job and the strategic position within ministerial circles. They can therefore evolve and can be improved with training. However, the transformation of these values cannot be so great as to modify the global conception that civil servants have of the relationship between public administration and political spheres, or the ranking of social values which determine their professional success. One cannot change civil servants' social values through administrative reform. Such a change requires extra-professional resources that only senior managers can enjoy. For instance, it is clear that senior civil servants support personal performance appraisal systems much more than clerical employees do. A recent study of Canadian deputy ministers clearly shows that the new performance appraisal system was largely accepted because it encourages the sharing of professional values and a corporate culture (Bourgault, Dion, and Lemay 1993). The legitimacy of the various managerial tools is not the same along the hierarchical line. Like any other administrative reform, managerialism affects the channels of authority, giving more weight to formal procedures through productivity criteria and users' satisfaction assessment ratios. This implies that the very cultural dimension of managerialism cannot be handled in the same way by the various kinds of civil servants. Business management is largely acceptable to senior civil servants as long as they can control the reform process and escape the formalistic dimension of the reform. As soon as these senior civil servants feel that they could be victimized, the reform will end. (Significantly enough, the new Canadian deputy ministers' appraisal system is based on peer review.) Employees do not respond in the same way. For them, the managerial reform is a direct threat to their bureaucratic security and they know very well that inertia is their best weapon to oppose the reform, since formal procedures can be overformalized to the point that they are rendered useless. They look for minimum quality standards and adjust their professional duties to these new guidelines. Any additional professional requirement would mean more public expenditures in order to reward the best performances, and this is precisely what the reform is supposed to avoid. Finally, the managerialist reform process has changed the strategic game. In the traditional bureaucratic system, there is no extra-legal quality measurement and careers respond only to seniority and individual resources. People coming from the upper classes chose the civil service as a career because they could find there a social power that was unattainable in business firms. People coming from middle or lower classes looked for good salaries as compared to those offered on the market, and for upward social mobility. With the managerialist reforms, employees now have a new interest in carefully respecting the minimum professional requirements, but they just look for job security, while senior civil servants are motivated to quit when they have outstanding professional achievements.

Administrative reform is therefore confronted with a paradox: if the government does not change the career rules for all civil servants, the reform will have little impact and the door will be open for more fragmentation. But the very existence of various subcultures within public administration prevents a global change. Administrative reform which is tailor-made for high-level executives cannot be expected to fit well for middle-level or front-line bureaucrats.

It seems that a total disappearance of the social specificity of the civil service would be fruitless, if not dangerous. When civil servants act (and are regarded) like private employees, there is room for more politicization, which is to say that political systems are not entirely built upon technical or managerial considerations. They also need a sphere where equity as well as other ethical values are in practice confronted with economic requirements. This is a functional necessity that no political system can escape. If civil servants are transformed into private sector employees, this need is no longer satisfied within public administration but elsewhere, in political or private spheres. In many respects, the victory of managerialism could mean that political power is privatized and that private interests control any political debate. Managerialism fosters a transfer of political stakes outside public administration. As a matter of fact, apparent bureaucratic inefficiency could be the price to be paid so that democratic values can be expressed in a public space. The perfect rationalistic public administration is just a fantasy. At the end of the decision-making process or at the top of the public sphere, there is no final equation: there is only the mutual adjustment of competing values. The very existence of a core civil service culture is evidence that democracies do not work as machines do. The blended mixture between professional inherited values and technical skills is necessary to give some degree of freedom to the political system.

NOTES

1 These results are drawn from a CSA/La Vie poll survey, "Les français et les services publics," 5 October, 1987, and a CSA/Le Parisien/FGAF, "Les français et les fonctionnaires," 29 April, 1987. The poll is based upon a national sample of 1,000 persons (quota method).

BIBLIOGRAPHY

Aberbach, Joel D., Robert D. Putnam, and Bert A. Rockman. 1981. *Bureaucrats and Politicians in Western Democracies*. Cambridge, MA: Harvard University Press.

Bodiguel, Jean-Luc, and Luc Rouban. 1991. *Le fonctionnaire détrôné?* Paris: Presses de la Fondation Nationale des Sciences Politiques.

Bourgault, Jacques, Stéphane Dion, and Marc Lemay. 1993. Creating corporate culture: lessons from the Canadian federal government. *Public Administration Review* 53, 1:73-80.

Brown, Angela, and Aaron Wildavsky. 1987. What should evaluation mean to implementation? In *The Politics of Program Evaluation*, ed. D.J. Palumbo, 157-72. Beverly Hills, CA: Sage.

Campbell, Colin. 1986. *Managing the Presidency*, 218-19. Pittsburgh: University of Pittsburgh Press.

Crozier, Michel. 1963. *Le phénomène bureaucratique*. Paris: Seuil.

Dalton, Russell J., and Manfred Kuechler, eds. 1990. *Challenging the Political Order*. Oxford: Polity Press.

Hood, Christopher. 1994. Public management changes in Great Britain and the goal of 'deprivileging' the civil service. *Revue Française d'Administration Publique* 70:295-308.

Levine, Charles, B. Guy Peters, and Frank J. Thompson. 1990. *Public Administration, Challenges, Choices, Consequences*. Glenview IL: Little Brown.

Mazey, Sonia, and Jeremy Richardson, eds. 1993. *Lobbying in the European Community*. Oxford: Oxford University Press.

Metcalfe, Les. 1993. Conviction politics and dynamic conservatism: Mrs. Thatcher's managerial revolution. *International Political Science Review* 14, 4:351-73.

Observatoire Interrégional du Politique. 1989. *Public Opinion Annual Survey*. Paris: Fondation Nationale des Sciences Politiques.

Perrineau, Pascal, ed. 1993. *L'engagement politique - Crise ou mutation?* Paris: Presses de la Fondation Nationale des Sciences Politiques.

Pierre, Jon. 1993. Legitimacy, institutional change, and the politics of public administration in Sweden. *International Political Science Review* 14, 4:374-87.

Pollitt, Christopher. 1990. *Managerialism in the Public Service*. Oxford: Basil Blackwell.

Rouban, Luc. 1994a. *Les cadres supérieurs de la fonction publique et la politique de modernisation administrative*. Paris: La Documentation Française.

_____ 1994b. *Le pouvoir anonyme, les mutations de l'État à la française*. Paris: Presses de la Fondation Nationale des Sciences Politiques.

Weber, Max. 1959. *Le savant et le politique*. Paris: UGE.

The Marketization of the State: Citizens, Consumers, and the Emergence of the Public Market

JON PIERRE

INTRODUCTION[1]

The days when it made sense to perceive politics and markets as separate spheres of society and as different systems of resource allocation appear to be gone forever. Neither politics nor markets exist in their ideal forms in current capitalist democracies. Instead, it makes more sense to speak of different mixes in politics and different "patterns of subordination" between the two spheres of society (Offe 1984:38-45). Thus, following a period of political intervention in different markets, market-driven theories are today penetrating the public sector of the Western democracies.

Some might find this to be a counter-intuitive or paradoxical statement. Many would probably argue just the opposite: that the past decade has seen politics and markets being increasingly separated. Indeed, a key feature of the fairly rapid process of "rolling back the state," including extensive market deregulation, privatization, and the introduction of customer-driven models of public service delivery (Daneke and Lemark 1985) has been a weakened political presence in the market. However, if we look at these developments in a longer perspective it becomes obvious that what is happening is the third step in a long-term process of shifting balances between politics and markets.

The first phase – comprising the immediate postwar period in most developed capitalist democracies – saw politics increasing its

55

influence over the economic arena. With substantial national variation, the overarching policy objective was to allow the public sector to gain some control over the growth generated in the private
sector and to use this growth to sustain the politics of redistribution and public services. In the second phase – from the late 1970s
up until the late 1980s – some of this public control was reduced
or abolished. This was partly because the growth in private markets was decreasing and partly because of a shift in the political
regimes in most of these countries.

In the third and current phase, politics and markets seem to be
converging again, only this time because economic theory and a
general market-based philosophy are penetrating areas that used
to be reserved for political control. Again, there appears to be a
significant shift in the political regimes towards a "marketization
of the state," namely, to employ market criteria for allocating
public resources and also to measure the efficiency of public service producers and suppliers according to market criteria. Additionally, the "marketization of the state" is strongly sustained by –
indeed, perhaps even a part of – what is normally referred to as the
"new public management," which is shorthand for business-style,
result-oriented, public sector management (Hood 1990). Finally, the
"marketization of the state" includes allowance for individuals to
choose in a market-like fashion between different service suppliers.

In most countries, the public administration and the public service
have become the main turf for this tug-of-war between the political
sector and the market (Hood 1990; Maier 1987; Schwartz 1994). An
important consequence of the administrative reforms that have swept
across the Western world during the past years has been the changing nature of state-society interaction and exchange. Reforms such as
privatization or "contracting out" of public services, the introduction
of private sector- type management strategies and objectives into the
public sector, the allowance for private involvement in the delivery of
public services, and the perception of the recipients of such services
as "customers" have contributed to this change in the relationship
between the public and the private sectors.

More specifically, most of these reforms have aimed at facilitating
the powerful entrance of a market-based ideology into the sphere of

public administration. This ideology – a set of political beliefs and objectives – is derived from and capitalizes on two different trends. One is the general move away from collective or public solutions to the societal problems facing most governments, for example social welfare, care of children and the elderly, and medical care. The other major trend is the fiscal crisis facing almost all advanced capitalist democracies. The current predominant ideology in most of these countries occurs at the nexus of these two trends and legitimizes extensive cutback programs in public services and the emergence of private suppliers of many of these services.

This ideology has not only changed state-society relations; it has also questioned existing criteria for public sector efficiency, urged that private providers of public services become legitimate actors on the "public market" – a concept which will be discussed later in this chapter – and introduced new models for public sector management. In short, the public sectors in most countries in Western Europe and North America appear to be gradually transforming from Weberian organizational structures into private sector-modelled organizations.

Needless to say, there are many different aspects of this development: organizational, economic, political, etc. This chapter is mainly concerned with one of those aspects, namely the transformation of the concept of the citizen into that of the customer and the consequences of this change. The discussion in this chapter will show that in some ways this reconceptualization of citizenship is unfortunate, because many of the qualities associated with citizenship are critical to the relationship between the individual and the polity at large. Also, the introduction of the concept of the customer opens up the possibility of inequalities between individuals, which essentially run counter to the equal and universalistic entitlements and obligations associated with citizenship.

Furthermore, we will see that, although much of this change in perspective appears to be rhetorical rather than a reflection of actual changes in public administration and public management techniques, conceiving of citizens as customers does indicate an important change in the state's perception of the individual. The key problem, it seems, is that while perceiving citizens as customers may indirectly serve important purposes (increasing public sector efficiency and responsiveness towards individual choice and preferences), this reconceptualization distorts a delicate and sensitive system of mutual entitlements and obligations between the state and the individual (King 1987). Given the increasing volatility of people across regions and borders, it appears – perhaps somewhat paradoxically – that what is needed is not so much customer-based models of public service as a reaffirmation of the legal, social, and political dimensions of citizenship. To be sure, the juxtaposition of "citizens" and "customers" is unfortunate, because it neglects the material aspects of citizenship. Citizenship, as we will argue below, denotes a system of entitlements that are complementary, not contradictory, to those related to the concept of the customer.

The 1980s and early 1990s witnessed policy makers in a large number of countries paying increasing attention to the concept of citizenship. More specifically, following the growth of the public sector of most countries in Western Europe during the postwar period, there seems to have developed a growing need to delineate the rights of citizens in relationship to the state. Thus, in July 1991 Britain adopted the "Citizen's Charter," a document describing the obligations of state institutions vis-à-vis the citizens (Lovell 1992). This "Charter" has been adapted and specified with regard to different service sectors and policy areas. Similarly, in 1982, Canada adopted the "Charter of Rights and Freedoms," outlining citizens' rights in a fashion similar to that of the "Citizen's Charter."[2] Similar "Charters" have been published in France and Belgium (Bouckaert 1993). In Sweden, the final steps towards codifying human rights in the Constitution were taken in 1979. More recently, the idea of adopting a manifesto similar to the "Citizen's Charter" seems to have gained support, not least among the political elite. The idea of creating a "welfare contract" was recently put forward by the Liberal Party leader, also the Secretary of Social Affairs (Westerberg and Nordh 1993:53-7). There are several other examples of a political reassertion of citizenship.

This new debate about the political nature of citizenship is placed right at the centre of the state-society discourse. Following a long period of growing influence of the state over civil society, much of the debate during the past few years has revolved around the problem of how to reaffirm the political rights of citizens in their exchange with the state. As we will argue later in this chapter, if the debate on these issues during the 1980s aimed at clarifying – indeed often also codifying – the significance of citizenship, the 1990s have seen this debate take one more step in this direction. The current debate appears to be concerned mainly with other means of empowering citizens in their relationship to the state. By perceiving citizens as customers, it is argued, individual persons are given the right to choose between different public services, or between public and private services. Converting citizens into customers means placing purchasing power in their hands and creating a "public market" in which this purchasing power can be unleashed, as a choice between different (types of) suppliers of public services.

CITIZENS, CUSTOMERS, AND THE STATE: CLEARING THE JUNGLE

There appear to be several contributing reasons for the recent reaffirmation of citizenship, some of which are only remotely associated with the political dimensions of social membership and state-individual relationships. Turner (1993) advances two different hypotheses regarding this development. According to the first hypothesis, it is the ongoing globalization that "raises problems about the relationship between the individual and macro societal structures" (Turner 1993:1-2). The second – and probably less important – of Turner's hypotheses states that citizenship has become an important issue because of recent advances in modern medicine. Given the rapid development of transplant surgery and the many ethical issues associated therewith, citizenship has come to address the increasingly salient questions about "the relationship between the human body and social membership" (Turner 1993:2).

For Turner, a sociologist, it is natural to look primarily at these two aspects of citizenship in modern society; indeed, he explicitly argues that he wants to avoid the "opposition between the two notions of civil society and citizenship" (Turner 1993:4). For most (non-Marxist) sociologists, a key problem associated with citizenship is how political democracy can be accommodated and sustained within a capitalist economic system. For these theorists – the most prominent being Marshall (1977, 1981) – the welfare state became the answer to their question. Welfare states ensure redistribution of the wealth generated by the capitalist system. They both spread the fruits of growth to all socio-economic groups and bring the potentially alienated social groups into the community (cf. Turner 1986).

For most political scientists, however, the relationship between the three concepts and notions of citizenship, state, and civil society is a more familiar and comfortable point of departure for analyses of citizenship (cf. King 1987). In particular, such a perspective helps us highlight the political dimension of citizenship. Therefore, this approach should help us generate theories of why the debate on citizenship emerged so rapidly in the mid- to late 1980s. First, we could assume that this process reflects the changes in the political regimes and the *Zeitgeist* of the late 1980s and early 1990s, compared to that of the 1960s and 1970s. In most of Western Europe, the early post-war period saw the public sector expanding, taxes being raised, and political control over various sectors of civil society being strengthened. However, as we mentioned in the introduction to this chapter, politics and markets appear so far to be just as intertwined in the 1990s as they were in the 1960s and 1970s, but with the important difference that this time it is the market philosophy dominating politics, not the other way around as was previously the case. Along with the "rolling back of the state," there evolved a "vacuum" with regard to the rights of individuals; as the material elements of citizenship were abolished or transformed into services provided under private auspices, citizenship had to be redefined and reaffirmed. Moreover, since such a reaffirmation of the individual in relationship to the state was at the heart of the individualistic culture that characterized the 1980s, there were a number of different political forces pulling in the same direction.

Secondly – and complementary to the first hypothesis – we can assume that the globalization which Turner discusses has a special dimension pertaining to the discussion about the rights and duties of individuals and the state. The past few years have witnessed a dramatic increase in immigration and migration, compared to only a decade or so earlier. Some of this volatility of individuals and social groups is triggered by the rapid trans-nationalization of corporate organizations, or by the economic integration as we see it happening within the EC and to some extent also NAFTA. Moreover, most of this migration is caused by political and military conflict forcing tens of thousands of people to abandon their habitats to seek shelter in other countries. However, for both the corporate employee working "abroad" – a concept directly related to that of citizenship and now becoming just as hard to define – and the political refugee, citizenship becomes an important question. If citizenship denotes social identity and membership in a community, then we are talking about something much more significant than merely the colour of a passport. Individuals living in a country without being a citizen of it are deprived most seriously of their political capabilities and their rights vis-à-vis the state.

These issues and problems have been exacerbated by the fact that political refugees are often seeking asylum on a collective basis. If granted such status, they will maintain a strong social community but they will also remain deprived of the social connections to the society of which they have yet to become an integrated part. In many countries in Western Europe and even more so in the United States, this transnational volatility of social and ethnic groups seems to be a growing problem, mainly because of the tremendous challenge it poses in terms of assimilation and accommodation in the new country. Citizenship, according to the ancient Greek definition of the concept, was essentially a political codification of social membership in a society characterized by a minimum of social differentiation (Walsh 1989:213). Current citizenship, on the other hand, reflects the increasing social and ethnic heterogeneity of most countries and thus tends to play different political and administrative roles, and, most importantly, different social roles.

Most definitions of citizenship tend to stress the inclusion of individuals in a social community and the entitlements and responsibilities associated with this membership; see for example, the definitions suggested by Turner, Ranson and Stewart, and Walzer:

Citizenship may be defined as that set of practices (juridical, political, economic and cultural) which define a person as a competent member of society, and which as a consequence shape the flow of resources to persons and social groups (Turner 1993:2).

The citizen is both an individual and a member of the collectivity. Indeed, citizen has to be understood as "individual as a member of" the public as a political community (Ranson and Stewart 1989:11).

A citizen is, most simply, a member of a political community, entitled to whatever prerogatives and encumbered with whatever responsibilities are attached to membership (Walzer 1989:211).

In an analysis of the differences between citizen- and customer-driven models of public service delivery, a key dimension of citizenship is the material entitlements that are associated with it. Here, we need to take on board and briefly address the distinction between the individual good on the one hand and the general good – or what the Americans would call "the public interest" – on the other. According to American political philosophy, the "public interest" comprises the sum of individual goods. As Meicklejohn (1965) argues, citizenship does not indicate the right of the general good to take precedence over individual preferences. Indeed, there does not exist any conflict between the individual good and the public interest (Meicklejohn, 1965:81). Meicklejohn conceives of the general good – or the public interest – as

not another different interest superimposed upon our individual desires and intentions. It is compounded out of them. It includes nothing which is not included by them. The common purpose is made up of the separate purposes of the citizens (Meicklejohn 1965:81).

In this model of citizenship and the state, it becomes the task of government – the sum of individuals in the body politic – to reconcile the tensions between the individual preferences of individuals and to promote the general or common good (Meicklejohn 1965:80):

On the one hand, each of us, as a citizen, has a part to play in the governing of the nation. In that capacity, we think and speak and plan and act for the general good. On the other hand, each of us, as an individual or as a member of some private group, is rightly pursuing his own advantage, is seeking his own welfare . . . Our constitutional agreement is that each man's individual possessions and activities shall be subject to regulation by laws which he is bound to obey. His private rights, including the right of "private" speech, are liable to such abridgements as the general welfare may require.

Thus, in Meicklejohn's political philosophy, government and its regulations of individual behaviour are justified to the extent that they are based on the consent of the people and to the extent that they promote the public interest.

The Western European political philosophy tends to look at the relationship between individual and general interests in a slightly different way. Here, citizenship has a more extensive material connotation than in the United States. The notion of "social citizenship" (Esping-Andersen 1985; King 1987) refers to citizenship as comprising both the constitutional and membership aspects typical of the American debate on this topic, as well as a codified system of material rights, like freedom from poverty. Next to this, "social citizenship" also includes entitlements in the form of benefits from the many welfare state programs. What makes "social citizenship" an important concept in these countries is the comprehensive and nonselective nature of extensive welfare state provisions.

An important consequence of these differences in the definition of citizenship is that introducing customer-driven models of public services will mean different things and have different effects and outcomes in different national contexts. In individualistic political cultures, with limited welfare state service programs, the impact will probably be less significant than in more collectivistic cultures, where there are extensive and universal welfare state programs.

A plausible cause of the recent overt reaffirmation of citizenship – in addition to the vacuum created by the "rolling back of the state" and the globalization discussed earlier – is that these measures are introduced as compensation for the substantial reductions of social citizenship. In countries where citizenship has had a significant material component, which has been dismantled by cutback programs, "Charters" and other means of strengthening citizenship may help redefine the relationship between the state and the individual.

FROM CITIZENS TO CUSTOMERS

From this brief discussion on the nature of citizenship as a form of codified social membership and a system of entitlements and obligations between the individual and the state, we can now take a closer look at how citizenship relates to the concept of the customer. Table 1 presents some of the basic differences between citizens and customers in relationship to the state.

The common denominator between citizenship and the customer-based model is that both outline a model of exchange of goods and resources between the individual and the state. What essentially differs between the two models is the source of the individual's entitlements; citizenship in its traditional form can be described as an immaterial relationship between the individual and the state. In some countries, this relationship has also been given a material dimension, as we saw earlier.[3] Customers, on the other hand, derive their entitlements from purchasing power, some of which may be transferred from the state, some of which may come from other sources. Thus, while citizenship denotes a constitutional model of equal individuals' relationship to a government made up of the collectivity of these individuals, customer-based models draw on market behaviour, which by definition is anonymous, unequal, and individualistic.[4]

As Table 1 suggests, there is a consistent difference between the citizenship and customer models. The former model aims at incorporating the individual into society. A citizen differs from an individual primarily with regard to a formal membership in a larger social group, a community. Citizenship brings with it political capabilities that individuals do not enjoy. Thus, citizenship could be referred to as *political empowerment.* The customer model, on the other hand, appears to disperse and weaken this collectivity. It

TABLE 1

Citizen- and customer-driven models of public-private relationships and service delivery

Dimensions	Citizens	Customers
Source of individual resources	Legal rights	Purchasing power
Types of entitlements	Universal	Selective
Types of responsibilities	Civic, political	None
Base for social membership	Collective	Individual
State-individual relationship	Inclusion	Exclusion
State-individual communication	Verbal ('voice')	Non-verbal ('exit')
Policy objective	Social welfare	Individual empowerment
Public administration management objectives	Legal security, efficiency	Customer satisfaction, market-like resource allocation

strongly emphasizes individualism and a state-individual relationship where the customer has only certain rights but few or no obligations. The model is focused on *"economic empowerment"*; it transfers resources from the public sector to the individual to be used to purchase services according to the customers' preferences. Some, and mainly neoliberal thinkers, tend to believe that economic empowerment is equal to political empowerment, because it gives the individual the right to choose in market-like fashion between different public services, or between public and private service providers. However, the important point here is that political empowerment relates to the political dimensions of citizenship, with all that entails of universalism. Economic empowerment, on the other hand, essentially refers to strengthening the position of a customer in a market. As we have seen above, this is a much more selective and individualistic measure than political empowerment.

The idea of perceiving citizens as customers is assumed to play different roles within the public service provider on the one hand, and in the exchange between the organization and its external environment on the other (Lovell 1992). Inside the service-producing organization, customer-driven models are supposed to boost efficiency as well as a service-minded approach and management style (Osborne and Gaebler 1993; DiIulio et al. 1993). However, the most important differences refer to various relationships between the service provider and its environment.

One obvious purpose of this strategy is to strengthen the legitimacy of the public sector and the services it delivers.[5] The predominant *Zeitgeist* of the 1980s and 1990s has been derived so far from market strategies, behaviour, and conceptualizations. In this ideology, the public sector has been portrayed as a rigid, expensive, and self-sufficient set of structures, more or less indifferent to what citizens think about the services they are delivering. Instead of being responsive to the recipients of these services, public institutions are responsible and responsive only to the preferences and ideals espoused by policy makers and elected officials; this is the essence of the market-based criticism of the public sector. Interestingly, much of the modern theory of public administration seems to agree with this criticism. For many scholars, the traditional service-providing role of modern public administration is believed to be obstructed both by elected officials, who place inconsistent and contradictory demands on the bureaucracy, and also by special interest groups who penetrate the civil service (Moe 1989; Peters 1987; Rockman 1992). In both cases, the civil service becomes a vehicle to promote the interests of small segments of society, not the public *tout court*.

Much of the indifference of the public bureaucracy vis-à-vis citizens, according to the critics, stems from the fact that, short of moving, the clients of the bureaucracy have no place else to go to in order to receive special types of services (Osborne and Gaebler 1993:167). Moreover, since most of the financial resources given to agencies is not directly related to the quality of the services it is delivering, there is little incentive to "try harder." Thus, public service providers do not have a financial incentive to try to cater to their clients in a market-like fashion; nor does the intraorganizational career take the service attitudes of employees into consideration.

Following a comparison between a fairly stereotypical description of public bureaucracy on the one hand and a commercial service sector business operation on the other, Osborne and Gaebler (1993:166-9) arrive at a couple of recommendations that serve to make public institutions more customer-responsive. The basic idea is to move financial resources from these institutions to those receiving the services, thus allowing the latter to choose between different services and service providers. This system creates what we call a "public market," that is, a competitive arena within which public and/or private service providers compete for customers of various services. Competition, in turn, is believed to be the best way of increasing efficiency and a public bureaucracy delivering services more in tune with what the citizens or customers demand.

However, the "marketization of the state" also means the depoliticization of the state. While the traditional system of public services produced goods designed and redesigned through a communication channel from citizens via policy makers to the bureaucracy, the customer-driven model aims at opening up a channel directly from the citizens/customers to the providers of the public services. Following Montin (1995), this model can be described as "democracy without politics"; in theory at least, it enables citizens/customers to send signals to service suppliers without having to go through traditional political channels and through elected officials who, in turn, are supposed to try and encourage the service provider to improve its performance (cf. Osborne and Gaebler 1993:180-6).

Let us now look more closely at the "public market" and how it compares with more traditional systems of public service delivery.

THE "PUBLIC MARKET"

In order to understand the implications of transforming citizens into customers we must look briefly at the market in which these customers are supposed to engage in market choice and also at the nature of the goods exchanged there. Without deliberately adding to the conceptual confusion associated with many of the issues addressed in this chapter, we would like to advance the concept of the "public market." The "public market" refers to processes of resource allocation between the public and private sectors of society, with special regard to services delivered under some form of public auspices, for example, regulatory, administrative, or financial control (Daneke and Lemak 1985; Lundqvist 1988; Saltman and von Otter 1992). The "public market" sees citizens choosing between different public providers of different services, or between public and private providers of similar types of services. However, as we will see below, although the proponents of the "marketization of the state" normally depart from a public-choice model of public services, the "public market" displays a couple of important features that question its allocative efficiency.

The "Public Market": Exchange Processes

The "public market" differs from other types of markets in three important respects. First, it is not a market in the traditional sense, because entrance to the market for providers (or suppliers) is restricted by legislation or other public rules. However, the "public market" is not a monopolistic market in the traditional meaning of that concept, because the scarcity of suppliers is not the result of market competition but rather of public regulation. Given this predominant role of public actors and rules, creating a very special type of market, it is difficult to assess the competitiveness of public and private suppliers. On the one hand, we would expect the "public market" to give public suppliers a competitive edge over private suppliers, because they are closely associated with those institutions that define the basic parameters of the market, parameters such as the number of suppliers, costs, types of commodities, customer purchasing power, etc. On the other hand, since the purpose of creating "public markets" is to bring the market as a mechanism for allocation into the public sector, we would predict that private participants will turn out to be more competitive than public ones.

Secondly, the "public market" differs from other types of market with respect to demand structures, price mechanisms and the determinants of purchasing power. In this type of market, purchasing power is not primarily derived from individual financial resources but rather from public entitlements of rights to individuals. Most of the resources available to the customers have been transferred from the state to the individual to be used to acquire public services, or similar types of services delivered by private suppliers. This transfer of resources from state to individual occurs through an administrative procedure and according to some political norm or standard of allocation. With regard to prices, these will only indirectly reflect actual costs. More importantly, since purchasing power is based on vouchers or cheques, price becomes largely irrelevant as a competitive edge for the suppliers. Thus, in the "public market," public and private suppliers compete on supposedly similar terms with similar or identical products. However, the very basic element of classic market theory – that price is the outcome of the relationship between demand and supply – is not the case in the "public market." Indeed, in this type of market price, demand, and supply are only remotely related. Generally speaking, the "public market" is characterized by strong political control. This control, however, differs in an important way from political control in traditional markets. As Saltman and von Otter (1992:18) argue in their analysis of "planned markets," "the state designs the market before it appears rather than attempting to restrain it after it has run out of control."

The "Public Market": Goods and Commodities

The provision of collective goods can never be a perfectly rational process, at least not according to the economists' definition of rationality. There are two main reasons for this. First, collective goods can be thought of as utilities that individuals or social groups utilize at more or less irregular intervals, but when utilized the services should be of high quality. We do not request the service of the fire brigade, schools, or health services on a very regular basis, but when we do we expect them to deliver efficient, top-quality services. Along with the political dimension about who should carry the financial burden of these services, economic logic tells us that organizing such services as collective goods is similar to the private insurance system, where you make financial contributions to the system regardless of whether or not you use the services in question. Thus, quite apart from any political notion of what should, normatively speaking, be collective and what should remain individual, there is also a clear economic rationale for having the production of some goods organized collectively.

Secondly, collective goods can be thought of as utilities where there exist significant potential economies of scale that cannot be exploited at an individual level. We cannot have individual fire brigades, schools, or health care systems simply because of the overwhelming costs that would be entailed for each individual or household. However, since there is a substantial economy of scale present here, and also because these services are critical to society as a whole and not just individual citizens, both political and economic logic tells us that they should be organized collectively. Conceived of in this perspective, the process of delivering collective goods or services is likely to have some indigenous inefficiencies. The issue here is not so much whether or not there exist such inefficiencies but rather whether these inefficiencies are bigger than the costs of alternative systems of public service production and delivery.

Thirdly, the "public market" differs from other markets with regard to the type of commodities it allocates. The "public market" allocates services and goods that are nominally public, that is to say, they have at some previous time been delivered by public organizations but have now become subjected to competition and can thus be delivered by either public or private suppliers. Introducing private suppliers of public goods can also introduce different problems. One such problem is that privatized utilities tend to remain perceived as public as long as they deliver public goods. Citizens might look at a particular type of service and perceive it as "public," regardless of whether a private or public organization is delivering the service.

This problem is in part related to the difficulties in dividing public goods into private, individual, and commodified goods. As Ranson and Stewart (1989:7) argue, "public goods . . . are collective goods. Provided for one, they are necessarily provided for all." Furthermore, Pascal (1986:43) notes that commodifying public goods like fire protection and police is not a very good idea, even from an economic point of view: "If public goods are to be provided at all, they must be supported by the general resources of the community – local taxes and intergovernmental grants." This suggests that the commodification of public goods violates a basic property of such goods, namely their collective and universal nature. Although not all public goods are collective goods by definition in the economist's sense, the key distinction here is between public and private goods, and as has been shown here this distinction is far more difficult and complex than might be assumed.

Finally, competition between different public utilities in the "public market" does not reflect the type of competition other markets display. Different public utilities may require very different capabilities to enter such competition. Schools in socially distressed areas, to give an example, often lack the resources necessary to become successful in the competition for students. Moreover, even if they were able to generate the funds necessary to be able to deliver top-quality services, their competitiveness would still be reduced by their location.

To sum up, the concept of the "public market" is employed here to indicate the commodification of public services, new forms of the production and distribution of public goods and services, and the notion of the beneficiaries of such services as "customers" rather than citizens. It goes without saying that many of the recent changes in public administration, as discussed earlier, seem to aim at replacing the traditional exchange between the individual and the state, based on needs, obligations, and entitlements, with a market-like exchange process. In this exchange process, service providers under different auspices are assumed to be in competition with each other. Customers choose in a rational fashion between different services and different service providers, thus sending signals regarding the quality of different services.

The "marketization of the state" and the services it delivers raise a number of significant problems. One set of problems is political-democratic. The emergence of the "public market" means that the system of accountability is shifted from that which involves elected officials, political parties, and political institutions to accountability measured primarily in terms of customer satisfaction. However, unlike the relationship between citizens and the state, which is based on equality and universal rights and duties, the market relationship is based on – or at least generates – inequalities determined by purchasing power, knowledge, information, and so on. The point here is that the "customerization" of citizens introduces the notion of selective public services as utilities not distributed equally to all. This is clearly in conflict with the traditional meaning of citizenship.

Another political problem associated with the "public market" is its nonverbal and nonpersonal nature. Since politics and markets – conceived of as different systems of resource allocation – differ in most significant respects, so do market behaviour and political behaviour. Thus, after discussing the basic differences between economics and politics, Hirschman (1970:15) concludes that "exit belongs to the former realm, voice to the latter." Since citizens are essentially political creatures and customers are economic creatures, redefining citizens as customers will deprive citizens of their right to use "voice." Thus, direct communication – or at least communication in some form – is the typical instrument in the political arena. Conversely, exiting or entering arenas typifies market behaviour.

How does this relate to the "public market"? Since customer behaviour in the "public market" is characterized primarily by choosing between different suppliers and not between whether or not to consume in the first place, exit – the established way for customers to communicate with suppliers, according to Hirschman – does not appear to be a very viable option in most cases. Given the types of goods allocated in the "public market," this observation raises questions about the efficiency of the "public market" and also about the inequalities it can create or reinforce. As Lipsky (1980) observes, in most core welfare policy areas, clients cannot exit without incurring financial or other losses. To be sure, if the general purpose of exiting is to find better products or to "send a signal" to the supplier that their commodities are of inferior quality compared to those of their competitors, then – given the oligopolistic and regulated nature of the "public market" – exit in the "public market" will probably inflict more damage on the customer than on the provider.

Thus, slightly ironically, the claim of the "public market" advocates that it will facilitate two-way communication between service providers and service recipients is in fact inconsistent with the very logic of the market. In fact, introducing the concept of the (public) market in the context of public services may mean that an established channel of communication between the public and the private sectors – the democratic process – is largely abolished and replaced by the silent communication typical of markets.

Another set of problems may be found at the organizational level. Public organizations, it must be remembered, were never designed to engage in market competition but rather to guarantee legal security and administrative efficiency (Chandler 1988). Although these public organizations have now been subjected to the major challenge that characterizes market competition, these basic objectives remain as salient as before. Thus, these organizations find themselves having to make decisions about what aspect – efficiency or legal security – to compromise. It is not very surprising, therefore, to see that organizational development and change have been key components in the administrative reform of most Western countries during the past few years (Aucoin 1990).

A third group of problems relates to public sector management, control, and systems of resource allocation. According to the logic of the "public market," it is the recipients of the public services, through their choices, who allocate goods and resources, not the providers of these services. This is accomplished primarily by the use of cheques or vouchers for specific services. By distributing such cheques and vouchers to individuals, the state puts purchasing power in the hands of the "customers" and enables them to choose between services provided by different suppliers. Indeed, a key purpose – as advanced by the advocates of the serve-the-customer model – is that it will give public service providers information about how their services or the "product" are evaluated at the receiving end. The empowering of citizens is supposed to be accomplished by giving them the power to choose and thus to send signals via the market about the quality of different services. In this way, services that are not in demand will be discontinued.

Clearly, this is a model that, in theory at least, empowers citizens vis-à-vis the government. That said, it is equally clear that the model causes tremendous problems for public sector managers

(Lovell 1992). How are public organizations supposed to be able to conduct any type of planning in this new system, given the uncertainty introduced by the customer-choice-based model? How are these organizations going to be able to get some return from facilities set up in socially problematic neighbourhoods? How are they going to be able to cope with increasing demand, for instance, for schools in attractive neighbourhoods?

These questions are not merely theoretical arguments against a completely customer-based public service model. Let us look very briefly at a couple of illustrations of these problems. If for no other reason, they might serve as a partial counter-balance to the many success stories reported by Osborne and Gaebler (1993).

THE "PUBLIC MARKET" IN OPERATION:
SOME COMPARATIVE ILLUSTRATIONS

Today, almost all advanced capitalist democracies such as Australia, Britain, Denmark, France, New Zealand, Sweden, and the United States, have more or less developed "public markets." Numerous public services have implemented extensive reforms of privatization or "contracting out" of public services (see Schwartz 1994; Rouban, 1995). Also, in many countries – or locales – different voucher- or cheque-based systems have been introduced, enabling individuals to choose, for example, between different schools or day-care centres.

In the Swedish context (Häggroth 1993; Wise and Amnå 1993), there are several examples where the "marketization" of services has helped the government (national or local) save money and give the beneficiaries of the services some input into public service design. However, it is difficult to evaluate the long-term effects of these reforms, not least because they have been implemented at the same time as the effect of various cut-back programs began to be noticeable. There has been some discussion about the bias generated by the school-voucher system. In the city of Gothenburg, the media recently reported that a large number of high school students and their parents had simply abandoned a socially distressed part of the city and moved to schools in more attractive areas (Isemo 1994). This tends to cause problems in both parts of the city: in the poorer areas, because they are not competitive with schools in the more affluent parts of the city; and in schools in affluent areas, because they find themselves in higher demand than they can accommodate.

In Britain, the market penetration of the state – as well as the reaffirmation of citizenship – has gone much further than in Sweden (Hood 1990; King 1987; Lovell 1992; Metcalfe 1993). The creation of the "Citizen's Charter" is one of the clearest manifestations of a reaffirmation of citizenship in the Western world. Interestingly, the entitlements codified in the "Citizen's Charter" seem to refer also to previously state-owned but now privatized utilities. British Rail, for instance, which will soon be privatized, is covered by the Charter. Thus, for the public – as well as for policy makers and bureaucrats, apparently – services once delivered by public authorities remain public also after privatization. There seems to be a clear distinction between the auspices under which services are delivered and the nature of the utility. If the service is "public" to the extent that it serves a common good, then it is subject to the Charter, regardless of who organizes the service.

Space forbids a more extensive list of examples of "public markets." Here, suffice it to say that "public markets" tend to create some types of problems while resolving others. In fairness it should be said that these reforms are still quite recent and they have yet to sink in before they can be fully assessed and evaluated.

CONCLUSIONS: "MORE BANG FOR THE BUCK" OR "MORE BENEFITS FROM THE BALLOT"?

The new public management reforms and the "marketization of the state" are two sides of the same coin: they both illustrate the rapid emergence of market criteria in the public sector of most advanced democracies. This process, as has been touched upon earlier in this chapter, seems to build on a simultaneous depoliticization and politicization of the public administration. The depoliticization is reflected in the downvaluing of politics as a signalling device or a means of communication both within the public administration and also between the public service and policy makers. This in turn may depend on the downgrading of mass politics at large, as Peter Aucoin shows in his contribution to this volume. On the other hand, the politicization has, in an ironic way, become necessary in order to enforce the "marketization" of the public sector. Moreover, replacing a political signalling device with a market-based device is also a political process. Paradoxical as it may seem, depoliticizing the public administration is a highly politically charged project, because it includes, inter alia, altering the relationship between the public service on the one hand and civil society and policy makers on the other.

The "marketization of the state" is said to serve an essentially good purpose, namely to increase the quality of public services, bring private sector management into the public sector, and empower individuals in relation to the state. The ultimate goal, or the common denominator, is to increase overall efficiency in the public sector. According to the "marketization" advocates, there is no better way of accomplishing this than to open up for competition, or, in the words of Osborne and Gaebler (1993:80), "The most obvious advantage of competition is greater efficiency: more bang for the buck."

Few, if any, are very likely to oppose these objectives. Indeed, a reform aimed at increased public sector efficiency and citizen empowerment is likely to gain widespread political support. This needs to be mentioned in the present context to avoid any misinterpretation of the criticism against the "customerization" of citizenship delivered here. While the commodification of public goods, the conversion of citizens into customers, and the emergence of a market for public goods – three interrelated elements of the larger project of the "marketization of the state" – may serve these purposes, these reforms are also replete with problems of different natures and with different consequences. In particular, because of its emphasis on market behaviour on behalf of the citizens/customers, the process of "marketization of the state" seems to endanger the political nature of citizenship.

Thus, the question could be asked: do any other reforms exist that could serve the same purpose without generating the side-effects which seem to be endemic to "the marketization of the state"? As DiIulio and his associates argue (1993), public administration develops in two different ways: invention and evolution. Much of the development so far has been evolutionary, characterized by marginal changes rather than paradigmatic shifts in the performance of the bureaucracy. More recent proposals, on the other hand, are seen as development caused by invention.

As has been argued throughout this chapter, citizenship denotes a system of mutual entitlements and obligations between the individual and the state. The concept of customers, on the other hand, is associated with markets and economic theory. The reason why they have become almost synonymous in the current public administration reform jargon is that they both denote the individual in an exchange process. However, the concepts of citizens and customers refer to two different aspects of the individual; we are citizens in the political realm of society and customers in the economic realm. Thus, it appears misleading to juxtapose them and exclude the qualities associated with citizenship from the current debate on public sector reform.

These problems are compounded by the apparent inability of the "public market" to perform the tasks normally attributed to markets, that is, optimal resource allocation and optimal pricing of commodities. A major reason for this is related to the special roles of the state in the market. The state plays three different roles in different markets.[6] First, it is a vendor of services and goods. These services and goods are what we traditionally refer to as public services. Secondly, the state is a purchaser of different services and goods; to be sure, in many countries, the state is a leading actor in most domestic markets. Finally, the state is a competitor, in relationship both to private business and to other governments. The former aspect is highlighted in the "public market" as discussed earlier. The latter aspect may appear less salient but is becoming increasingly important as economies become globalized or internationalized.

For these reasons, the question above as to what should be the overarching objective of public administration reform – increased public sector efficiency or a strengthened citizenship – could perhaps best be answered "both." The two objectives are not inconsistent or contradictory; indeed, they relate to different spheres of society. It might be a bold policy objective to go for both objectives.

NOTES

1 This chapter has benefited immensely from comments on an earlier version of this paper from the participants in the "Governance in a Changing Environment" project and also from Herman M. Schwartz.

2 Technically, the Charter of Rights and Freedoms is part of the new Canadian Constitution adopted in 1982. The Charter has tended to move much of the process of interpreting and implementing legislation from the executive branch of government to the legal system. In this respect, the Charter brought the Canadian system closer to that of the United States than had previously been the case.

   The provinces are not automatically subject to the Charter but have – according to the "notwithstanding rule" – the right to disregard elements of the Charter. The provinces of Quebec and Alberta have exercised the right a couple of times (personal communication, senior official at the Canadian embassy in Stockholm).

3 Some critics of the citizen-empowerment school have argued that citizens are stronger, not weaker, individuals vis-à-vis government than are customers. Thus, George Frederickson (quoted in DiIulio et al. 1993:48) argues that citizens are the owners of government, not its customers. Interestingly, Osborne and Gaebler (1993:73) make a very similar observation: "The ultimate form of ownership is not ownership simply of problem solving or of services, but of government. In theory, our representative system of democracy gives us that ownership." However, they add that, "In reality, few Americans feel that they 'own' or 'control' their governments."

4 It should be noted that "collective" in the table does not refer to any compulsory, political aggregation of individuals into collective bodies. Instead, it refers to the promotion of the general good and the process through which citizenship transforms individuals into members of a social community.

5 Much of the organizational change and overall strategies and modus operandi of the public sectors in most Western countries during the past few years seems to have been triggered by the decreasing legitimacy of public institutions; cf. Metcalfe 1993; Peters 1993; Pierre 1993; Rouban 1993.

6 I am grateful to Phillip Cooper for drawing my attention to these different roles of the state in markets.

BIBLIOGRAPHY

Aucoin, Peter. 1990. Administrative reform in public management: paradigms, principles, paradoxes and pendulums. *Governance* 3, 2:115-37.

Bouckaert, Geert. 1993. Charters as frameworks for awarding quality: the Belgian, British and French experience. Paper presented at the seminar on Concepts and Methods of Quality Awards in the Public Sector, 21-22 October, at University of Leiden, the Netherlands.

Chandler, Ralph Clark. 1988. The commercial republic re-examined: a critique of the economization model of public policy making. In *Market-Based Public Policy*, ed. Richard C. Hula, 181-203. New York: St. Martin's Press.

Daneke, G. A., and D. J. Lemak. 1985. *Regulatory Reform Reconsidered.* Boulder, co: Westview Press.

DiIulio, Jr., John J, Gerald Garvey, and Donald F. Kettl. 1993. *Improving Government Performance: An Owner's Manual.* Washington, DC.: The Brookings Institution.

Esping-Andersen, Gösta. 1985. *Politics Against Markets.* Princeton: Princeton University Press.

Häggroth, Sören. 1993. From corporation to political enterprise: trends in Swedish local government. Ds 1993:6.

Hirschman, Albert O. 1970. *Exit, Voice and Loyalty.* Cambridge, MA and London: Harvard University Press.

Hood, Christopher. 1990. De-Sir Humphrefying the Westminster model of bureaucracy: a new style of governance? *Governance* 3, 2:205-14.

Isemo, Alf. 1994. Skolelever väljer bort Göteborg [High-school students opt out of Gothenburg]. *Göteborgs-Posten* 13 March 30.

King, Desmond S. 1987. *The New Right: Politics, Markets and Citizenship.* London: Macmillan.

Lipsky, Martin. 1980. *Street-Level Bureaucracy.* New York: Russell Sage Foundation.

Lovell, Roger. 1992. Citizen's Charter: the cultural challenge. *Public Administration* 70:395-404.

Lundqvist, Lennart J. 1988. Privatization: towards a concept of comparative policy analysis. *Journal of Public Policy* 8, 1:1-19.

Maier, Charles S. 1987. Introduction. In *Changing Boundaries of the Political*, ed. Charles S. Maier, 1-26. Cambridge: Cambridge University Press.

Marshall, T. H. 1977. *Class, Citizenship and Social Development*. Chicago and London: University of Chicago Press.

_____ 1981. *The Right to Welfare and Other Essays*. London: Heinemann.

Meicklejohn, Alexander. 1965. *Political Freedom*, 2d ed. Oxford and New York: Oxford University Press.

Metcalfe, Les. 1993. Conviction politics and dynamic conservatism: Mrs. Thatcher's managerial revolution. *International Political Science Review* 14, 4:351-72.

Moe, T. M. 1989. The politics of bureaucratic structure. In *Can the Government Govern?*, ed. J.E. Chubb and P.E. Peterson, 267-329. Washington, DC: The Brookings Institution.

Montin, Stig. Forthcoming. Kommunala organisationsförändringar. In *Kommunal Förvaltningspolitik*, ed. Lennart J. Lundqvist and Jon Pierre, 13-40. Lund: Studentlitteratur.

Offe, Claus. 1984. *Contradictions of the Welfare State*. London: John Hutchinson.

Osborne, David, and Ted Gaebler. 1993. *Reinventing Government*. New York: Plume/Penguin.

Pascal, Anthony. 1986. How useful are user charges? In *Managing Cities*, vol 2, part B, *Research in Urban Policy*, ed. Terry Nicholas Clark, 39-51. Greenwich, CT. and London: JAI Press.

Peters, B. Guy. 1987. Politicians and bureaucrats in the politics of policymaking. In *Bureaucracy and Public Choice*, Vol. 15, *Sage Modern Politics Series*, ed. J.E. Lane, 256-82. Beverly Hills, CA and London: Sage Publications.

_____ 1993. Searching for a role: the civil service in American democracy. *International Political Science Review* 14, 4:352-86.

Pierre, Jon. 1993. Legitimacy, institutional change, and the politics of public administration in Sweden. *International Political Science Review* 14, 4:387-401.

Ranson, Stewart, and John Stewart. 1989. Citizenship and government: the challenge for management in the public domain. *Political Studies* 37:5-24.

Rockman, Bert A. 1992. Bureaucracy, power, policy, and the state. In *The State of Public Bureaucracy*, ed. L.B. Hill, 141-70. Armonk, NY and London: M. E. Sharpe.

Rouban, Luc. 1993. France in search of a new administrative order. *International Political Science Review* 14, 4:403-18.

_____ 1995. Public administration at the crossroads: the end of French specificity? In *Bureaucracy in the Modern State: An Introduction to Comparative Public Administration*, ed. Jon Pierre, 39-63. Cheltenham: Edward Elgar Publishing.

Saltman, Richard B. and Casten von Otter. 1992. *Planned Markets and Public Competition*. Buckingham and Philadelphia: The Open University Press.

Schwartz, Herman M. 1994. Small states in big trouble: state reorganization in Australia, Denmark, New Zealand, and Sweden in the 1980s. *World Politics* 46, 4:527-555.

Turner, Bryan S. 1986. *Citizenship and Capitalism*. London: Allen & Unwin.

_____ 1993. Contemporary problems in the theory of citizenship. In *Citizenship and Social Theory*, ed. Bryan S. Turner, 1-18. Newbury Park and London: Sage.

Walzer, Michael. 1989. Citizenship. In *Political Innovation and Conceptual Change*, ed. Terrence Ball, James Farr, and Russel L. Hanson, 211-20. Cambridge: Cambridge University Press.

Westerberg, Bengt, and Sture Nordh. 1993. *Välfärdsstatens Vägval och Villkor*. Stockholm: Brombergs.

Wise, Charles R., and Erik Amnå. 1993. New managerialism in Swedish local government. *Scandinavian Political Studies* 16, 4:339-58.

Globalization, Nation States, and the Civil Service

DONALD J. SAVOIE

Looking back, one could easily conclude that the national civil services in many Western countries lost their way in the 1980s. It is considerably more difficult, however, to pinpoint precisely the reasons. Still, we know that public bureaucracies came under attack for a variety of reasons and from different quarters; the global economy is such that nation states exist today in an increasingly interdependent and competitive environment, with some experts insisting that "the nation state has become too small for the big problems of life and too big for the small problems of life" (Bell 1986:6). The political leaderships of the 1980s became openly hostile to their public services, hurling all kinds of accusations at them, notably of being "fat, bloated, inefficient, uncreative, and too powerful" (Savoie 1994); and fiscal imperatives pushed governments to reform the machinery of government with a consequent enthusiasm for privatization and other ways of commercializing government activities (Boston 1991). The public services have remained on the defensive ever since, uncertain of their policy advisory role and even of their program delivery function.

Globalization – the catchphrase of the 1980s – is one force that is having an important impact on the public service as an institution, but it has not received the attention it deserves. The global order itself is constantly in the throes of a major period of contradictions and reconfiguration. American sociologist Daniel Bell has likened this process to an "accordion-like expanding and contracting at particular moments" that is rarely anticipated by national governments of the day (Bell 1986). We know that the international economy and the telecommunication sector are increasingly integrated. The emergence of global corporations, and new trade, financial, and communication links are dramatically changing the policy context for national governments in a shrinking world. "Globalization" is thus more than a catchphrase. The pace of the international division of production, which is now almost oblivious to national boundaries, has been remarkable, as has the speed with which financial capital can move about the globe. Yet we also know that many polities are fragmenting, fuelled by the emergence of regionally based nationalism, and by linguistic or religious groups challenging the legitimacy of the nation state. The nation state is, accordingly, being challenged from diametrically opposed directions – from above and from below.

The Club of Rome recently reviewed the challenges of globalization in a report entitled *The First Global Revolution: A Strategy for Surviving the World*, and concluded that: "The deficiencies of governance are at the root of many of the strands of the *problematique* and hence improved governance is an essential aspect" of the solutions (King and Schneider 1991:160).

The purpose of this chapter is to look at the challenges of governance for nation states. It reports on the powerful forces at play redefining the role of government and the public service in nation states, reviews how some national public services have dealt or are dealing with the challenges, and speculates on future requirements and future direction.

THE GLOBAL ORDER AND NATION STATES

The dominant political thinking for much of the twentieth century was independence and national sovereignty. New sovereign states were established as numerous Third World countries broke free from colonial rule. Meanwhile, in the industrialized world, the Keynesian revolution captured one Treasury after another and national governments gave themselves the tools to manage their national economies. By the end of the Second World War, the public's belief, at least in Anglo-American democracies, in the ability of national governments to intervene and to manage the national economy was high. Not only did the Allies win the war, but governments had run the war economy well. Unemployment had fallen to zero, yet prices had been held down. When the war ended, the public became determined never to permit another depression of the kind witnessed in the 1930s; people looked to their national governments for strong leadership – even in countries with a highly decentralized federal system of government (Savoie 1990, chap. 1). In turn, national governments by and large looked inward to national fiscal policies, to economic development measures, and to national industrial strategies to develop "their" economy and in relative isolation from the international community. In short, Keynesian economics turned politicians loose on national economies (Buchanan and Wagner 1977:4).

Recently, however, the dominant words in our political vocabulary have been neoconservatism, globalization, and interdependence (Simeon 1990:1). One keen observer argues that these words call "into question not so much the existence of the nation state, but its continuing effectiveness and viability as an institution through which individuals and communities can meet economic, environmental, social and a host of other challenges" (Simeon 1990). How is it then – to employ Harlan Cleveland's expression – that the nation state is "leaking away at the edges" and leaking away in a number of different directions? (Cleveland 1985:195).

We know that there is an upward flow of influence and power into the supranational institutions: examples include the European Community, the IMF, the World Bank, the Group of Seven Industrialized Nations, the General Agreement on Tariffs and Trade (GATT) and regional trade agreements such as the United States/Canada Free Trade Agreement (FTA) and the North American Free Trade Agreement (NAFTA). Indeed, we are witnessing an unprecedented voluntary transfer of decision-making authority and sovereignty to these supranational institutions. This is true even in cases where national governments do not join regional trading blocs. The global economy requires the sacrifice of sovereign discretion to international rules where, for example, trade policy is increasingly being shaped by international agreements.

At a minimum, what we are witnessing is a "pooling of sovereignty in alliances," enabling policies to be struck and decisions to be made to move the global economy. This is true not only with respect to trade policies and practices but also to a host of other policy fields, notably monetary policy. As is well known, there is nothing more insecure and, accordingly, more mobile when threatened than a million dollars. The levers once available to national governments to control the flow and mobility of capital are less and less available or, if they are, the price to be paid to manipulate them is prohibitive. It can be argued that Reagan's 1981 tax cuts, for example, initiated a worldwide shift to lower corporate and income taxes. Firms and even individuals have access to highly sophisticated means of communication, and they respond quickly to higher levels of taxation, new labour laws, or tougher pollution legislation. In addition, the 1980s saw "traditional banking go out the window" with the world banking community becoming increasingly "deregulated" and "decartelized" (The Economist 1993a).

We also saw strong pressure to harmonize a wide variety of laws and policies from one nation state to another. Robert Reich brought this point home when he wrote that the well-being of Americans depends on the value that they can add to the global economy and no longer only on the profitability of their own corporations (Reich 1991). Reich also argued that the global economy will leave in its wake large differences in economic well-being at the regional level. Regions are inserting themselves differently into the global economy, and their links with the outside world will accordingly become more important relative to the economic linkages within their own nation state. The argument goes that Reich, in effect, sounded "the death knell of the economic nation state" (Courchene 1992:759-91). In short, the conventional wisdom is that there will be a limited role for the nation state as we see the emergence of an internationalization of "rugged individualism."

To be sure, there are some views that run counter to the above, with some observers arguing that globalization in fact calls for a stronger role for governments. Michael Porter, for example, argues that, "Differences in national values, culture, economic structures, institutions, and histories all contribute to competitive success" (Porter 1990:74). What this suggests, however, is a stronger role for local, state, or provincial governments, given that they are usually responsible for areas such as education and infrastructure, while global pressures will increasingly constrain the policy instruments of national governments such as monetary, fiscal, trade, and redistributive policies.

The rise of the "global" corporation also holds important implications for nation states and "national" economies (King and Schneider 1991). Few large, technologically advanced firms call themselves "national" any more. Ownership of such firms is increasingly spread among several nations, and the various components of major products are each produced in different countries. These corporations operate more and more on the basis of a worldwide or global footing than even a multicountry one. Some observers insist that these corporations, rather than national governments or even international institutions, will be shaping the international economic environment (Ostry 1990). Global corporations favour the denationalization of enterprise and are particularly alert to attempts to restrict the flow of capital or the location of economic activities. They all have well-staffed government relations units and the necessary resources to retain powerful lobby groups, not only to ensure *stable* and *unencumbered* trade rules, but also to push for a freer movement of goods, services, and capital, if not labour, and an environment where governments treat firms equally, independent of their nationality. This is not to suggest that all of this has occurred, but the march is on and some important movement has already taken place.

Indeed, there is no denying the remarkable rise of global corporations and the increasing importance of cross-border investment. Between 1983 and 1990, for example, corporate investments across borders grew four times faster than world output and three times faster than world trade. (The Economist 1993b:5) This has served to integrate more fully the world economy where businesses walk across borders with minimal effort. The result is that capital, goods, and services go to places where their home nation states may not like them to go. Some $1 trillion are now traded round the clock on foreign exchange markets – triple the figure of 1986. It will be recalled that Great Britain felt the sting of these markets in the autumn of 1992.

The influence and power of nation states is thus flowing sideways to those global corporations that do not carry national flags and often operate unregulated at the global level. These corporations increasingly shape the pace and location of national economic activities, while leaving national governments limited opportunities to go their own way. Low-wage countries with a weak socioeconomic infrastructure are attracting new manufacturing and production capacities; accordingly, pressure to harmonize public policies is leading to less government intervention in the economy rather than more. In any event, regional trade deals and globalization are introducing "straitjackets limiting the ability [of government] to intervene in the pursuit of social and economic goals" (Simeon 1990:3). The result is that, unlike the old multinationals, which entered nation states subject to national regulations and requirements controlling their activities, global corporations now increasingly enter countries under rules that apply to domestic firms. For this reason, economists claim that we can no longer speak of a "national" production economy. To bring home the point, they will point out that the Chrysler Corporation has more Japanese than American components in its cars, while Honda has more American parts than Japanese. International ownership and international management control the stateless corporations with an allegiance to shareholders and senior management, but not to a country. They will locate new activities where profits can be maximized, will establish "headquarters of convenience," and will seek out the most favourable monetary and fiscal zones (Valaskakis 1992:B4).

Finally, the authority of nation states is leaking down to regional and local governments, to minorities, and single-issue constituencies. As is well known, regional forces are running strongly in Eastern Europe. In Western Europe, notably Italy, Spain, France, and Belgium, new political authority is being transferred to local governments. Regional forces are being fuelled by all kinds of factors, such as regional imbalances in economic well-being, alienation from a "central" and "remote" government, and ethnic, religious, cultural, or racial differences. These forces can sometimes tear nation states apart, as they have done in the Soviet Union and Yugoslavia and as they sometimes threaten to do in Canada. Thus, at the same time as the world economy is becoming integrated, we see that the attachments to race, religion, language, and cultural and regional identities remain strong and in many cases are getting stronger. The point here is that while people may want to break free from the shackles that inhibit their ability to buy goods and services from any country they like and to invest wherever they wish, they continue to rely on race, religion, language, culture, and their community or region for their identity.

We are also witnessing a sharp decline in the deference of citizens to their governments. Calls are made for more public consultations and for a greater say in politics than simply the opportunity to vote for politicians every four years or so (Kaass 1972:243-59). In addition, we are seeing, in many countries, a shift towards an American style "rights-oriented society" (Cairns 1992). The application of the "Charter" in Canada and calls for a "Bill of Rights" in Britain are evidence of this. It is important to remember that those who put forward claims under a charter or a bill of rights do so under the "most powerful of all moral considerations" and are in no mood to compromise (Parklington 1982:815). This movement is happening at a time when historically marginalized groups, such as women and visible minorities, are gaining prominence on the political agenda. This "politically focused cultural pluralism" has given rise to radically different types of cleavages in society, putting new pressures on the structures of government (Williams 1991:6).

The information revolution is also having far-reaching implications for the nation state. In the past, government had a near-monopoly position on the information it generated, which served to strengthen its hand considerably in its dealings with interest groups and the public. This no longer holds. New communications technology and easier access to government information provide to outside groups and individuals a capacity to develop positions on a whole range of issues and to challenge government policy.

The breathtaking speed of modern communications, especially television, is putting enormous pressure on government to make decisions quickly for fear of appearing indecisive and not in control (Taras 1990). Newspapers were and remain, in large measure, local or territorial, but this is not so for the modern means of communications. Television, for example, gave its viewers a ringside seat during the Gulf War. The modern media are global, increasingly critical and widely accessible, even to the illiterate (Meyrowitz 1985). Within minutes, they can zero in on any issue anywhere in the world and compare virtually any given situation in one country to a similar one in another. Above all, they have a capacity to intrude into the political arena and the operations of government and to inform the public quickly, visually, and with considerable impact about what is not working. The media are, accordingly, "privileging" or "empowering" people in their dealings with governments.

In short, globalization and the modern media are changing the art of governing. The postwar years provided reconstruction, strong economic growth, a firm belief in the ability of government to intervene in the economy, and a tremendous expansion of government spend- ing. They were also quiet and stable years; countries were relatively free to shape domestic policy in isolation, even of neighbouring countries. The media were not nearly so critical of government, especially in the pre-Watergate days. It might have been an environment ideally suited to the Sir Humphreys of the world, but this is no longer the case. The world depicted in George Orwell's novel *1984* has been turned upside down (Williams 1991:29). It is not a government elite that uses advanced technology to control the behaviour of citizens. Rather, it is politicians and, albeit to a lesser extent, government agencies, that are continually "watched, even hounded, as they attempt to go about their daily affairs" (Pollitt 1988:178). To sum up, then, the world of relatively isolated national economies, linearity, and discrete variables – even common sense – inhabited by government officials is giving way to a new world. The new order is much more challenging and less deferential. Government officials will require a strong capacity to adapt to change and to deal with a more probing and better-informed media, policy communities, interest groups, and the public.

THE RESPONSE

How are national governments preparing their civil services to respond to the new world? There is little doubt that there is worldwide frustration among political leaders with their civil services. Gerald E.Caiden, B.Guy Peters, and Christopher Pollitt, among many others, have documented the numerous reform measures introduced during the 1980s (Caiden 1991; Peters 1993; Pollitt 1988). Osborne and Gaebler insist that the reinvention of government is a "global revolution" (Osborne and Gaebler 1992). Scandinavian countries are busy "renewing" their national administrations, France is attempting to decentralize its civil service, the Reagan administration implemented its Reform 88 initiative, the Clinton administration is trying to "reinvent" the government, and British Commonwealth countries have introduced a host of reform measures in search of a new "Public Management" (Savoie 1994).

This is not to suggest that all these reforms were designed to prepare civil services to assist nation states to meet the challenges of the new world. They were certainly not part of a grand design to rethink the civil service as an institution (Savoie 1994). On the face of it, one could conclude that the reforms were incoherent, at times contradictory and even spiteful.

Accordingly, hand in hand with the new powerful force shaping the global economy, national civil services in most countries were asked in the 1980s to welcome a political leadership to office that was, if not openly hostile, then certainly prepared to challenge both what they did and how they went about their work. Indeed, the political rhetoric of the 1980s had many targets, including government as an economic manager, and the civil service was singled out for criticism.

The political agenda dealing with national civil services for much of the past twelve years or so in most of the industrialized world has been centred around two themes: the civil service has become too powerful in setting government policy and government officials are poor managers. The goal was clear: reduce the influence of permanent officials on policy and the policy process, and strengthen the capacity of government officials to manage. Concerns over globalization or the ability of national civil services to play an important role in managing the new forces at play does not appear even yet to carry much weight in this new agenda.

How did the political leadership go about implementing their agenda? Rhetoric as well as a firmly held view that government managers should emulate the private sector played key roles. Indeed, "bureaucrat-bashing" was often the order of the day throughout the 1980s. One heard of the need to "deprivilege the civil service," to teach "bureaucrats a thing or two about political leadership," to cut an "overgrown and overweight" bureaucracy down to size, and not to let oneself be "educated by bureaucrats" (Hennessy 1989; Savoie 1994). The overall image of the civil service that emerged was that of a bloated and misdirected "behemoth staffed by incompetent zealots, hardly an image likely to encourage bureaucratic self-esteem" (Solomon and Lund 1984:14). Whether intended or not, the rhetoric served to undermine the confidence senior civil servants had in their institution. There is ample evidence to show that morale in the civil service plummeted in the 1980s in most Western countries (Savoie 1994).

It was widely believed during the 1980s, even among left-of-centre politicians, that permanent government officials were invariably wedded to the status quo, unwilling or unable to change direction, to be creative, and to challenge conventional wisdom (Williams 1980:81). Thus, the objective for the political leadership in office became the need to avoid the "Yes, Minister" syndrome, where public servants allegedly take hold of the agenda and direct the scope and pace of change – often giving the appearance of activity while, in fact, standing still.

How has the political leadership sought to attenuate the influence of permanent officials over policy? It has largely built its strategy of containment around the notion that only politicians should define and move the political and policy agenda and, of course, giving a much greater role to the private sector in the economy. It also sought to redefine the role of bureaucracy so that senior civil servants would be managers rather than policy advisers or administrators. The political leadership sought to recapture authority over policy by reforming the machinery and by appointing noncareer public servants to key positions. All in all, one can detect a declining faith in the neutral competence of public servants, with a good number of politicians and observers suspecting bureaucrats of "being biased rather than neutral in their policy perspectives and at times willing to sabotage policy proposals that political leaders want to put into effect" (Rourke 1992:540). As a result, expertise on public policy issues began to flourish outside of government offices in lobby firms, think tanks, public opinion surveys, ministerial offices, single issue groups and so on. In many ways, public policy expertise has been privatized.

But that tells only part of the story. Hand in hand with efforts to attenuate the influence of permanent officials on policy issues were determined efforts to see senior public servants become managers rather than policy advisers or administrators. The political leadership sent out not-so-subtle messages that they wanted "fixers," "doers," or those with "a bias for action," rather than "tinkerers" and "can't do" types (Metcalfe and Richards 1987; Pollitt 1988; Savoie 1994). Over the years it had been thought that the glamour of government work was in policy, not in management. Indeed, senior officials had been happy to live with elaborate rules and regulations, as long as they were free to play a policy role. The view in some quarters is that the functional units were there to worry about rules dealing with personnel, administration, and financial matters, whereas the senior officials' job was to concentrate on politicians and policy issues. Some go so far as to argue that in government, the managing of major departmental or agency programs traditionally has been a job for "junior personnel or *failed* administrative-class people, who are seen by the mandarins as not being able to make it to the top levels" (Williams 1988:62).

To strengthen the management of government operations the only strategy was, essentially, to look to the private sector for inspiration. The political leadership virtually everywhere in the Western world, even in countries with left-of-centre parties in power, concluded that management practices in the private sector were superior to those in the public sector and that whenever possible the public sector "should either emulate the private sector or simply privatize the function" (Pollitt 1988:vi). Many governments set out to restructure their operations. The process was essentially designed to test a number of public sector activities by exposing them to competition or by privatizing or contracting out government activities, and to empower government managers to manage their operations in a more businesslike manner and front-line government employees to respond directly to "clients." It is interesting to note that, at the same time as nation states are losing some control through globalization, national governments are losing some control over their operations through privatization, contracting out, and the empowerment of government managers and front-line employees.

At the risk of making too sweeping a statement, senior public servants adopted a defensive posture. They became uncertain about their policy role and, in particular, how to respond to the charge that they exerted too much influence. To a much greater extent than before, the political leadership brought in their own partisan policy advisers and for the past fourteen years or so it has been as if civil servants were saying to politicians and their partisan advisers: "OK now, you drive."

For their part, senior civil servants focused their efforts on management matters. We have seen wave after wave of management reform measures introduced in most Western countries. As Peter Aucoin writes: "The internationalization of public management parallels the internationalization of public and private economies" (Aucoin 1988:134). A review of the work of the OECD, for example, over the past twelve years or so reveals a strong preoccupation with such issues as "management development," "performance pay," and "services to clients." Rethinking the policy advisory function of the permanent civil service was rarely on the agenda in international meetings, nor did it figure prominently in the various reform measures introduced in most national governments.

In short, then, market forces as well as the management superiority of the private sector over the public sector would drive the reform agenda for national civil services. Partisan policy advisers – or, as one former senior Canadian civil servant labelled them, the "new Clark Kents" of the policy world – would fine tune policy direction when required (Massé 1993:6).

Though civil servants may have appeared to be defensive, they have also seen, first hand, far-reaching changes to their own work environment. In Europe, they have felt the impact of a growing community structure, the application of various community standards, and the establishment in Brussels of administrative and coordinating units relating to their work. In North America, they have felt the impact of the Canada-United States Free Trade Agreement and the discipline it imposes on government operations. Elsewhere, they have seen the march – albeit at times uncertain – towards a freer global trade environment.

They have had to cope also with other powerful forces. These forces include vastly improved means of communications, the free flow of ideas between nation states, the widely held view that the private sector is far more efficient than the public sector, growing government debts, and the push to make government information accessible to interest groups and the public. The interdependence of nation states and of policy issues and far better informed and much stronger interest groups are seeing government officials spending more time being "policy networkers" than policy specialists in their own right. That said, governments have not instituted many changes in the way they receive policy advice from their civil service.

Civil servants have also seen a new vocabulary introduced to describe their work, much of it borrowed from the private sector. These phrases include "empowerment," "total quality management," "pay for performance," and "improved services to clients." This new vocabulary holds far more implications for government operations and civil servants than one may initially assume. Clients and customers, as opposed to citizens are, of course, more demanding, and less deferential, and this attitude can give rise to the view that financial resources move from individuals to the state or, in some instances, from the state to individuals and back to the state, for the consumption of goods in a competitive environment, with the competition being between the public and private sectors and even public providers. In addition, it is important to remember that while citizens can have common purposes, clients and customers are sovereign.

Civil servants have on the whole embraced this new vocabulary. Indeed, a review of developments in various countries suggest that civil servants played a key role in promoting the new public management agenda. The successful implementation of the privatization agenda in Britain and Canada and the shift towards contracting out of government activities in many countries were possible because of the work of senior civil servants. Senior civil servants played a key advisory role in selling public assets and in successfully putting in place a process to transfer assets to the private sector, to contract out government activities, and to deregulate the economy.

LOOKING BACK

What have we accomplished over the past fourteen years or so, and are national civil services better prepared to meet the challenges of the global economy? To what extent have we been able to get at the "deficiencies of governance" which, according to the Club of Rome, are at the root of the problem in the fast-changing global economy?

The political leaderships tried "this" and "that" in their attempts to reform the civil services. Lacking a grand design or a carefully crafted plan, the political leadership in various countries in the 1980s improvised from their first days in office. To be sure, the level of activity in reforming bureaucracy has been intense and far-ranging. The 1980s left us with a series of new buzz words and names: empowerment, Rayner, Grace, Nielsen, privatization, contracting out, IMAA, Next Steps, Special Operating Agencies, Total Quality Management, corporatization policy (New Zealand), PS 2000, pay-for-performance schemes, and also a new emphasis on service to clients. There have been cuts in personnel, reductions in the number of government departments (Australia), and a drive to separate policy advice from operational activities.

The reforms have also given rise to several models of organization. Guy Peters reports on four. He points to the market model, which calls for splitting up large departments into smaller entrepreneurial "agencies" or units. This model argues that public sector agencies confront the same managerial and service-delivery tasks as private sector firms. The participatory model, on the other hand, considers that hierarchical rule-based organizations inhibit effective management; it looks to the lower echelons of workers as well as clients for solutions and calls for flatter organizations. The temporary model enables government to respond more quickly to a crisis or rapidly increasing demands for services. By looking to temporary task forces or agencies, this model also deals with public perceptions of waste and empire-building in government organization

(Peters 1993). The fourth model, of course, is privatization, including contracting out, and new organization models to strengthen the hand of politicians over policy matters (e.g., chiefs of staff position and new policy units in ministerial offices, including the Prime Minister's Office in the case of Britain).

Though still short of a grand design, we do know that governments have been looking to the private sector for inspiration and to each other for guidance. Measures introduced in one country (e.g., executive agencies in Britain) were soon introduced in another (e.g., Canada and Special Operating Agencies). The same is true for virtually every other measure introduced in the 1980s to reform government operations. There are remarkable similarities in the approaches tried in various countries, despite different institutional structures and public service cultures. Some of the more important similarities include "the assumption of public sector inefficiency, the recourse to the private sector's expertise, the stubborn belief in the usefulness of merit pay, the tremendous emphasis on new accounting procedures" and sustained efforts to distinguish the policy formulation role from that of management (Pollitt 1988:181). On the policy side, however, the only thing that appeared to have been "fixed" was to attenuate the influence of permanent officials. Reducing their influence was relatively straightforward – import your own policy advisers, or look to partisan advice for help.

Ideology, fiscal pressure, and the self-fulfilling prophesies of bureaucratic bashing led the political leadership to focus reform efforts on management. Lack of rigorous management was seen as the culprit, rather than the policy advisory capacity of the civil service or the considerable discretion given to government departments in applying policies and delivering programs. In short, the focus was on the boiler room aspects of governance. That is, efforts to strengthen the management capacity of government were directed at what James Q. Wilson and Henry Mintzberg have labelled "production or machine-type organizations" rather than to departments with a high policy content (Wilson 1989).

It is still too early to reach firm conclusions about improvements to government operations. In any event, a good number of observers question whether it is possible to measure qualitative performance in government operations. Still, a survey of reform measures in several countries reveals that the reforms had the greatest impact on machine- or production-like organizations, precisely those elements of government that already appeared to work best (Savoie 1994, chap. 9). These organizations produce a tangible product and the workload and level of productivity can often be measured. One wonders, however, how much more efficiency can be squeezed out of the Land Registry Office, Her Majesty's Stationery Office, Inland Revenue, the Passport Office, or the IRS. These agencies have not reduced staff; furthermore, they continually claim that they have insufficient financial resources to meet "client expectations."

The reforms, however, have had a negative impact on several fronts. As pointed out earlier, morale in the civil service has suffered greatly throughout the Western world in the 1980s. There is plenty of evidence, including a number of surveys, to suggest that a mood of frustration gripped many civil servants, that it gave rise to a crisis in morale, and that the confidence civil servants have in their institutions was badly shaken (Carroll et al. 1985:805-14). To career officials, the message from the political leadership was clear and hardly positive: a good part of the civil service had no intrinsic values, since much of its work could be turned over to the private sector or to agencies employing people expected to behave as though they were in the private sector. When it came to policy matters, civil servants were felt to be of limited help. Best to turn to partisan policy advisers, to think tanks, and to lobby firms for advice. All of this shook the values of public servants and their views of public service as well as what they considered to be the more noble side of their profession. One American official summed it up when he observed: "I might break and enter for my country but I would never do it for K-Mart or CitiCorp" (Business Week 1991:100).

It may well be that the civil service as an institution would have been challenged in the 1980s regardless of which political leadership was in office. The fact that both right-of-centre political parties (e.g., Britain, the United States, Canada) and left-of-centre ones (e.g., Australia, France, and New Zealand) introduced similar reform measures speaks to this point. Indeed, the fact that a left-of-centre party, the Labour government in New Zealand, made the most radical use of the market-based model to reform the country's civil service suggests that fiscal problems, together with a widely shared sense that public bureaucracies were no longer appropriate for the challenges of the new world, were as important, if not more so, than political ideology.

LOOKING AHEAD

Globalization, as noted earlier, requires above all a capacity to adjust rapidly to changes in the world economy (Porter 1990). It has become trite to write that the pace of change is breathtaking and that we are far more confident about what has gone before than about what lies ahead. The economic restructuring flowing out of globalization appears to be successful at the micro level. We are seeing the emergence of more efficient "individuals" (at least some), "firms," and "governments." However, things are different in the macro level where we see fewer people employed, a decline in the work force, and regions and ethnic groups feeling alienated from their governments. Accordingly, we can no longer look to a world of more or less "stable regularities about which easy generalizations can readily be advanced" (Williams 1991:10). Modern political theory and our traditions of governance have been built on a number of ideas, including – among others – a view of the nation state existing in relative isolation from other states except in war, diplomatic affairs, and some trade issues; a mechanistic understanding of problem solving; and a relatively clear understanding of the roles, responsibilities, and boundaries separating the rules and citizens. These ideas no longer hold.

Where do nation states, in particular their civil services, fit in the new scheme of things? There is no denying that the role of nation states is being challenged, as we pointed out earlier, from various directions: from above, from global corporations, and from below. At the same time we see the ability of nation states to implement new policy initiatives increasingly constrained because of international or regional trade agreements, and we see subnational regions growing restless and looking elsewhere for leadership. One such example is the Pacific Northwest Economic Region (PNWER). The enterprise is comprised of five American states (Washington, Oregon,

Montana, Idaho, and Alaska) and two Canadian provinces (British Columbia and Alberta) that have agreed to "collaborate" across national boundaries in six areas – expanding environmental products and services, creating markets for recycled materials, tourism, telecommunications, education, and improving the region's labour force and expanding markets for selected products (University of Washington 1991). The two national governments remain, thus far, inconsequential actors in the initiative and in the process.

Alvin Toffler points to one of the most disturbing features of our "strange new world" – regional differences increasing economically, culturally, politically, and technologically. He goes on to argue that as regional differences increase, it will be more and more difficult for national governments to manage economies with the traditional tools of a central bank, fiscal policy, and national programs (Toffler 1990:240-1). Therein lies the rub. Keynesian economics gave nation states the ability to manage national economies. It also, of course, fundamentally reshaped what governments do. Before Keynesian economics, the work of government was essentially of a routine nature, with government offices staffed largely with clerks processing application forms of one kind or another. By the end of the Second World War, however, governments everywhere expanded dramatically. Yet we did not initiate a fundamental rethinking of the workings of government. New departments, new programs, and new units, including new policy groups, were added to the existing machinery of government, with the hierarchical nature of government remaining intact. In short, we established new agencies, hired new people (mostly young university graduates), and in the spirit of Keynesian economics we told them to be creative, to challenge the status quo, and to come up with new solutions to old problems. Yet we did not attempt to remove the creative or policy shackles inhibiting government bureaucracies, to look to new ways of doing things, or to jettison dated government programs and activities. In hindsight this may well have been a mistake, and in this sense a good number of our present-day problems with governance may well predate the globalization phenomenon. There is a school of thought that suggests that Keynesian economics did not fail: the failure was in its application. Politicians were unwilling to cut back government spending in good economic times and government bureaucracy became too rigid, unable to rid itself of redundant units, and too uncreative to chart a new course when it became necessary – hence John Kenneth Galbraith's suggestion that "bureaucracy has given government a bad name."

The never-ending attempts to reform the civil service, beginning in the 1950s with the Hoover Commissions in the United States, carrying on in the 1960s with the Glassco Commission in Canada, Fulton in Britain, and the PPBS and PAR reforms in the 1970s, among others, speak to the inability of the machinery of government to accommodate the requirements of Keynesian economics. Calls for "letting the manager manage" and for putting in place objective evaluation criteria to assess the performance of programs ran up against the reality of government operations where things can never be so simple and where things cannot always be measured. The requirements of partisan politics, officials fighting for turf, and accountability issues are just some of the things that shape government decision making.

Neoclassical economic theory and globalization are now redefining the role of government, much as Keynesian economics did forty years ago. There are, of course, large differences between the two. Neoclassical theory tells us that a liberalized world economy is more efficient and more productive than a controlled or managed economy. The theory, however, tells us nothing about something that is key to its success, that is, how to get there, or how to make the transition from a managed economy to a liberalized one. The reforms of the 1980s and early 1990s either overlooked these issues or sidestepped them. By and large, they sought to make government operations more efficient and to make them less rule-driven. They also sought to instil the notion of competition in public service thinking, and that with competition quality would get better and costs would come down.

If these reforms, in fact, give rise to more efficient government operations, so much the better. But the reforms do not go far enough in preparing nation states to make the transition to a more liberalized world economy. The challenges for nation states are becoming clear – new cleavages are emerging, flowing out of a growing gap between the economically distressed and the economically secure, and between subnational regions as they integrate themselves differently in the global economy. The global economy, however liberalized, will require the will and ability on the part of nation states to oversee its evolution. There is no global government ready to formulate and apply the necessary regulations; thus it is left to nation states to pick up the pieces as best they can and to provide the link between the global perspective and subnational regions, regions that are becoming increasingly frustrated over their inability to influence not only forces operating beyond their borders but even those shaping their own local economies.

In attempting to play a new role in the emerging scheme of things, nation states will have to look at the functioning of their democratic institutions and their requirements. If we have learned anything during the past thirty years, it is that attempts to reform the civil service as if political institutions do not matter invariably force reformers to work at the margin. Governance starts and ends with our democratic institutions, to which a civil service is at least partially accountable. The wave of reforms we have seen have either begun with a deliberate decision not to ask fundamental questions about political institutions (e.g., Fulton) or have simply proceeded without asking how the reforms would be made workable in the political environment.

The time may well have come for public servants to say to Parliament, Congress, Cabinet, and Cabinet committees "heal thyself" first before further civil service reforms can be attempted. Our political institutions were designed when things were simple and when nation states operated in relative isolation of one another. If the global economy now requires a well-honed capacity on the part of a national public service to innovate, to challenge the status quo, to take risks, to change course quickly, and to have the capacity to speak simultaneously to both the global perspective and to subnational regions, political leaders must attach some question marks to the workings of their own institutions, to what they do, and to how they do it.

There are still precious few rewards for calling a spade a spade or for risk taking in government bureaucracies, and plenty of career punishments for creating or mismanaging a political crisis or for a bureaucratic faux pas, particularly the ones reported in the media. Bureaucracy, as is well known, was designed to give priority to due process, to applying rules and regulations fairly, to responding to political direction from above, and to ensuring a full public accountability of its decisions and activities. In the hierarchical world of central bureaucracies, one looks upwards in order to serve political masters, the permanent secretary or other senior permanent officials as best one can. There is always a political crisis to manage, a "turf" war to be won, and centrally prescribed rules and processes to observe. Talking about the need for greater emphasis on service to clients and establishing new executive or special agencies will only carry civil service reforms so far. Real reforms can take place only if political institutions are themselves reformed. In short, the search for less bureaucracy without less government may only be possible if politicians also look at the reform of their own institutions.

The quality of governance in the new global order, however, extends beyond national political institutions and their civil services. New means of communication are making the public stronger actors in the governance process. As we noted earlier, people are being empowered. This is not to suggest for a moment that they have the necessary knowledge to pressure politicians and their governments to pursue the "general public good." Robert A. Dahl's recent essay on the "problem of civil competence" speaks eloquently to this issue (Dahl 1992). If the objective in the global economy is to see people and regions reduce their reliance on government and to see the qualities of citizenship "restored" (Massé 1992), then public servants may well need to become teachers of public policy and governance. They may be called upon to act as "knowledge-based" advisers explaining the required trade-offs, and to assist in determining and explaining the parameters within which solutions must be found. This, in turn, will require redefining the relationship between politicians and career officials.

National civil services themselves must also look internally and strengthen their capacity to be creative, to challenge the status quo, and to recommend and implement change. It is not too great an exaggeration to suggest that on the policy side, the quality of a civil service "corresponds to the discretion available to be creative" (Aberbach and Rockman 1992:145). Again, recent reforms did not deal with this issue. The emphasis in the 1980s was on removing administrative – or better yet, management – shackles rather than policy shackles. If anything, the attempts to rediscover the politics/ administration or management dichotomy served to undermine the policy role of civil servants. With the exception of cuts in the numbers and size of policy units, the policy machinery in government looks exactly as it did in the late 1970s. Perhaps the fear of strengthening the policy role of officials prevented the political leadership from reforming the policy formulation, coordination, and evaluation machinery in government. Still, we know that the hierarchical nature of government departments, the dysfunctions of permanence, and the "system" are inhibiting creative talents in government.

There is also, of course, the ongoing bureaucratic dilemma in which the urgent drives out the important, a dilemma which remains unresolved. Policy fire-fighting is the norm in policy units. Their criteria for success is how well senior officials and politicians are being served on the policy front. The problem here, of course, is that senior officials and politicians are rarely in a position to compare the work of their policy units with another across the street. Standards can change whenever there are changes in senior personnel or in politicians. In addition, in a collegial system, the expectations include securing the respect of other units in the department or other government departments. This is hardly conducive to developing a capacity to be creative or to challenge the status quo. Some officials in "policy shops" readily admit a reluctance to tackle "big" issues for fear of challenging the operational side of the department (Savoie 1994:214). One official explained that his policy shop had "become irrelevant by attempting to be relevant and supportive of the operational side of the department" (Savoie 1994). Another reports that an inordinate amount of time was spent "keeping fingers in all areas to ensure that our side is protected in the interdepartmental game" (Savoie 1994). Again, we have seen precious few efforts thus far to deal with such problems. To achieve changes, political leaders will have to indicate to their civil services that there is a market for objective, nonpartisan policy advice.

At the risk of overstating the case, there was far more evidence in 1980 that the policy side of government and the ability of bureaucracy to be innovative and self-questioning needed more attention than did the machine- or production-like agencies (Rourke and Schulman 1989:133). If nothing else, we needed a fundamental review of the merits of advising on policy from a sectoral or departmental perspective. The current machinery of government tends to compartmentalize thinking in government. It was, no doubt, appropriate at the turn of the century to establish vertical sectoral lines and deal with problems in agriculture, transportation, and industry in relative isolation. Issues and challenges confronting nation states, however, now increasingly cross departmental lines. If key policy issues are more and more horizontal, then the bureaucratic policy formulation and advisory structures must become horizontal as well. Civil servants will have to bring a far broader and more informed perspective to bear on their work, since issues are now much more complicated and interrelated.

The idea of looking at government operations from a framework that encourages the different assessment of different kinds of activities also holds promise. Such a framework could distinguish: (a) developmental agencies that design or create changes, or advise on them; (b) clerical delivery agencies, whose operating employees require relatively little training in providing certain services; (c) professional delivery agencies, which provide governmental services of a more skilled nature; and (d) control agencies, which act in some kind of control capacity vis-à-vis segments of the population (e.g., regulation), the population at large (army, police, etc.), or government itself (e.g., Treasury Board). In addition, new agencies should be distinguished in their "start-up" years from long-established ones.

Each of these could use a different kind of structure to make it more effective. Developmental agencies seem to function best with "adhocracy" type structures, which must be highly flexible, decentralized, and provide relatively quick access to senior officials and to political authority. Professional delivery agencies, as well as many control agencies, tend to require a "professional bureaucracy" structure, which could be decentralized. Neither of these structures, however, lends itself to performance measurement. Clerical delivery agencies appropriately rely on the traditional structure of "machine bureaucracy" that is centralized in power and formalized in procedure. They lend themselves to some form of performance measurement.

All in all, new approaches, particularly ones designed to strengthen the policy capacity of national civil services, are required for nation states to meet new challenges. Indeed, the challenges at hand have a great deal more to do with creativity, quick response to emerging problems, and with a capacity to reconcile various interests both at home and even abroad than with squeezing more productivity out of the machine-like departments or administrative units. It only takes a moment's reflection to appreciate some of the challenges ahead for nation states. Globalization and the legacies of the new "public management" are raising important issues of organizational complexity, including the problem of overlapping organizations dealing with overlapping issues, the need to strike a new balance between the public and private sectors, the ensuring of accountability in both public and private sectors, and the management of multi-organizational approaches to program delivery (Farazmand 1994:29).

It is also wrong to assume that the global economy, the rise of local or regional governments, and the burgeoning international bureaucracy (e.g., United Nations) will leave in their wake little for national civil services to do. To be sure, the emerging world order is reshaping the international power structure and the impact on national civil services will be profound. The world is no longer divided along ideological lines, with two superpowers dominating the political landscape and military orientations. New problems are constantly being added to the political agenda, yet, many of the old ones still remain. It may be, however, that nation states and their governments will need to focus on new targets and to look to new policy instruments. For example, in the past, national industrial policy often looked to firms as its target for development. Given the rise of global firms, it may be that in future national industrial policy should instead look to capital markets to meet public policy goals. Similarly, grants to businesses may no longer be an appropriate regional development policy instrument. It may be appropriate in future to focus on the community or the individual rather than on the private firm.

Though there is no denying that regional or local forces, often fuelled by ethnic, religious, cultural, and economic differences, are running strong everywhere and are challenging nation states, it remains that national governments will still be the ones asked to resolve old and new problems, albeit with new approaches and new policy levers. A recent incident off the coast of Newfoundland speaks to this issue (Troubled Waters 1992). The Canadian government imposed a two-year moratorium on groundfish, following the virtual disappearance of the northern cod off the coast of Newfoundland and Labrador. The moratorium extended to two hundred miles off the coast of Newfoundland and Labrador, or the area over which Canada holds jurisdiction. Spanish fishermen, however, have continued to fish on the "nose" of the Grand Banks, which – at least as far as Newfoundland fishermen are concerned – is an important spawning ground for northern cod. The nose, however, is located just beyond the two-hundred-mile limit. A number of Newfoundland fishermen, with the full support of the Newfoundland provincial government, set out to sea in a large fishing trawler in the summer of 1992 to confront the Spanish fishing fleet. A television crew captured the confrontation, which unfolded as follows: the Newfoundland ship came within fifty yards or so of a Spanish trawler and a spokesperson for the Newfoundlanders called the Spanish captain to express his displeasure and to ask him to leave the area. The Spanish captain replied that he was in international waters, that there were precious few fish left elsewhere, and that he and his crew had to make a living. The Newfoundlander replied that although the Spanish ship was beyond the two-hundred-mile limit, overfishing on the nose of the Grand Banks had serious implications for the local fishery and explained that he and his colleagues were also trying to make a living. At that point both sides agreed that they had a lot in common – they were fishermen, they wanted to continue to be fishermen, and they should make every effort to protect the fishery. They also agreed to a solution: they recognized that they could not resolve the problem themselves and concluded that both their "national" governments would have to meet to resolve the problem. The Government of Newfoundland and Labrador sought to raise the issue at a U.N. sponsored conference "on high-sea fishing" but it was told that the problem was too "minor" to be dealt with at the United Nations (Citizen 1993:5).

This story illustrates well the role nation states will have to play in future. The global economy can set the stage for national and local economies to compete and lay down the rules under which economies and firms must operate. It is hardly possible, however, to imagine a global economy taking shape without conflicts between firms, sectors, regions, and nations or without far-reaching adjustments in some sectors and regions. The designers of the new order will have to be national politicians and national public services. They alone have the legitimacy. In short, national governments will have to take the lead in managing and resolving these conflicts, in paving the way for adjustments to take place, and in integrating regional economies. To do so they will need "national" civil services with the capacity to be creative, to seek out compromises, to educate, and to initiate and manage change. The challenge at hand is one of redefining the role of government in major policy areas, identifying new levers, and designing policy to deal with the new political and economic forces emerging.

Though no one can deny that the globalization of the economy, the information revolution, ecological awareness, and population migration appear to be making national borders porous, the nation state has not run its course. The suggestion that it is becoming a relic of the twentieth century appears to be premature. The instant creation of a united Germany, the continuing cohesion of many nation states such as China, Japan, and the United States, and recent developments in the Maastricht process suggest that the nation state has strong staying power. It requires, however, a stronger capacity on the part of its civil service to manage change and economic adjustments, to deal with strongly felt local, regional, and political identities and loyalties, and the ever-expanding scope of the "global" economy.

BIBLIOGRAPHY

Aberbach, Joel D., and Bert A. Rockman. 1992. Does governance matter – and if so, how? Process, performance and outcomes. *Governance* 5, 2 (April).

Aucoin, Peter. 1988. Administrative reform in public management: paradigms, principles, paradoxes and pendulums. *Governance* 3, 2.

Bell, Daniel. 1986.The world and the United States in 2013. *Daedalus* 116, 3.

Boston, Jonathan. 1991. The theoretical underpinnings of public restructuring in New Zealand. In *Reshaping the State, New Zealand's Bureaucratic Revolution*, eds. Jonathan Boston et al. Auckland: Oxford University Press.

Buchanan, James M., and Richard E. Wagner. 1977. *Democracy in Deficit: The Political Legacy of Lord Keynes*. New York: Academic Press.

Business Week. 1991. Government. Hightstown, N.J. (14 October).

Caiden, Gerald E. 1991. *Administrative Reform Comes of Age* . Berlin: Walter de Gruyter and Co.

Cairns, Allan C. 1992. *Charter Versus Federalism*. Montreal: McGill-Queen's University Press.

Carroll, James D. et al. 1985. Supply-side management in the Reagan administration. *Public Administration Review* 45, 6 (November/December).

Cleveland, Harlan. 1985. The twilight of hierarchy: speculations on the global information society. *Public Administration Review* 45, 1 (January/February).

Courchene, Thomas J. 1992. Mon pays, c'est l'hiver: reflections of a market populist. *Canadian Journal of Economics* xxv, 4.

Dahl, Robert A. 1992. The problem of civil competence. *Journal of Democracy* 3, 4 (October).

Farazmand, Ali. 1994. The new world order and global public administration: a critical essay. In *Public Administration in the Global Village*, ed. Jean-Claude Garcia-Zamor. Westport, CT: Greenwood Press.

Hennessy, Peter. 1989. *Whitehall*. London: Fontana Press.

Kaass, Max. 1972. The challenge of the participatory revolution in pluralist democracies. *International Political Science Review* 5, 3.

King, Alexander, and Bertrand Schneider. 1991. *The First Global Revolution: A Strategy for Surviving the World*. A report by the Council of the Club of Rome. London: Simon and Schuster.

Massé, Marcel. 1993. Getting government right. An address at the Public Service Alliance of Canada – Regional Quebec Conference, 12 September, at Longueuil.

_____1993. The John L. Manion Lecture: partners in the management of Canada: The changing roles of government and the public service. Ottawa: Canadian Centre for Management Development.

Metcalfe, Les, and Sue Richards. 1987. *Improving Public Management*. London: Sage Publications.

Meyrowitz, Joshua. 1985. *No Sense of Place*. New York: Oxford University Press.

Osborne, David, and Ted Gaebler. 1992. *Reinventing Government: How the Entrepreneurial Spirit is Transforming the Public Sector.* Reading, MA: Addison-Wesley.

Ostry, Sylvia. 1990. *Governments and Corporations in a Shrinking World.* New York: Council on Foreign Relations Press.

Ottawa Citizen.1993. Fisheries crisis too small for U.N., E.C. official says. (14 July).

Parklington, Tom. 1982. Against inflating human rights. *The Windsor Yearbook of Access to Justice.* Windsor, ON: University of Windsor.

Peters, B. Guy. 1993. *The Public Service, the Changing State, and Governance.* Ottawa: Canadian Centre for Management Development.

Pollitt, Christopher. 1988. *Managerialism and the Public Services.* Oxford: Basil Blackwell.

Porter, Michael E. 1990. The competitive advantage of nations. *Harvard Business Review* (March/April).

Reich, Robert B. 1991. *The Work of Nations.* New York: Alfred A. Knopf.

Rourke, Francis E. and Schulman. 1989. "Adhocracy in policy development. *The Social Science Journal* 26, 2. (They argue that "bureaucratic think tank comes close to being an oxymoron.")

Rourke, Francis E. 1992. Responsiveness and neutral competence in American bureaucracy. *Public Administration Review* 56, 6 (November/December).

Savoie, Donald J. *The Politics of Public Spending in Canada.* Toronto: University of Toronto Press.

_____ 1994. *Thatcher, Reagan, Mulroney: In Search of a New Bureaucracy.* Pittsburgh: University of Pittsburgh Press.

Simeon, Richard. Globalization and the Canadian nation-state. A paper presented to a conference sponsored April 1990 by the C.D. Howe Institute, Toronto.

Solomon, Lester M., and Michael S. Lund. 1984. Governance in the Reagan era: an overview. In *The Reagan Presidency and the Governing of America,* eds. Lester M. Solomon and Michael S. Lund. Washington, DC: The Urban Institute Press.

Taras, David. 1990. *The Newsmakers: The Media's Influence on Canadian Politics.* Scarborough, ON: Nelson Canada.

The Economist. 1993. A survey of multinationals. (27 March).

_____ 1993. A Survey of International Banking. (10 April).

Toffler, Alvin. 1990. *Powershift: Knowledge, Wealth and Violence at the Edge of the 21st Century.* New York: Bantam.

Troubled Waters. 1992. A Burma-Olser Production, 29 April. St. John's, the United Allied Food Workers, January 1993.

University of Washington: Northwest Policy Centre. 1991. Strategies for the Pacific northwest economic region.

Valaskakis, Kimon. 1992. A prescription for Canada inc. *The Globe and Mail*. Toronto. (31 October).

Williams, Doug. 1991. Problems of governance, political participation and administration of justice in an information society. Ottawa: Department of Justice.

Williams, Shirley. 1980. The decision makers. In *Policy and Practice: The Experience of Government*. London: Royal Institute of Public Administration.

Williams, Walter. 1988. *Washington, Westminster and Whitehall*. Cambridge: Cambridge University Press.

Wilson, James Q. 1989. *Bureaucracy: What Governments Do and Why They Do It*. New York: Basic Books.

PART THREE

THE POLITICAL PROCESS

AND GOVERNANCE

Politicians, Public Servants, and Public Management: Getting Government Right

PETER AUCOIN

INTRODUCTION

The malaise in contemporary governance, which began with the politics of restraint in the 1970s, sparked off a revolt against government that has yet to run its course. Everywhere governments continue in their efforts to roll back the state through some combination of privatization, contracting out, deregulation, expenditure reduction, program termination, downsizing the public service, and measures to contain pressures on the public purse. In many, but not all, Western democracies, bureaucracy-bashing accompanied the politics of restraint. In the Anglo-American democracies in particular, career public services were subject to an assault by politicians that was unprecedented in this century. Relations between politicians and the public service turned sour and public service morale plummeted. The combination of policies to restrain government and bureaucracy-bashing during the 1980s appeared to be a formula for electoral success. Government, as Ronald Reagan put it, was "the problem." Hence even incumbent politicians could run "against government," if they identified bureaucrats as the source of the problem "in government."

Much has changed over the course of the past decade, however. Three of the political leaders most identified with bureaucracy-bashing, namely Margaret Thatcher in Britain, Reagan in the United States, and

Brian Mulroney in Canada, have now departed (Savoie 1994). Although the Conservatives still govern in Britain, John Major is clearly not a Thatcherite in his relations with the British public service (Wilson 1991). In the United States, George Bush tempered the effects of Reagan's demoralization of the American career public service (Aberbach 1991); the Clinton Democrats promised to restore public confidence in government by "reinventing" it (Gore 1993). In Canada, the Conservatives under Mulroney's successor as Conservative prime minister, Kim Campbell, were humiliated at the polls in 1993, winning only two seats in a House of Commons with 295 members, and thereby losing their status as a recognized parliamentary party.

As the Democratic presidential candidate, Bill Clinton, had done in the American presidential election the previous year, the Canadian federal Liberal party, headed by Jean Chrétien, promised to restore public confidence in government and rebuild relations between politicians and the public service. Its leading spokesperson on the public service, in a campaign speech approved in advance by Chrétien, declared that: "Good government requires a close and congenial relationship between public servants of every level and politicians. In particular, ministers and deputy ministers [in Canada, the senior public servant in each government department] have to work together intimately and must share a mutual trust" (Massé 1993a:6).

Among the first decisions of the newly elected Liberal government were: (1) a major downsizing in partisan-political ministerial offices, including the prime minister's office, which had been significantly enlarged under the Conservatives (Aucoin 1986); (2) the elimination of the post of "chief of staff" as the head of each of these ministerial offices – senior positions first created by the Conservative government in 1984 when it assumed office (Plasse 1994); and, (3) the creation of a new cabinet portfolio for "public service renewal."

The prime minister's statement in announcing the first two changes was explicit: "The important role played by ministerial staff [in Canada, almost exclusively partisan appointees from outside the public service] should not duplicate the role of the department. Ministers should look to their Deputy Ministers for professional advice and support, on both policy and operations, across the full range of their responsibilities" (Canada 1993:2). The appointment of Massé, a former deputy minister-turned-Liberal politician who was personally appointed a Liberal candidate by Chrétien, was equally explicit. It was meant to signal the government's intention to reverse the philosophy and practice of the Conservative government in regard to its relations with the federal public service, a public service that Massé proclaimed as second to none internationally. For Massé, these changes were critical to "getting government right."

If it is necessary to get government "right," what had gone wrong in the first place? Massé's campaign answer to this question was twofold. First, "Over the last eight years the Tories have been trying to persuade this country that the private sector can solve almost any problem. They see no particular role for government." Second, "Reinforcing simplistic biases, government and the people who work in it are always portrayed by the Tories as inefficient, bureaucratic, and unreliable. The best thing the public service could hope for when the Tories were elected, said Mulroney, was 'pink slips and running shoes'" (1993a:4).

More than six months into government, however, it became clear that "getting government right" for the Liberals meant essentially three things: (1) "redefining" the role of the federal government to make government "affordable," that is, to get government expenditures under control by subjecting federal programs to review; (2) eliminating "overlap and duplication" in federal and provincial programs, through collaborative efforts with the provinces; and, (3) assessing the continuing relevance of a wide variety of nondepartmental agencies, boards, and commissions (Massé 1993b). The strategic plan of the new Liberal government, in short, looks very much like that of the Conservatives when they assumed office in 1984, minus, of course, the rhetoric of bureaucracy-bashing and the number and status of partisan-political staff in ministerial offices. "Public service renewal," however, has meant a continuation of the restraint measures introduced by the Conservatives, including, ironically, many of the very initiatives Massé blamed for poor morale under the Conservatives (Swimmer, Hicks, and Milne 1994).

If the Liberal's strategic plan continues to be to roll back the state, what changes, other than a change in government, brought about this apparent need to restore the traditional model of "close and congenial" relations between politicians and public servants? Second, to the extent that the Conservative government was following the examples of other political regimes, especially those the Tories most sought to emulate, namely the United States under Ronald Reagan and Britain under Margaret Thatcher (Savoie 1994), does the Canadian reversal mirror experience elsewhere?

In the analysis that follows I argue that, over the past decade, career public servants across several jurisdictions have demonstrated that they are able and willing to be responsive to changes in political priorities and policy objectives demanded by politicians intent on restraining government; and, that career public servants, again during the same period and across several jurisdictions, have demonstrated that they are able and willing to adjust to political demands for improved public management. Although the value of partisan-political assistants as well as external consultants has been demonstrated over this same period, politicians have come to recognize, once again, that career public servants are essential to good government. In the process, however, political leaders have learned, first, that career public services will be responsive only to the extent that politicians themselves engage the state apparatus and, second, that improved public management will occur only in so far as management regimes and practices demand results.

CHALLENGING THE ADMINISTRATIVE STATE

Notwithstanding the universal acceptance of career public service as a condition of good government in the modern development of Western democracies, different constitutional structures affect relations between public servants and elected officials in executive and legislative branches in different ways (Peters 1989). The creation of career public services throughout what are now the Western democracies occurred at different times, took different forms, and were the consequence of different constellations of political forces. In each case, the flowering of career public services paralleled the rise of the modern "administrative state." The administrative state emerged as a consequence of the significant expansion of government interventions in the economy and society in Western industrial nations. With this expansion, the size and complexity of government operations, coupled with the increasing time demands on elected officials to manage the political dimensions of governance, resulted in public service elites with significant influence and power in governance. This development was not unique to government; it paralleled the emergence of managerial elites in the private sector, as the twentieth century corporate form of organization separated ownership and management.

In the Western systems of representative government, accordingly, those who advised political decision makers and implemented their policies could not but challenge the supremacy of their political masters in government. This state of affairs was tolerated, if not always welcomed, by politicians in power so long as the dominant policy paradigm accommodated, and therefore was seen to serve, their political priorities and policy objectives. To this extent, politicians could accept both their limited control over the career public service as an institution of governance and the significant role of public servants in governance, not only in administering the law and managing government programs but in advising on public policy.

Although this equilibrium was questioned at various times, particularly with changes in government, over the past three decades it has been challenged in fundamental ways. In large part this has been the result of declining confidence in, and thus support for, the efficacy of the paradigm of an interventionist-welfare state in securing both economic growth and continuous improvements in public services. To the degree that politicians regarded their public services as wedded to this paradigm, they began to question the value of a career public service to good government. When, in the 1970s, politicians, first on the right but soon after also on the left, began to roll back the state, they could not but challenge their public services directly.

In the Anglo-American democracies, the principal theoretical challenge to the idea of a career public service as a condition of good government came from the combined assault of public choice theory and, its close relation, agency theory (Boston 1991; Pollitt 1990). Both theories assume that public servants, like all others engaged in politics and government, have their own self-interests to promote; that these will often be at odds with those of elected representatives and those they represent; and, that because of the power of bureaucrats relative to that of elected politicians, the interests of the former will win out over the objectives and priorities of the latter. The second theory also assumes public servants have their own interests to pursue. But it presents a clearer thesis as to why bureaucrats are so powerful. Under this formulation, public servants are viewed as the "agents" of elected representatives, who are their "principals." In this structure of relations, it is posited, the former invariably have the upper hand over the latter: they have an inherent "information advantage" in the formulation of public policies and their subsequent behaviour in policy implementation is largely unobservable (Boston 1991). Public choice theory thus speaks to the limited capacity of politicians to direct the state apparatus; agency theory speaks to the limited capacity of politicians to hold their public administrators accountable.

There is, of course, an obvious element of reality portrayed by these theories, even though there is little, if anything, new. They portray both a reality and conundrum long recognized by scholars and experienced practitioners alike. However, the popularization of these theoretical assertions via "Yes, Minister" mythology, especially in the Anglo-American systems, has done much to spread public as well as political cynicism concerning relations between politicians and public servants (Borins 1988). In the *real-politik* of governance, these ideas may have served to temper a naive enthusiasm for, or self-serving promotion of, career public service as a "vocation" (Campbell 1988a). But, to the degree that they served only to embellish bureaucracy-bashing, they undermined the "congenial relations" between politicians and bureaucrats required to secure the "mutual trust" essential to good government.

In any event, the seeds of discontent implicit in this mythology fell on fertile ground. The fiscal crises of Western democracies that emerged in the 1970s reduced the capacities of these states to provide public services at levels to which citizens had become accustomed. At the same time, however, most, if not all, governments quickly learned that taxpayer tolerance for increased taxation had also diminished. In addition, in what was increasingly becoming a global economy, governments themselves either resisted or were hesitant to impose additional impediments to the competitiveness of their national economies. Both expenditure and regulatory restraint became the order of the day common across governments, whatever their ideological dispositions.

In some jurisdictions, of course, government restraint was accompanied by the rebirth of "limited government" ideologies, best represented by the Thatcher Conservatives in Britain and the Reagan Republicans in the United States, strongly supported, financially and intellectually, by an increasingly politically active business class (Pollitt 1990). Support for limited government was also fueled by the significant rise in scepticism about the effectiveness and efficiency of the interventionist-welfare state on the part of the increasingly educated and better informed middle classes of Western democracies. The coalitions that had brought about the interventionist-welfare state everywhere began to collapse into various states of disarray.

These transformations in the political orders of Western democracies have also been fostered by the extent to which increasingly aggressive mass media, legislators and legislative agencies (especially auditing agencies) have enhanced public awareness of the shortcomings extant within governance and public administration. While there may be little that is novel in these accounts for those knowledgeable about government and public administration, public perceptions of a general disregard for economy in government, limited attention to the pursuit of administrative efficiency, and the futility of many government undertakings in achieving their socioeconomic objectives have clearly increased. Among other factors, greater access to government information has also resulted in a diminution in deference to authority, including the technical expertise of public services. Demands for greater public consultation, more transparent government, and increased public accountability constitute a widespread public reaction to the closed character of the modern administrative state.

While dissatisfaction with government increased, political participation did not decline. Rather, it shifted focus in at least two directions. On the one hand, political activists in increasing numbers rejected the primary traditional institutions of political participation, namely political parties, and opted to expend their time and energies in interest groups or social movements. On the other hand, there emerged in a number of political systems an increasing interest in new political parties and political movements that sought to challenge the existing structures of representative government. For the latter, representative government had come to mean government by and for special interests and elite groups. These two strands of opposition to the established order, albeit ranging across the political spectrum, are joined in common cause, at least in part, in the increasing public support for the institutional mechanisms of direct democracy, especially referenda and citizen initiatives.

In this new environment, as fluid as its dynamics were (and continue to be), it is not surprising that politicians almost everywhere, and of all partisan stripes, sought to reassert their authority over the state apparatus. Their public services had to be tamed and brought under control if the politics of restraint were to be applied to self-regulating, "budget maximizing" bureaucrats (Blais and Dion 1991).

ENGAGING THE STATE

For perhaps the same reasons that it has always been the least secure of the Western career public services, the American federal public service experienced the most explicit assault by politicians (Hill 1992). In addition to the massive negative political rhetoric to which it was subjected for almost two decades, a significant expansion in the number of partisan political appointees to the administrative apparatus of the federal bureaucracy, beginning in the Nixon administration and reaching its zenith in the Reagan presidency, severely reduced the power and influence of career public servants. An extension to presidential authority, enacted under Jimmy Carter, combined with Reagan's excessively partisan view of governance, resulted in a degree of politicization unprecedented even for the United States. This took its toll on the federal public service as an important institution of governance (Ingraham, Eisenberg, and Thompson 1993).

The political assault on career public service systems that this kind of politicization represented, however, constituted only one approach to reasserting political direction over the state apparatus. Governments in the Westminster tradition have been no less inclined to deploy direct challenges to their career public services, although not all evinced the same degree of bureaucracy-bashing experienced in the United Kingdom or Canada. Under the Westminster system, with Cabinet separate from, yet dominant in, Parliament, ministers, and especially prime ministers, bent on asserting political control are able to effect change more easily than in the American system. In Britain under Thatcher, in Australia under Bob Hawke, and in New Zealand under David Lange, governments from the two ends of the political spectrum asserted political authority to the fullest (Wilson 1991; Campbell and Halligan 1992; Boston 1991). Political assistants in increasing numbers were appointed to support ministers, including the prime minister. But in no case was there a partisan politicization of the career public service in the American style. Rather, prime ministers and ministers became more active in determining senior appointments, using either traditional powers, as in Britain, or newly devised apppointment powers, as in Australia and New Zealand.

Notwithstanding Thatcher's rhetoric it was only in Canada, under Mulroney, that an explicit attempt was made to emulate the American model within a Westminster system. With the creation of ministerial chiefs of staff, as well as a major expansion in the staff of the prime minister's and ministerial offices, a new design was effected: partisan political appointees were to constitute a counterweight to the public service. Within two years of assuming office, moreover, all deputy ministers who remained in government had new positions (Bourgault and Dion 1989). In almost all cases, however, the Mulroney government appointed its deputies from within the federal public service. The expected infusion of private sector executives into the senior ranks of the federal public service failed to materialize. For some potential recruits the pay was not attractive; for others, the assumption that ministers and their political officials, rather than deputies, were to be in control made the positions much less attractive. Although Mulroney and many, if not all, of his ministers, never tired of bureaucracy-bashing, the Conservatives' efforts to emulate the American model failed (Zussman 1986). Their political aides, especially at the outset, were best known for their inability to master the arts of governance; indeed, the Prime Minister's Office itself had to be rescued by a career public servant, seconded from the Department of External Affairs (Aucoin 1988; Campbell 1988b).

A third approach to reasserting political authority was exhibited in those continental European democracies, most notably France and Germany, where a longstanding relationship between political elites and career public servants has enabled the latter not only to participate in partisan politics but also to identify with governments in a partisan manner. As a consequence, there has been much less bureaucracy-bashing in these systems, due in no small measure to the fact that the political elites in these two regimes contain many former career public servants. In addition, ministers are able to appoint experienced public servants who share their partisan affiliation to staff their ministerial offices and to head government ministries. Asserting political control in these circumstances meant extending the range of partisan appointments from within the public service to senior positions in the public service (Mayntz and Derlien 1989; Derlien 1991).

Given these several different approaches to reasserting political control, there is a need, as Campbell concludes in his analysis of the political roles of senior government officials, to "cast around for new terms to capture the 'politicization' of bureaucracy" (1988a:271). Campbell's account of these developments is especially instructive. He carefully distinguishes the politicization that accompanies the use of external appointments to the regular state apparatus or to ministerial/executive offices in order to tame the bureaucracy, as practised in the United States, especially during the Reagan era, or in Canada under Mulroney, from the more strategic efforts to utilize professional political and public service expertise to enable the political executive to engage the state apparatus in pursuit of its political priorities and policy objectives. Viewed in this manner, the first approach derives neither from a sound understanding of the dynamics that make bureaucracy difficult to control, let alone to direct, nor from an appreciation of what is necessary to establish the critical linkages between political responsiveness and technical competence that are essential to good government.

Securing these critical linkages means recognizing that good government requires the strategic deployment of partisan professionals, whether these are recruited from outside the public service or from the public service itself, as in the case of France or Germany. In most Western systems, the number of professionals outside the public service competent to assist ministers in the management of the state has increased over the past few decades. This is a result of several factors, including: a universal increase in higher education in fields related to public policy; increased professionalization in the staffs of organized interest groups as well as private corporations; and the growth of research institutes, party foundations, and think tanks concerned with matters of public policy. The second and third of these developments have also been influenced by the growing numbers of public servants who have left the public service to work in these settings as well as the growing numbers of others who have worked temporarily for governmental bodies, especially quasi-independent advisory agencies, commissions of enquiry, and task forces.

In addition to the value added by these partisans on purely technical grounds (namely securing the broadest possible inclusion of the options that ought to be considered by politicians), political assistants, consultants, and "minders" (Walter 1986) serve to link politicians to the broader political environment in ways that go beyond both the policy networks and experiences of nonpartisan public servants. Although nonpartisan career public servants have long considered it their responsibility to advise on public policy and its implementation in ways that encompass a knowledge and understanding of the political implications of the options and issues confronting political executives, partisan strategies and communications lie beyond the pale of a neutral public service. Even the Chrétien government, with its stated intention to rebuild political-public service relations, for instance, did not dispute that there is a necessary and legitimate role for partisan political assistants to ministers.

If politicians require partisan political assistance to manage the political dimensions of governance, how does this relate to a restoration in relations between politicians and public servants? Campbell's prescription here is relevant. He argues that "the most compelling method for those committed to the improvement of governance" is the "blending of partisan responsiveness and continuity in the form of *policy competence*" (1988a:271, emphasis in original). For this to occur, "political leaders [must] seek to engage the state apparatus and direct it towards their partisan priorities rather than simply overriding it." This means at least "three strategies":

First, such leaders . . . continue to improve the control and guidance systems available to bureaucracy. These include policy and planning units operating at the cores of line departments and central agencies functioning at the heart of the executive branch. Secondly, these leaders . . . base their selection of partisan appointees on their credentials as policy professionals . . . Thirdly, those selecting career officials for service either in the key coordinative positions in departments or in central agencies . . . base their choice on the candidates' proven skill at crosscutting executive-bureaucratic gamesmanship (272).

This prescription is important from two perspectives. First, it recognizes that politicians cannot effectively engage the state apparatus if public servants do not occupy critical positions in policy and planning units, both at the centre and in departments. Public servants need not monopolize these positions, but they must be present in sufficient numbers. In the experience of the past decade, the best empirical evidence to support this prescription comes from the extent to which politicians in those regimes where there has been a conscious effort to decouple responsibilities for policy management on the one hand and operational management on the other, most notably in Britain and New Zealand, have continued to value the participation of public servants in policy management. Although these changes offered politicians an opportunity to limit the role of public servants to managing operations, they have continued to assign public servants major roles in policy management.

Second, the continued crucial role of career public servants in policy management has been shown to be a function of the degree to which politicians have strategically staffed senior positions. Strategic leadership applied to staffing the state apparatus has not precluded the appointment of outsiders, either as an exercise of traditional executive prerogative powers or as a result of open competitions for senior administrative positions. But success in strategic leadership in this respect requires that outsiders be competent in the arts of governance. This was perhaps best illustrated in the achievements of Sir Derek Rayner as a chief adviser to Thatcher. However, only to the extent that political leaders are themselves competent, at least in their capacities to recognize competence in others, will strategic leadership be present. The simple fact is that good government is unlikely to be forthcoming where political leaders lack this minimal competence, yet, at the same time, determine who shall, and who shall not, participate in policy management. The inexperience of both Reagan, at least in national government, and the Mulroney government, combined with their distrust of their career public services, goes a long way to explain their early shortcomings in governance (Savoie 1994).

These developments indicate that the idea of career public service is being transformed. While this transformation may have the effect of diminishing the traditional idea of a "career" public service as necessary to good government, it does not devalue the need for a "professional" public service staffed by persons who are experienced in public service per se. Indeed, recent experiences demonstrate, in ways that nostalgic appeals to tradition could not, that governments are poorly served when they seek to govern without reliance on those who are experienced in the arts of public administration (Savoie 1994). A public service that possesses both institutional memory and experienced staff is not a sufficient condition for good government, but it is a necessary condition.

If the past decade teaches anything, it is that the critical distinction in political-public service relations is not between the continuation of a career public service and a politicized bureaucracy. Rather, it is between a professional public service, however constituted, and a public service that lacks the necessary balance in professional competence and political responsiveness. In these regards, the crucial evidence relates not so much to formal systems, but to actual practice. For instance, over the past decade there has been little hard evidence to indicate any overt partisan-politicization of the senior public services in Australia, Britain, or Canada (Weller 1989; RIPA 1987; Bourgault and Dion 1989), each constituted basically on the same model. Yet relations between the senior public services and ministers (and their partisan political advisers) in each of these countries have been subject to relatively different patterns of interaction, mutual confidence, and trust. In Australia, the political leadership has effectively engaged the public service and the evidence suggests that results have been forthcoming (Campbell and Halligan 1992). In Britain, the political leadership, at least under Thatcher, was more demanding but also more hostile; the results, while impressive on some fronts, were inconsistent. In Canada, under Mulroney, the political leadership failed to engage the public service effectively; the results were less than satisfactory (Savoie 1994). In the Canadian case it was more than partisanship that led the Liberal party to claim that a new bargain between the public service and its political masters was required.

While it is increasingly recognized that the political leadership requires an effective working relationship with the professional public service, it is also acknowledged that political leaders require partisan-political assistance in managing the state. It matters little whether these partisans come from the public service, as in Germany or France, or from outside government, as in other regimes. Just as in the last century, when politicians accepted the need for a career public service to assist them in the administration of public affairs, as they become increasingly preoccupied with legislative politics (Parris 1969), political leaders now require a strengthening of the political arm of government if they are to cope with the demands of the transformed political systems that they must govern. These transformations have extended the political dimensions of governance well beyond traditional party politics. More than partisan loyalty is thus required of political assistants or partisan appointments to government offices; even partisans must now be competent in governance. They too must be able to engage the public service in the pursuit of good politics.

REFORMING PUBLIC MANAGEMENT

At first blush, it appears to be one of the great ironies of our age that the very politicians who have challenged the idea of career public service have also sought to enhance the capacities of public servants to perform their public service *management* functions. Although the influence of the "new public management" varies across Western democratic regimes, everywhere there is a recognition of the need to reduce the micromanagement of government operations by legislatures, the executive, and central administrative agencies (OECD 1993).

This recognition has resulted in the adoption of management regimes in which there is an increasing deregulation of operational management, with fewer controls imposed by the centre of government. A reduction in government-wide and standardized administrative rules, delegation of authority over the deployment of financial and human resources, and decentralization from the centre of operational agencies to front-line managers and personnel are the essential organizational design features of the new public management (Auditor General of Canada 1993).

The purpose of public management reform is to increase the degree to which public servants manage their operations in ways that enhance economy, efficiency, and effectiveness. Public servants are expected to become more cost-conscious in their use of inputs (financial and human resources), on the one hand, and more concerned with outputs (service quality and results), on the other (Scott, Bushnell, and Sallee 1990; Keating and Holmes 1990; Kemp 1990). The instruments to achieve these outcomes are increased flexibility for managers, down the line and out in the field, coupled with more explicit performance measures and service standards. The result implies a new bargain between politicians and their public servants involving organizational and management systems that simultaneously "let the managers manage," in order to promote economies and efficiencies, and "make the managers manage," in order to achieve effectiveness in serving citizens. Not surprisingly, these two developments cannot but introduce a fundamental paradox in changing political-public service relations (Aucoin 1990).

The twin goals of letting managers manage and making managers manage derive not only from the need to cope with fewer financial resources, but also from the tendency on the part of many politicians and citizens, and even some public servants, to compare the models and practices of management in the public sector unfavourably with those in the private sector. In one sense, the rhetorical contrast is one in which public management cannot but appear deficient, so long as management and service are conceived entirely in terms of narrow definitions of economy and efficiency in operations and quality service to a limited range of paying customers. The pursuit of the public interest in governance requires that politicians secure political support for public policies – the bottom line of democratic government. This, in turn, results in politicians pursuing competing values, whatever the consequences for incoherence in policy direction, stress on public finances, or limitations in service responsiveness. As Peter Hennessy puts it, government is "the sump into which all the impossible problems ultimately fall" (House of Commons, United Kingdom 1993:88). These conditions apply in all democratic regimes, regardless of the extent to which politicians are committed to state intervention in the socio-economic order.

In another sense, however, the new public management adheres to traditional values of public service in democratic governance; economy, efficiency, and effectiveness are not merely contemporary concerns introduced by a new focus on "management" within government. Moreover, some measure of discretion has always been exercised, indeed must be exercised, by subordinate public servants, including those on the front lines. This discretion is exercised in the name of political authorities, precisely because they have neither the time nor, in most instances, the practical knowledge to administer public policies across the entire range of particular cases to which they apply. While the time factor, perhaps, does not rule out an entirely politicized public service, in the Jacksonian mode (Riggs 1994), the factor of practical knowledge does, if good government is to be pursued.

The major consequence of increased decentralization in government for relations between politicians and public servants is that public servants, and especially public service managers, become more visible – to the public, to the media, and to politicians in the legislative branch of government. Given that legislatures in most jurisdictions have become more aggressive in challenging political executives, that independent legislative auditors (financial and otherwise) are more comprehensive in their audits, that media scrutiny everywhere now subjects governments and their administrators to more searching reporting and critical analyses, and that citizens are less deferential to and more demanding of governments, greater visibility for public servants is inevitable. In addition, in so far as public management reforms entail published service standards and performance targets and measures, the visibility of public servants, and thus their answerability to an increasing number of authorities and interests, is further increased. In many systems, the reality, if not the theory, of public accountability is beginning to emulate the longstanding practices of American government with its multiple sources of demands for administrative accountability (Wilson 1989).

In the Westminster systems, in particular, these developments have been viewed with alarm in some quarters as constituting a regressive step in public accountability (Sutherland 1991). The official response in most cases is that no change has occurred: public servants, however visible in their new roles, remain subordinate to ministers, even if, as with the newly devised "chief executive" positions in New Zealand, for example, they are delegated full responsibility for the delivery of the outputs of their organizations. Ministers still remain publicly accountable to Parliament.

There is perhaps no way to resolve this difference of opinion, precisely because the very concept of individual ministerial responsibility (in contrast to the system of collective government responsibility, whereby a government can be forced to resign or call an election by the legislature) depends almost entirely on the constitutional norms and political dynamics extant in a given political system. In any event, it appears unlikely that concerns for preserving traditional interpretations of public accountability will slow down public management reform. Greater public exposure to criticism from politicians, the media, and citizens is part and parcel of the bargain between executive politicians and public servants implicit in the new public management. To the degree that such exposure requires public servants to defend themselves publicly, tensions, and even conflicts, between public servants and their political masters are bound to occur.

Moreover, the new public management, by pushing for greater decentralization and thus a further separation of policy and operational responsibilities, cannot but result in increased organizational differentiation. To the degree that program designs and implementation strategies come from those at the operating core as "emergent" policy (Mintzberg and Jorgenson 1987), the new public management has an important contribution to make to good government, precisely because those down the line and out in the field will have increased opportunities to "reinvent government" (Osborne and Gaebler 1992).

Although swings in the centralization-decentralization, regulation-deregulation, and control-delegation pendulums are to be expected, it is unlikely that major reversals will be forthcoming in the near future where regimes have made fundamental changes, such as the decentralization initiative in France, the executive agency structure in Britain, or the New Zealand division of policy and operational departments. These and other reforms, such as the major changes to cabinet and portfolio structures in Australia (Halligan 1987) and Canada (Aucoin and Bakvis 1993), may not constitute the revolution in public management that some of their adherents would claim, but they have become integral parts of reformed management systems. Moreover, public servants have demonstrated that they are more than capable of adjusting to the demands for improved public management that these new systems require. Equally important, it is increasingly recognized that, while major economies require decisions from the centre of government (prime minister/president, finance/treasury/budget ministers and departments) to effect expenditure reductions, the driving force of decentralization is the need to manage operating budgets in ways that not only contain spending but deploy resources as efficiently as possible. Central controls and standardized administrative practices simply cannot achieve these results.

Reversing these changes would not only have enormous consequences for public service morale in most cases, they would signal a further collapse of faith in the capacities of government, and those who work in government, to provide public services in ways that are economical, efficient, and effective. The more likely scenario for the near future is continued efforts to redefine the business of government. More government functions will be privatized, others will be contracted out, and some undertakings will be terminated in whole or in part. In these respects, public service morale is likely to remain low for as long as governments continue to roll back the state (Peters 1991). Efforts to pull power back to the centre of government, however, will likely be resisted where newly empowered clients or local community partners are affected. Reinventing government also means reshaping government-citizen relations, as implied, for instance, in the Citizen's Charter in Britain (Doern 1992) or decentralization in France (de Montricher 1991).

CONCLUSIONS

Relations between politicians and public servants in public management have clearly been transformed over the past decade. The demands on politicians have intensified with the combined onslaught of the fiscal crises of Western democracies and the emergence of new challenges to traditional practices of representative government and public administration. The former did not cause the latter, but they have altered relations between politicians and the public service, in part because they require greater transparency and accountability in public management and greater participation by citizens in governance.

Politicians have responded by reasserting their authority within governance and public management, by seeking increased assistance from outside government, and by attempting to ensure that their public servants are responsive to their political priorities and policy objectives. Different regimes have approached this in different ways, in part because their institutional systems provide different degrees of discretion to mold their public services.

Although merit remains the basis for recruitment and for promotion through the ranks below the most senior positions in all career public services, it is highly unlikely that the self-regulating character of career public services, in selecting the members of their own elites, will be restored. The critical issue for good government, accordingly, is the extent to which politicians recognize the requirement to staff senior positions in the public service with competent and experienced professionals. This does not rule out selecting career public servants who are sympathetic to the political, policy, or management priorities of a government, however these sympathies are determined. Nor does it rule out the appointment of professionals from outside the public service in question, that is from the private sector or from other public services. The New Zealand approach, with open competitions managed by the State Services Commission, may offer an alternative to the kind of politicization experienced in Britain and Canada.

For the same reasons, good government also requires that politicians be assisted in the partisan-political dimensions of their work. The effective exercise of political power demands more than a simple reassertion of formal authority over the state apparatus. The new political dynamics of modern democratic government – more aggressive interest groups, media, legislators, and auditing agencies of various sorts – call for a greater attention to transparency, communications, consultations, and accountability than has been traditionally provided by the partisan dynamics of elections and legislative debate. Politicians can no more handle all this on their own than they could handle the administrative challenges brought on by the rise of the administrative state. But mindless partisan-politicization, as witnessed in the Reagan or Mulroney regimes, will be no more effective in meeting this challenge than the spoils system was in the last century.

In these respects it is clear that the Chrétien government, in seeking to restore relations between politicians and the public service, is, in fact, mirroring the experience elsewhere. Bureaucracy-bashing has diminished, even in the United States and Britain where it had reached its zenith. But in all three systems, it is equally clear that a new bargain has been struck. Career public servants no longer can expect either to monopolize the senior ranks of the state apparatus or to determine on their own who shall occupy these positions. They must expect competition from outside their ranks as well as greater attention paid by their political superiors to political and policy responsiveness as criteria in the selection of senior officials. In addition, they must also work with those who are appointed to assist ministers in their partisan-political roles, including, as is presently the case in Germany and France, partisans who come from the career public service itself.

Equally important are the changes taking place in the management of the operations of government. The new public management demands that much less emphasis be given to the command and control forms of administration that have traditionally served to maintain political supremacy and public service subordination. Instead, the new public management requires that increased authority be delegated to those who manage government operations on the front lines. Although there will always be selective recentralizations of authority to cope with exigencies, it is unlikely that the trend towards devolution will be reversed in the foreseeable future. The quid pro quo, however, is that much more emphasis is now placed on public service performance in the delivery of public services; public servants, accordingly, must accept increased responsibility for the exercise of authority delegated to them.

The critical change in the relationship between politicians and public servants in these respects is that public servants have become more accountable. While academics and practitioners may debate the extent to which this alters formal accountability regimes, the reality is that public accountability for government operations has been changed, if only in a de facto manner. Just as realists have always accepted the political and policy roles of public servants, they now understand that authority cannot be delegated without political judgments being made about the behaviour and performance of public servants who exercise discretion in managing their operations.

Public servants are now much more exposed to public scrutiny. But the change here is not simply a result of the new public management with devolved authority. Like their political masters, public servants too must cope with more aggressive legislators, media, auditors, and citizens. The challenge to public servants in these regards is not only to ensure that their performance meets the highest professional standards, but also to forge, with political executives and/or legislators, new understandings about public accountability. Good government requires that, as clearly and precisely as possible, distinctions be drawn between those matters for which public servants should be held accountable, and to whom they should be held accountable, and those matters for which political executives and/or legislators themselves should be held accountable.

Designing changes to accountability regimes to accommodate the new public management is not a simple task, as the efforts of many governments testify. But even where progress is made, a high level of "mutual trust" will still be required to restore a "close and congenial relationship" between politicians (and their partisan-political assistants) and public servants. At a minimum, this obviously means a cessation of bureaucracy-bashing. "Getting government right" in this respect, however, must ultimately mean restoring public service respect for their political masters. This is unlikely to occur until public confidence in the political institutions of democratic governance is itself restored.

BIBLIOGRAPHY

Aberbach, Joel. 1991. Public service and administrative reform in the United States: the Volcker Commission and the Bush administration. *International Review of Administrative Sciences* 57, 3 (September):403-420.

Aucoin, Peter. 1986. Organizational change in the Canadian machinery of government: from rational management to brokerage politics. *Canadian Journal of Political Science* 19, 1 (March):3-27.

Aucoin, Peter. 1988. The Mulroney government, 1984-88: Priorities, positional policy and power. In *Canada Under Mulroney: An End-of-Term Report*, ed. A.Gollner, and D.Salee, 335-56. Montreal: Vehicule Press.

Aucoin, Peter. 1990. Administrative reform in public management: paradigms, principles, paradoxes and pendulums. *Governance* 3, 2 (April):115-37.

Aucoin, Peter, and Herman Bakvis. 1993. Consolidating cabinet portfolios: Australian lessons for Canada. *Canadian Public Administration* 36, 2 (Fall):392-420.

Auditor General of Canada, 1993. *Report of the Auditor General of Canada in the House of Commons*, chap. 6, 159-85. Ottawa: Minister of Supply and Services Canada.

Blais, André, and Stéphane Dion, eds. 1991. *The Budget-Maximizing Bureaucrat: Appraisals and Evidence*. Pittsburgh:University of Pittsburgh Press.

Borins, Sandford. 1988. Public choice: "Yes, Minister" made it popular, but does winning the Nobel Prize make it true? *Canadian Public Administration* 31:12-26.

Boston, Jonathan. 1991. The theoretical underpinnings of public sector restructuring in New Zealand. In *Reshaping the State: New Zealand's Bureaucratic Revolution,* eds. Jonathan Boston, John Martin, June Pallot, and Pat Walsh, 1-26. Auckland: Oxford University Press.

Bourgault, Jacques, and Stéphane Dion. 1989. Brian Mulroney a-t-il politisé les sous-ministres? *Canadian Public Administration* 32, 1:63-83.

Campbell, Colin. 1988a. The political roles of senior government officials in advanced democracies. *British Journal of Political Science* 18 (April):243-72.

_____ 1988b. Mulroney's broker politics: the ultimate in politicized incompetence. In *Canada Under Mulroney: An End-of-Term Report,* ed. A.Gollner, and D. Salee. Montreal:Vehicule Press.

Campbell, Colin, and John Halligan. 1992. *Political Leadership in an Age of Constraint: Bureaucratic Politics Under Hawke and Keating.* St. Leonards: Allen and Unwin.

Canada, Office of the Prime Minister. 1993. Release. November 4.

Doern, G. Bruce. 1992. *Implementing the U.K. Citizen's Charter.* Ottawa: Canadian Centre for Management Development.

de Montricher, Nicole. 1991. "The career public service in France: problems and prospects. *International Review of Administrative Sciences* 57, 3 (September):373-84.

Derlien, Hans-Ulrich. 1991. Historical legacy and recent developments in the German higher civil service. *International Review of Administrative Sciences* 57, 3 (September):385-401.

Gore, Albert J. 1993. Creating a government that works better and costs less. *The Report of the National Performance Review.* New York: Plume/ Penguin.

Halligan, John. 1987. Reorganizing Australian government departments. *Canberra Bulletin of Public Administration* 52 (October):40-7.

Hill, Larry B., ed. 1992. *The State of Public Bureaucracy.* New York: M.E. Sharpe.

Ingraham, Patricia W., Elliot F. Eisenberg, and James R. Thompson. 1993. Political management strategies and political/career relationships: where are we now in the federal government? Paper prepared for the Annual Meeting, September, American Political Science Association, Washington, DC.

Massé, Marcel. 1993a. Getting government right. The Liberal Party of Canada (Quebec). Address 12 September to the Public Service Alliance of Canada, Longueuil, Quebec.

_____ 1993b. Getting government "right": the challenge of implementation. Address to the National Conference on Government Relations, 1 December. Ottawa: Office of the President of the Queen's Privy Council for Canada.

Mayntz, Renate, and Hans-Ulrich Derlien. 1989. Party patronage and politicization of the West German administrative elite 1970-1987 – towards hybridization? *Governance* 2, 4 (October):384-404.

Mintzberg, Henry, and Jan Jorgensen. 1987. Emergent strategy for public policy. *Canadian Public Administration* 30, 2 (Summer):214-29.

Organization for Economic Co-operation and Development. 1993. *Public Management Developments: Survey 1993*. Paris: OECD.

Osborne, David, and Ted Gaebler. 1992. *Reinventing Government*. New York: Plume/Penguin.

Parris, Henry. 1969. *Constitutional Bureaucracy*. London: Allen and Unwin.

Peters, B. Guy. 1989. *The Politics of Bureaucracy*. 3d ed. New York: Longman.

_____ 1991. Morale in the public service: a comparative inquiry. *International Review of Administrative Sciences* 57, 3 (September):421-40.

Pollitt, Christopher. 1990. *Managerialism and the Public Services: The Anglo-American Experience*. Oxford: Basil Blackwell.

Plasse, Micheline. 1994. *Ministerial Chiefs of Staff in the Federal Government in 1990: Profiles, Recruitment, Duties and Relations with Senior Public Servants*. Ottawa: Canadian Centre for Management Development, Minister of Supply and Services Canada.

Riggs, Fred. 1994. Bureaucracy and the constitution. *Public Administration Review* 54, 1 (January/February):65-72.

Royal Institute of Public Administration. 1987. *Top Jobs in Whitehall*. Report of a RIPA Working Group. London: RIPA.

Savoie, Donald. 1994. *Thatcher, Reagan, Mulroney: In Search of a New Bureaucracy*. Toronto: University of Toronto Press.

Sutherland, S.L. 1991. Responsible government and ministerial responsibility; every reform has its own problem. *Canadian Journal of Political Science* xxiv, 1 (March):91-120.

Swimmer, Gene, Michael Hicks, and Terry Milne. 1994. Public service 2000: dead or alive? In *How Ottawa Spends 1994-95: Making Change*, ed. Susan Phillips, 165-204. Ottawa: Carleton University Press.

United Kingdom, House of Commons, Treasury and Civil Service Committee 1993. *Sixth Report*, Volume II, 21 July. London: HMSO.

Walter, James. 1986. *The Ministers' Minders*. Melbourne: Oxford University Press.

Weller, Patrick. 1989. Politicisation and the Australian public service. *Australian Journal of Public Administration* 48, 4 (December):369-78.

Wilson, Graham. 1991. Prospects for the public service in Britain. Major to the rescue? *International Review of Administrative Sciences* 57, 3 (September):327-44.

Wilson, James Q. 1989. *Bureaucracy: What Government Agencies Do and Why They Do It*. New York: Basic Books.

Zussman, David. 1986. Walking the tightrope: the Mulroney government and the public service. In *How Ottawa Spends, 1986-76: Tracking the Tories*, ed. Michael Prince, 250-82. Toronto: Methuen.

Policy Advice and the Public Service

JOHN HALLIGAN

The senior public service has not been immune from the tide of public sector reform with conscious action taken to target both the status of officials and their policy advisory role. The provision of policy advice was affected by readjustments in the central relationships that governed and shaped the conduct of public affairs. As a result, politicians have placed greater demands on senior bureaucrats. The increasing complexity of the policy environment has also been critical for the conduct of advising government. There has been a broadening of sources of advice, with the expanding involvement of actors both within and beyond the governmental system. Moreover, advice has become more contested and competitive. There are new conceptions of what advice should be and the need to apply a performance framework and quality standards to policy work. The consequence is that the policy adviser is under greater pressure than ever before to ensure the "product" reflects government's needs (Waller 1992:444; OECD 1990).

The central issue in this chapter is the continuing role of the public service in policy advice and the changing conditions under which it operates. Two questions of particular importance have been the main trends that have affected the provision of policy advice and their impact on the public service and policy advice. From the latter can be derived subsidiary questions about where the public service fits in, its importance relative to other bodies,

and how its own handling of the advisory process has been changing. In short, the concern is with the characteristics of the policy
advisory system in the 1990s.

POLICY ADVICE AND ANALYZING TRENDS

Conceptions of policy advice vary according to focus and scope.
Two recent conceptions are both broad-based but in different
ways. The first focuses on the public servant adviser and regards
policy advising as covering "analyzing problems and proposing
solutions." It specifies structuring of the problem, information
gathering, analysis, formulation of options, and communication of
the results (Waller 1992:440-1; Edwards 1992:448). In this case
policy advising has been equated with the policy formulation
process. As an official's depiction of policy advising it is assumed
that even if the senior advisers do not undertake all these roles
they will be responsible for their performance. The other conception views the process as the open-ended reception of advice by
government: "How do governments deliberately acquire, and
passively receive (and, sometimes, deliberately resist and ignore),
advice on decisions and policies which may be broadly called
informative, objective or technical?" (Peters and Barker 1993a:1).

The first definition draws attention to components of policy
advice. Distinctions have been made between strategic and infor-
mational and operational advice, and between policy and political
advice. A focus on stages in the policy process yields distinctions
between advice about formulation and advice about implementation – most particularly "production engineering," the giving of
"operational shape and impact to the minister's objectives" (Pollitt
1994:1). Changes in the relative significance of all forms have been
detected over the last decade or so. For example, political advice
has often been accorded more attention compared to conventional
policy advice from public servants; and strategic policy development has reappeared as significant after a quiet ten years (e.g.,
OECD 1990:2-3).

The second conception points to the broader context of advice
in which there are flows of information and influence. A number

of elements may be relevant, including the extent to which the government can exercise direct control over its policy process. Another approach is to ask whether advice is solicited (and presumably subject to some degree of formal influence) or unsolicited (but still has to be taken into account). Other relevant questions include the extent to which advisory systems are institutionalized or informal, open or closed and temporary or permanent (Seymour-Ure 1987; Peters and Baker 1993a:11).

In this case we can make sense of the subject and how it is changing by distinguishing two central dimensions of the policy advisory system. The first is the location of policy advice: whether the sources of advice are internal or external to the governmental system. The second dimension is the degree of control exercised by government over policy advice. The two dimensions are depicted in Table 1. The internal processes are divided between those which are internal to the public service – the mainstream departmental advisers – and those which are part of the broader governmental system. This internal-to-government category covers political units and alternative advisory structures that are separate from the formal public service. The external dimensions take several forms: government work that has privatized elements, the competing expertise from nongovernmental organizations, public consultation, and the influence of international processes and organizations.

The Advice System

The advice system comprises several types of bureaucratic and political adviser. The core is the single advice provider (the public service) for a specific client (usually the cabinet minister). There is generally provision for central advice (both the first minister's unit and central agency) and some other form of policy instrument is commonly employed (e.g., special administrative unit or task force; political advisers). Less agreement would be reached on some elements: the emphasis on the various components (e.g., role of political operatives or the legislature); the significance of different organizational options; the role of specialized political units; and the flexibility, with regard to strategic processes, for managing specific policy issues.

TABLE 1
Location of advice and degree of government influence

| Location | Government Control | |
	High	Low
Public service	Senior departmental policy advisers Central agency advisers/ strategic policy units	Statutory appointments in public service
Internal to government	Political advisory systems • Ministers' offices • First minister's office Temporary advisory policy units Parliaments (e.g., a House of Commons)	Permanent advisory policy units Statutory authorities Legislatures (e.g., u.s. Congress)
External to government	Private sector/NGOs on contract Community organizations subject to government grants and appointments Federal international organizations	Trade unions, interest groups etc. Community groups Confederal international communities/ organizations

The advice system is subject to the preferences prevailing within a political system. It can be dominated by public servants, hence the characterization of the administrative state, and the concern with its quasi-monopolistic role. A second possibility is domination by politicians, where there is a reliance on political appointments and the sharing of the spoils of power, particularly under conditions of one- or multi-party government. Under an open governmental system, there will be more access points for external interests and a tendency to rely more heavily on a broader and more diverse range of contributions.

The settings in which public servants have operated have been shaped by at least three sets of factors. The type of governmental system is important, particularly the fundamental distinctions between parliamentary and presidential, and unitary and federal systems. One can indicate wide variations in the structure according to whether a government has substantial responsibility or formal authority is diffused among branches and levels of government. Similarly, the extent to which government is open to external influence is important. These comments simply imply the obvious: that different countries have distinctive features. The United States, to take one model, has relied on a broad range of policy actors. The characteristics of its government – federalism, fragmentation, and checks and balances – encourage "coalition building, bargaining and group politics," which "dominate the policy-making and implementation arenas" (Ferman 1989:211; Peters 1986). In contrast, the "Westminster" tradition is more executive-centred and has placed greater emphasis on the public service.

The structure of advice systems also varies between policy domains, e.g., the scientist compared to the mainstream policy specialist (Barker and Peters 1992; Smith 1992). Variations in organizations and interests among policy sectors have come to be identified as different types of policy networks (Lindquist 1991). A third set of factors centres on the personal styles of leaders and how they interpret and apply the principles that operate within their systems of government. Leadership style plays a significant role in how the chief executive engages the bureaucracy (Campbell 1983).

Trends

Recent developments in policy advice internationally can be traced to three sources of thinking – managerial, economic, and political theories – that have been influential in public service reform. They account for most of the impetus for change generally and also for the complications in working it through. The managerial challenges, derived from private sector experience and writings on generic and business administration, have emphasized debureaucratization, evaluation, accountability, decentralization, and performance. New applications of economic theories, which derive from market theory and public choice theory (Self 1993), accord prominence to notions about the market, deregulation, and competition. An illustration of how there are direct implications for thinking about policy advice is the following argument from a practitioner: "Concern about market-related concepts such as quality and value-added need to take account of the structure of the market in which policy advisers now work. Across the generality of government activity that market has become much more contestable and competitive" (Waller 1992:444). Market-type mechanisms have assumed centrality in the 1990s (OECD 1993), and extend to both internal as well as external markets.

Political ideas have also been important. The direct challenge to the strength of the civil service and, therefore, to the policy advice role has come from politicians. Two important themes have been the concern with the degree of influence exercised by public servants, a position captured by the American notion of the administrative state and the British "Yes, Minister" syndrome; and the argument that public servants are not value-free in their behaviour and their influence on policy advice should not go unchallenged (e.g., Wilenski 1986). Such challenges may be rationalized in terms of democratic principles and models with old theories being resurrected: thus the Westminster model is rediscovered by leaders as a means of sanctioning the authority and directive capacity of the political executive (Halligan and Power 1992).

In practice it may be difficult to distinguish the three sources so explicitly, and in any case conceptions of them differ. In different contexts the terms cover similar things. The economic and managerial approaches overlap in some respects. For example, decentralization is common to both approaches, although its expression is different. The latter, for example, supports the reduction in the size of head office, the former stresses provision through multiple units and competition. Public choice theory focuses on the workings of democratic government but comes to rather different conclusions than traditional democratic theory, although both agree on the need to revive the authority of the political executive. Thus, one can view the political side in the context of public choice (Aucoin 1990) but equally link it with the managerial side (Halligan and Power 1992).

With apparent international convergence among a number of OECD countries about so much of public management, a mix of all three approaches is commonly present. This does have one interesting outcome, as Aucoin (1990:125) argues: the different perspectives produce tensions and contradictions when they coexist in practice.

Fiscal stress focused governments' collective minds on resource constraints and led to the discouragement of new policy. The concerted reduction in policy analysis in the u.s. (Williams 1990; Aberbach and Rockman 1989) under the "anti-analytic" presidency was related to broader, ideologically driven attitudes towards the public sector and the civil service. Elsewhere it was a product of converting policy specialists to managerialists: the need to pay more attention to resources and their management either drew executives from policy work or required them to concentrate on managerial roles.

The application of new (and also old) principles influenced policy advice provision within the public service in the areas of internal organization, departmental capacity, evaluation of performance and the character of policy advisers. The overall tendency was for a shift towards greater use of sources beyond the public service. This was most pronounced in the u.s., where the role of officials in policy formulation and implementation, according to Rourke,

has progressively diminished. Increasingly in recent years, bureaucratic organizations in every area of governmental operation have lost the position of primacy once enjoyed in providing information and advice to policy makers both in the Oval Office and in Congress. Their place has been taken by a variety of advisory institutions and sources in both government and the outside world in helping appraising old policies or designing new programs (1992:226).

Internal Reorganization

New cultures and philosophies have led to major changes in operating frameworks. The rhetoric has been decentralizing and generally the trend has been in this direction, although this has rarely occurred without being accompanied by some centralizing impulses. The latter has been important for strategic and cross-sectoral policy as opposed to department-centred and operational policy. There is something of a trend towards policy-focused departments as opposed to broad-based, multiple function units, but the pattern is mixed.

The most interesting development has been the experiment with separating policy formulation from implementation. This has taken the form of either systemic separation of the two or pragmatic application of the principle. The best-known has been the British Next Steps, which involves creating executive agencies within a policy framework established by departments. In other words, there is meant to be structural differentiation of advice and operations. New Zealand has decoupled policy advice and service provision by the use of small policy ministries and large delivery departments. It has also linked policy output with chief executives and outcomes with ministers (Boston 1991; State Services Commission 1991:49).

Australia and Canada have applied this type of notion on an "as needs" basis. Canada has adopted the concept of Special Operating Agencies (SOAs) under the influence of the British experiment but has not proceeded very far with its application. A number of SOAs have been introduced and the experiment has been assessed by an interagency working group (Dingwall 1993; Savoie 1994:231-3). Australia has maintained a more pragmatic approach to this question. It has created a number of agencies with delivery roles, but has not sought to proclaim these cases as part of a system-wide reform program, although the overall effect may not be too dissimilar. "The Australian experience suggests . . . that it is not axiomatic to create agencies in order to provide a climate in which central control is reduced" (Department of Finance n.d.:6).

Policy Capacity in Departments

In terms of the overall balance of responsibilities the trend has been towards expanding those of the line department at the expense of the central agency (the most recent echo of this being Gore 1993). This has had greater implications for operational than substantive policy.

The roles and relative strengths of central agencies continue to differ between countries. There has been the demise of central policy units, for example, the Central Policy Review Staff in Britain (Plowden 1991) where their role has not been integrated and legitimized. Central agencies have strengthened their strategic roles in policy, but much has depended on their developing effective relationships with line departments and the competence of the government. Despite the rhetoric of decentralization, central agencies may be more interventionist in policy under fiscal austerity (cf. the case of the Department of Finance in Australia: Campbell and Halligan 1992).

The policy advisory group flourished in the 1970s (Prince 1979:275), but its fortunes nose-dived in the 1980s. The reasons go beyond fashion and reflect the rise and decline of policy analysis in bureaucracies as a result of political change (Aberbach and Rockman 1989). The existence of policy units in departments "strengthened in-house policy analysis skills relative to external research capabilities" (Prince 1983:188). One would expect the reverse to apply also. Under the impact of managerialism, the departmental policy unit has been buffeted and often disappeared. One issue has been whether distinctive units should exist within departments or whether the policy function should be "mainstreamed" across divisions. The pattern in the 1990s would appear to be more variable, with units re-emerging when the full impact of managerial reform has receded. The termination of policy units and the spread of their capability among departmental divisions has contributed to the weakening of internal capacity and the increasing use of the external consultant.

The Policy Adviser

The role of the public servant has been subject to fresh interpretations with direct implications for policy advice. Although much public sector reform was targeted on the public service monopoly, civil servants still tend to take the most senior departmental positions in countries with British traditions, though now their experience may be somewhat broader (and the chief executives of executive agencies often have more diverse backgrounds acquired outside), and the operating contexts have changed. There has been a tendency to bring in more outsiders – although this diversification has yet to go very far in parliamentary systems.

In the U.K., the Whitehall mandarins reverted to type. After a period of managerialism, they were able to discard management through the device of the Next Steps agencies and could again focus on policy.[1] The extent to which the recent White Paper on the Civil Service (British Government 1994) will lead to substantial changes to Whitehall's policy role is unclear at this stage.

In the Australian federal context, where departments are often still a mixture of policy and delivery, departmental secretaries perform the dual roles of manager and adviser. From 1987 and the development of the mega-department, the policy specialists have had to become managers of large organizations. The strategic focus was also fostered by requiring experience in a central agency as a prerequisite for the most senior positions (Campbell and Halligan 1992).

A different tactic is to change the adviser. The turnover of advisers was higher in the 1980s under managerialized systems, such as Canada (Bourgault and Dion 1989) and Australia. The practice of contract employment continues to expand, applying in New Zealand at the senior executive and chief executive levels, and from 1994, to Australian departmental secretaries.

The nexus between policy specialization and department was broken. The favouring of this mix of generalist manager, economic rationalist, and central agency can-doer possibly had the greatest impact on the policy specialists in line departments. The top managements of departments have been displaced by persons without a background in or commitment to their policy concerns (Campbell and Halligan 1992). These developments are closely linked with the move to the generic manager in some countries, and a favouring of economists internationally, at least during periods of fiscal austerity, although no country appears to have gone as far as Australia in fostering them to the point of dominance at senior levels (Pusey 1991).

Evaluating Policy Advice

Countries intent on comprehensive reforms have left few aspects of public management untouched, and where prominence is accorded to performance it is inevitable that this must eventually extend to policy advice. The most attention so far seems to have occurred in Australia and New Zealand, where official reports have been produced, although a survey was recently undertaken by the International Institute of Administrative Sciences (Nicholson 1994).

Pressure for greater scrutiny of policy advice has come both from the drive to managerialize the public service and from external sources. With regard to the first, the argument is that no part of the public service should be immune from some form of evaluation. The advocates of this position argue that "policy advising and formulation function, is in large measure, opaque. In essence, the function is a 'black box'." However, it is still possible that "external evaluation can throw light on the quality of the policy-advising process." Regardless of its viability, the market in which advisers work was far more contestable and competitive because of the pressures to meet government requirements (Waller 1992:443-4).

These pressures are being increasingly exerted by external review agencies eager to demonstrate consistency in the application of the rhetoric of managerialist reform. For example, the pressure for more systematic assessment of policy work has come from Australian Senate committees, which have shown interest in the "value-added" offered by central agency advice (Waller 1992:444). The type of external review that may now apply is illustrated by the Australian Auditor-General's critique of Treasury for not relating input data to outcomes, and for having insufficiently developed performance indicators for measuring "the quality and level of policy advice" in conformity with practices which had to be followed in the rest of the public service (Auditor-General 1992:3).

Despite these pressures, the development of appropriate performance indicators has been slow. Experience in the U.K. holds also for other countries: progress has been notable for executive activities but less so for policy formulation (Gray and Jenkins 1992:172).

INTERNAL TO GOVERNMENT

The assault on the public service monopoly in general has led to the greater use of alternative advisory systems within the governmental system. Something of a redistribution of power occurred between elements of government: politicians and bureaucrats; the executive and legislative branches; and the mainstream departments and other bureaucratic organizations.

Political Advice

Politicians have adopted at least three stances. There are those who have sought political control over the public service as an end in itself because it has acquired too much independence and discretion. (A more subtle variation is favoured by those who seek to influence the public service in order to implement party policy.) A second position is associated with new governments convinced that their opponents had acquired ownership of the public service. This may be seen in terms of the close identification of the public service with one political interest, as well as entrenched relationships between public servants and clients. The third challenge has come from leaders who concentrated on demeaning and debilitating the public relative to the private sector, convinced of the superiority of the latter. At its crudest, this simply involved public service bashing (e.g., Hennessy 1988; Levine 1988; Savoie 1994).

The political response has been to pursue these agenda by redefining relationships and weakening the status and autonomy of civil servants. The two most significant strategies have been to make political appointments to positions traditionally reserved for careerists, and to augment the resources of the politicians in dealing with civil servants. While these strategies represent quite different paths, they can be combined in practice.

With regard to appointments, in Westminster-derived systems the consistent pattern is for the political executive to seek top civil servants who will be responsive to its requirements. Mrs Thatcher's intervention in the appointment of senior civil servants is well known. The Australian and Canadian political executives have also relied increasingly on being able to appoint their preferred candidates to the civil service. There is usually greater scope than in the past for appointing outsiders to senior positions (Bourgault and Dion 1989:127; Hennessy 1988:190-1).

Studies of politicization offer insights into systems, such as the u.s., which have taken a more extreme approach to influencing the bureaucracy:

Presidents are now able to use their appointing power to infiltrate their own appointees deep within the ranks of bureaucracy in each executive agency throughout the government. Such presidential surrogates become heavily involved in the internal affairs of these organizations and can eventually control day-to-day decisions throughout the bureaucracy (Rourke 1992:226).

The other strategy mentioned previously involves countering bureaucratic influence with the employment of more political resources from outside the public service. There is a well-established tradition in some European countries of providing the political executive with special resources in the form of staff, the best-known example being the French cabinet. This type of practice has been adopted in other countries, with units or advisers being appointed to assist ministers. Australia has concentrated on this route as a means for redistributing power within the executive branch. The important differences in practice have revolved around the extent to which career civil servants have been used as well as partisans, and the extent to which appointees are policy specialists as opposed to operatives involved in the policy process (Halligan and Power 1992). The most extreme case occurred in Canada, where Mulroney appointed chiefs of staff whose status was coequal with that of deputy ministers. On the other hand, the u.k. has yet to move properly down this track, despite some tentative experiments (Hennessy 1989:172-5, 188, 189; Plowden 1991).

At the centre there have been various experiments with expanded advisory and support services for the chief executive. When prime minister of Canada, Mulroney augmented the resources of his personal office to an extent without parallel in other countries with British traditions (Aucoin 1988). In the u.k., the Prime Minister's Policy Unit, established by Thatcher, made use of advisers from outside the civil service. Under the u.s. presidency, an elaborate advisory system has been evolved that is independent of the civil service.

Alternative Advisory Systems

These systems are internal to the formal institutions of government but often relatively autonomous. The expansion of the role of other governmental institutions has occurred, but they vary widely – depending on the degree of institutionalization – ranging from branches to various types of temporary and permanent appendage. Nondepartmental agencies may comprise between 40 and 60 percent of the public sector (Wiltshire 1993:121). Intergovernmental organizations have also become more salient in specific policy fields.

Legislatures have played more prominent roles in policy, with the contribution depending on the extent to which they have the capacity to engage effectively in policy processes. The u.s. Congress has been most active in policy making, often taking the initiative on issues. It has developed a "formidable advisory system" with Congressional offices staffed by a range of aides. Congressional committees have multiplied to the point of institutional overload (Rourke 1992:226).

Even parliaments have become more prominent. Although they have not been renowned for their policy-influencing capacities, the emergence of committee systems during the last two decades has offered new opportunities. Parliamentary committees have engaged in investigatory work in Australia and the u.k. (but less so in Canada). Such parliaments have the capacity to advise government about policy, and indeed may be used by government for some types of policy development. Another respect in which these changes impinge on the conduct of the policy process is through the increasing appearances of senior public servants at committee sessions. Parliament's role, however, remains substantially dependent on the influence exercised by the executive over the content of committees' references and on other factors, such as the composition of the upper houses.

A wide range of advisory bodies have been created by executives. In the u.s., "National policy makers have also fallen into the habit of creating advisory commissions or other temporary organizations within government to consider and give advice on major policy issues or problems" (Rourke 1992:226). Arguments continue in the u.k. about the need to go beyond advisory panels to assembling expert groups for policy formulation (Dynes 1993). Permanent agencies also exist in a wide variety of forms in many fields ranging from science through to social services. These organizations may examine policies on an ex post basis (specialized units in areas such as industry policy, agricultural economics, and transport economics), and have a considerable measure of independence from the government's departmental policy advisers (Waller 1992:444).

The establishment of such bodies does not invariably produce a loss of public service influence. For example, economic advisory councils were established in Australia, the u.k., and Canada for the provision of independent advice on the conduct of economic policy, but they failed "to participate effectively in the development and formulation of government economic policy" (Singleton, forthcoming). This failure raises the issue of whether such bodies can play a real role in the policy process in Westminster-style systems because of the tight policy community of central agency officials and ministers engaged in economic policy. At the most they might exercise indirect influence.

EXTERNAL CONTRIBUTIONS

The expanding role of external influence is driven by both demand and supply considerations. While public sectors have been substantially reformed, they are still seen to have distinctive limits because of the rules, regulations and control systems. It has also become unacceptable to ignore the need for broader expertise and knowledge base. As a result of

fast-paced change, in both our external and internal environments, it is no longer possible to understand immensely complex problems or devise sufficiently independent solutions without bringing together groups of people who spend much more of their time understanding their evolving environment and whose advice must be based on constantly updated knowledge (Massé 1993:6-7).

The influence of external trends on policy analysis and advice takes three distinctive forms. Each can be further differentiated according to whether the actors work for or operate independently of government. This can be illustrated in terms of the first trend, the expanding role of NGOs. On the one hand, they provide the clearest external challenge: the competing policy competence of organizations that have the capacity to contest internal knowledge and expertise. At the same time governments have sought to incorporate special skills by the use of external advisers and as an alternative source to the public service. Often there is overlap, for example, private consultants operate as competitors as well as external sources of expertise. The second trend recognizes the renewal of community and citizens as players in policy, which had largely disappeared in the recent past. The third trend is the role of international organizations and processes, whose influence continues to expand.

Privatizing of Public Service Responsibilities

The external challenge from NGOs has increased to the point of offering competing policy competence. There has been a marked expansion of the advisory capacity of external organizations. These may be lobbyists, community groups, trade unions, and other interest groups. Private sector consultants have also flourished in the age of privatization. In Australia, Access Economics (a consultancy founded by former Treasury officers) was producing advice in the 1990s which could compete with that of the government, an unprecedented development with parallels elsewhere.[2] Government budget agencies have lost their monopoly "over economic forecasting and over estimates of the budgetary implications of policy changes" (Kettl 1994:30). The most identifiable trend has been the emergence and growth of think tanks. Once regarded as a peculiarly American phenomenon, where they proliferated during the 1970s and 1980s, the think tank was taken up in other countries during the latter decade (Marsh 1990; Smith 1991:xv; Weiss 1992).

The use of external individuals and organizations for performing public tasks has become an integral extension of government. For some governments, this inclination has been ideologically driven (Sutherland 1993:96). More generally, under fiscal austerity, governments have sought to reduce staff and functions. Often this has involved the substitution of consultants for public servants because it has been more politically (and managerially) acceptable. But it has also become recognized as a legitimate way of incorporating specialized skills.

As a result, external organizations have been increasingly used for policy design and development. This has become a common practice in the u.s. with the "increasing tendency towards privatizing the process through which public policy is made and carried out ... Such privatization has been reflected in the growing involvement of private groups and organizations in both the design and implementation of national policies" (Rourke 1993:9). The u.s. is generally acknowledged to have taken this practice further than other countries, even extending it to "inherently governmental functions" (u.s. GAO 1991), although there has been increasing reliance on contracting out elsewhere.

At one extreme of the privatization continuum this practice may simply involve bringing in consultants on a short-term contract to take advantage of external expertise. Or it may extend to formally constituted bodies, with

increasing use of task forces, presidential commissions, or advisory committees to generate a new look at old policies, or to break new ground in some highly troublesome area of policy development such as social security or health care. Professionals drawn from the private sector have customarily played a prominent role in the deliberations of these "adhocracies" (Rourke 1993:10).

The role of nonprofit agencies has been particularly important in countries such as the United States where they have been relied on for policy design (Rourke 1993:10).

The royal commission has a well-developed tradition in some countries. This device has been used by governments for many purposes including the avoiding of decision-making responsibilities or confronting intractable problems suited to the inquiry process. The use of large and comprehensive inquiries fell into disuse in the 1980s in some countries outside North America. The reason for their decline in the U.K. under Thatcher can be attributed to politicians who had an explicit agenda (Bulmer 1993:40). An additional factor in Australia was the unwillingness to grant responsibility and discretion for much policy development to any organization that was independent of the political executive. Only in Canada has the royal commission continued to flourish, although it remains unclear what its impact on policy has been.

The extent to which governments have relaxed control should not be overstated. They may rely on private bodies, but frequently the degree of government influence over these organizations is still significant because the participation of "private parties in policy development can be covertly and closely controlled by the agency itself" (Rourke 1993:10-11). Similarly, other types of advisory commission have come under the influence of the bureaucracy (Wilenski 1986).

Debate continues about the quality and worth of the "advice" offered by these external organizations. An argument put forward by senior Canadian public servants in CCMD seminars was that the quality of the external input may have deteriorated in some policy fields.

Public Consultation

For some countries much of the 1980s was about directive government, as conviction politics and resource constraints favoured strong leadership styles. This was perhaps epitomized by Margaret Thatcher in the United Kingdom. But reformist governments elsewhere (those on the left in Australia and New Zealand), although lacking a leader of her style and politics, were making tough decisions with major impacts on their communities.

New Zealand, in particular, was astounding for the lack of either consultation or an electoral mandate for its actions (Mascarenhas 1990). Similarly, in the U.K. consultation during the policy process was viewed as delaying necessary change, and was limited: "The Government operated with a top-down process model of policy making in which it could . . . set the policy agenda and choose the policy options, unencumbered by the constraints provided by interest groups" (Rhodes and Marsh 1992:8). In Australia, if it was not the policy-centred politician, the economic rationalists based in Canberra were seen to be driving policy change and imposing their narrow agenda on the country (Pusey 1991).

Moving toward the mid-1990s, the approaches had become different. The "bottom-end" reaction, even retaliation, had become noticeable. But bottom-up pressure was combined with various mixtures of top-down political and managerial pushes (as central reformers incorporated this element in their programs). If contempt for the citizen had previously been apparent there was now a reawakening of the need for consultation, a redefinition of the citizen as client and consumer, and a greater sensitivity to electoral imperatives. Minority views were being asserted through legislatures in several countries.

First, consultation was being revisited through planned processes for bridging the gap between capital isolation and a dispersed community. Second, populism was reawakened and becoming seemingly rampant in North America, with minority movements and parties attaining credibility. In Canada, this produced the transformation of the composition of the national lower house in 1993. Third, the whole question of service delivery and quality assumed centrality. It was recognized by the OECD and given prominence by the United Kingdom through the Citizen's Charter (Doern 1992). By the early 1990s, even countries which had not given priority to service quality, such as Australia, were according serious attention to this question. Closely related was the centrality being accorded to the consumer (Gore 1993, ch. 2; Osborne and Gaebler 1992).

These developments posed challenges for policy makers in central governments. As Massé (1993:7-9) argues, "The governmental sector can no longer impose its decisions without a fuller consent by the governed. Government must become less a lawgiver and more an arbitrator," paying more attention to partnerships and accountability.

Internationalization

Policy making at the international level has also had an increasingly important influence on both the external and domestic policy of countries. This influence has assumed a number of forms ranging from setting parameters for policy debate, through providing standards, to imposing formal policies. There have been different vehicles including various types of international policy communities and networks, international organizations, and supranational governments. Consultancy companies based on multinational organizations have also been favoured for public sector work.

An important element in policy making at the international level has been the networks that facilitate regular interaction. In some cases this may amount to "shared experience of learning" about a problem by an international policy community and can, therefore, be regarded as a case of policy convergence (Bennett 1991:224). The increasing role of international organizations and transnational cooperation in the handling of policy issues has registered an impact in many policy fields. The "international regimes," have a "shared and long-term commitment to a set of governing arrangements" (Bennett 1991:226). One can also include less formalized arrangements that nevertheless exert great influence on member nations: institutional pressures for harmonization can lead individual nations to adopt what is deemed to be good practice.

The role of the epistemic community has been accorded increasing recognition: it is a "network of professionals with recognized expertise and competence in a particular domain and an authoritative claim to policy-relevant knowledge within that domain or issue-area" (Haas 1992:3). Its distinctive role centres on setting the context for discussion and influence on choices, and contributing to the process of policy evolution (including policy innovation, diffusion, and selection):

By identifying the nature of the issue-area and framing the context in which new data and ideas are interpreted, epistemic communities bound the range of collective discourse on policy, as well as guide decision makers in the choice of appropriate norms and appropriate institutions within which to resolve or manage problems (Adler and Haas 1992:375, 377).

Examples are drawn from arms control, pollution control, regulation of trade in services, environmental pollution, and telecommunication (Adler and Haas 1992:375-7).

International networks with an explicit governmental basis have also played a role in shaping policy. The interaction has taken the form of exchanges between members of a network, whether conceived as a policy community or otherwise, and supranational organizations operating independently of member countries. The formal networks based on the Commonwealth provided one key channel of communication. A series of coherent international networks have been centred on Canada, Britain, Australia, and New Zealand. These networks have had a basis in a common language, cultural legacy, and institutions, and they have established connections of great strength. The networks' operating features have included regular meetings of civil service elites, exchanges of information and staff among members, and routine scanning of innovations and reforms (Halligan, forthcoming).

The role of the transnational organizations has received recognition in many policy fields by providing institutional frameworks for building common responses and developing congruent policies (Bennett 1991, 226). The Organization for Economic Cooperation and Development (OECD) provided the basis for an important network in the 1980s by becoming an important forum for the exchange of information about policy change in member countries. The most significant organization however remains that which provides for supranational government. The participation in regional government has become a central consideration for the members of the European Community. It is within such a grouping that the full impact of international arrangements on domestic policy becomes most apparent.

THE PUBLIC SERVICE AND
THE POLICY ADVISING ENVIRONMENT

Modern governments have always drawn on all three broad sources for policy advice. The relative significance of the three categories has, however, changed. In terms of overall trends the internal government category has expanded at the expense of the internal public service. But, in turn, the rise of external forms has been at the expense of internal mechanisms.

The relative significance of specific sources has also changed. Some have fluctuated in importance: for example, public consultation has re-emerged. Others – international factors being a good example – seem to be expanding in significance over time. In other cases, the pattern is subject to the practice of the country and is less susceptible to generalizations: for example, the use of advisory bodies within government. There also appears to have been a greater use of external advisory bodies in the open governmental arrangements of the u.s. than in executive-centred systems.

Few policy advisers would have the misfortune to be subjected to all the trends previously referred to. Some are specific to particular policy domains; others are, however, systemic. Some of the patterns suggest that the trends have become part of longer-term cycles. The countries under consideration have experienced major change over the last decade. There has been a shift from conservatism and conviction politics, which are negative to the civil service, to governments that are more positive. Economic conditions have improved. "Dries" have become "wetter" when confronted with electoral setbacks. The excesses of one phase produce reactions that have led to different approaches and policies.

Policy Advisers in the Public Service

The core question concerns the role of the public service in policy advice. Where governments seek to rely on outsiders or their own appointees for advice, they may cut senior public servants out of the policy loop. For executive-centred systems this has occurred under particular regimes or ministers or following leadership changes, but this has not normally been sustained. In contrast, it appears to have been institutionalized in the United States, where the senior civil servant appears to occupy few policy positions of any significance.

The remainder of this discussion concentrates on the public service which retains a role in policy advice. The new public management has not invariably displaced traditional elements. In the executive-centred systems the public service remains central; there has been something of a reaffirmation of the need for professional policy advice, even though confined to a small group of public servants.

According to a New Zealand report, where the costs of outputs are distinguished, they account for around one percent of government expenditure (Boston 1994:5; State Services Commission 1991:5).[3]

The overall trends have, however, had major implications for policy advice and the impact on public service, and they can be summarized at this point. First, there is the professionalizing of policy competence outside the public service: this extends to a diverse range of actors from established nongovernment, organizations – advocacy groups, consultants, trade unions – to branches of government such as parliaments. Second, there is the pluralizing of the process – internally and externally – as more, and more diverse, sources are replacing what was once a monolith that pulled the strings (or strands) of policy. Third, the general process of "push and pull" is externalizing and moving responsibilities outside both the public service and government and, therefore, beyond its capacity to exercise direct and close control. Finally, the public service is having to play an increasingly political role in processing the wide range of advice that is received. This reflects the greater demand for policy advice as governments have been doing more, but also indicates that the supply of advice – solicited and unsolicited – is coming from diverse sources. The politics of consent has become more difficult as party caucuses become more demanding and interest groups more professionally combative. The public service must engage more in the politics of policy advice.

Managing Processes

The managing of policy processes under the current framework involves a greater focus by the public servant on consultation, networking across a range of sources, coordination, and process management.

At the input end, a key question is whether the job can be undertaken in-house or requires the injection of external expertise. An important consideration is the need for flexibility, in particular with regard to the choice of advisers for specific projects. As an experienced senior policy adviser comments: "To get and retain the right people for the job, flexibility in attitude is needed, allowing for novel approaches. Prior assumptions about appropriate management structures could be constraining, if not inefficient" (Edwards 1992:448).

Second, public servants must also give greater attention to managing partisan settings. The partisan pressures are greater as the boundaries around the public service have become more permeable. Attention must be paid to handling partisan operatives, most particularly those associated with the minister's office, who may be taking the initiative on behalf of the minister.

Third, there is strategic management: "A major issue in providing policy advice to the minister is to decide how to handle strategically the policy process." Such process management requires attention to much more than policy content because it is essential "to assess advice given on how to carry proposals through bureaucratic as well as political processes in order to get desired outcomes . . . Outcomes can depend as much on high quality advice about the process to be followed as on particular options" (Edwards 1992:448).

Senior executives also have to manage networks to a greater extent in policy domains that incorporate a wide range of actors. There is an inclination to draw on a wide variety of mechanisms: parliamentary committees, task forces, and other groups for policy development. There are well-established models for the organization of interdepartmental processes, such as "a standing officials group, an interdepartmental working party, a task force or an implementation group" (Hawke 1993:36), but network management also extends to other elements across a spectrum ranging from the local to the international community. However, "These networks are far more complex, more unstable, and less predictable than orderly bureaucracies, and this fact produces far greater risks for government workers" (Kettl 1994:36). An increasingly important challenge, therefore, is managing external advisory inputs ranging from the contributions of policy implementors that have been decoupled to those that have been privatized.

The rethinking of the senior public servant's role is now well advanced. As has been observed in the Canadian context: "Top government officials must become less administrators and implementors of programs and activities and more knowledge-based advisers who help determine and explain the parameters within which solutions can be found" (Massé 1993:7-9).

The conventional wisdom appears to be that a good advice system should consist of at least three basic elements within government: a stable and reliable in-house advisory service provided by professional public servants; political advice for the minister from a specialized political unit (generally the minister's office); and the availability of at least one third-opinion option from a specialized or central policy unit, which might be one of the main central agencies. It is also accepted practice to draw advice from external sources, but this varies widely with the policy issue among think tanks, interest groups, and consultancy companies.

Three principles are central to the good advisory system. The first is the provision of multiple sources of advice. The second is flexibility: to be able to choose a mix of adviser(s) and processes appropriate for satisfying the needs of a particular policy issue. Reflecting the times, many would now add the need to review and assess not only advice systems – which have been undertaken in the past – but also the effectiveness of advice.

This set of elements and principles would still be subject to variation among political systems, depending on the relative significance of each. The emphasis on elements such as the role of political operatives and external actors depends very much on whether the former are accorded seniority within the system of government and the access of the latter is facilitated by open government (both features of the u.s. system, but less so in other countries). Some indication of other variations are provided in the discussion below of specific issues. While there is considerable convergence among countries, they still retain their own preferences.

Structure. The verdict is still out on what structure works best for policy advice, and, of course, the answer would undoubtedly be that there are several possibilities, depending on contexts and intent. The question may come down to whether the separation of policy and administration, organizationally, is best applied across the civil service (as in the N.Z. or U.K. variants) or a more pragmatic approach is suitable (as in Australia and Canada). While some of the initial scepticism about separating the two has abated, other issues remain, in particular the blurring of policy responsibilities between departments and agencies in the U.K. revealed by the recent Trosa report ("Reassuring Sir Humphrey" 1994:66). There may also be further developments if the current interest of several countries in clarifying the core public sector leads to anything.

The tighter integration that prevailed under the centralized systems of the past has broken down in some cases. With the greater focus on either departments (as opposed to central agencies) or delivery agencies (as opposed to policy departments), the policy process has become more complicated. One result has been that different people are engaged in strategic policy advice as opposed to operational advice, but with different organizational bases. If handled properly this need not detract from the effectiveness of the advisory system. It does, however, involve more careful planning and coordination of the strategic requirements of major policy initiatives.

Servant or Adviser. The public service is now more than ever subject to political influence and direction. Recent experiences have reminded public servants how easy it is to be bypassed. They have not only become more subject to ministerial decision making, but have often become the implementors of decisions taken elsewhere. The senior public service is now less permanent and becoming more vulnerable in the 1990s as the "contract state" continues to expand. The provision of fearless advice is difficult to sustain where high responsiveness is demanded. This issue centres less on whether the public service is either to be relatively marginalized or to retain a key advisory role. A more important factor is how to define that role in a meaningful way, particularly where it involves a partnership of political advisers and public servants.

Hierarchy versus Market. The two competing models of hierarchy and the market continue to offer major challenges. Too great a reliance on hierarchy tends to produce a monopoly. However, the advantages of control and access that derive from maintaining a professional in-house advisory capacity continue to make this highly attractive to ministers, even if the type of monopoly that prevailed in the past is unlikely to reappear. At the other extreme, a reliance on the market offers the advantages of multiple advocacy and flexibility, but it raises questions about control and management and the quality of outside expertise. The challenge is to obtain the advantages of both: to have a well-established, but not dominant, public service with well-honed skills at drawing on outside advice.

Contracting Out Advice. More specifically, contracting out has strengths and weaknesses. It allows the use of the skills and knowledge of organizations not bound by conventional public service norms and procedures, and it offers the possibility of fresh perspectives on problems from specialists independent of government. With the running down of public services, it is more difficult to obtain the concentration of specialized expertise within, while the increasing complexity of government ensures that it cannot continue to maintain the requisite expertise across all areas. The government may still exercise control through its management of the contract arrangement, and it has the advantage of multiple potential providers who are in competition. The greater use for policy advice of either internal or external markets that rely on competitive tendering for contracts to supply advice is most likely to remain the exception (Boston 1994:3).

The weaknesses of contracting out derive from the impact it can have on the public service and its knowledge base. This is particularly an issue when the "inherently governmental" activity is affected (cf., Kettl 1993:12). The problems of managing the process may outweigh the advantages of this option. Much depends on the internal capacity of the public service to manage what can be unstable and unpredictable elements. The markets that the government may rely on for services are subject to major imperfections (Kettl 1993). On the other hand, there is an argument that "direct provision tends to be more flexible and adaptable, thereby enabling quicker and more effective responses to changing circumstances." This may be of special relevance where the "quality of a good or service is of critical importance" (Boston 1994:13).

Consultation and Accountability. It seems likely that greater attention will be given to policy where economies are picking up and managerialism's influence is receding. The move for greater consultation will place pressures on those who have been recruited for their abilities to pursue top-down policy under conditions of economic constraint. External accountability does not square well with the more hierarchical demands of managerialism.

Quality of Advice and Evaluation. The recent experiments and speculations about evaluating policy advice have illuminated the issues without being conclusive. The more guarded verdict suggests that there remain "few, if any, proven models of effective policy-advising assessment systems" (Waller 1992:445). The recent international survey of this experience reports that there has not been major progress, although there has been a willingness to push out the boundaries. The major connection between process and result still needs to be made: recent evaluations of policy advising by Australian central agencies indicated that none was "particularly insightful into the effectiveness of the policy advising function in . . . its impact on outcomes" (Nicholson 1994:16).

However, there is now a willingness "to address an issue which had previously been considered 'too difficult' by most" (Nicholson 1994:16). Pollitt (1994:5) has recently advocated a "Whitehall-wide unit or audit team undertaking regular internal and confidential analyses of the technical quality of advice". There is also some commitment to producing guides for action: in New Zealand there is sensitivity to performance measures (quantity, coverage, quality, time, and cost) and quality standards for policy (Hawke 1993:18-23). There is also an increasingly sophisticated debate about relevant policy issues (Boston 1994; Pollitt 1994). Still outstanding, of course, are the more intractable questions such as the following: "A major issue in the definition of the quality of good policy advice is managing the tension between defining the quality of policy advice in terms of ministerial approval and in terms of peer review" (Hawke 1993:20).

Cohesive Policy Making and Coordination. Cross-portfolio issues still present problems for public administration (Waller 1992:445). One approach is via the development of capacity and competence of central agencies (although that can have its risks). Another option is to seek policy coordination through horizontal consolidation (Aucoin and Bakvis 1993; Craswell and Davis, forthcoming). Policy consolidation has costs for the internal range of policy advisory sources because diversity and competition may offer more policy options (Craswell and Davis 1993:182). This may have the further effect of externalizing policy development in order to obtain the interorganizational competition that may be missing. It remains unclear whether the revival of interest in strategic policy development will assist with intersectoral coordination. The questions of policy coordination continue to produce new challenges with the increasing interdependencies of policies and the internationalization of domestic policy (OECD 1990). These developments have implications for the policy cohesiveness of government and attempts to redefine the core.

CONCLUSION

The policy advisory role of the public service has been at the front line of reform turbulence. The public service was subject to assaults from politicians, who either wanted their own appointees to assume responsibility or at least to resume control of major policy. This role was central to the debate about managerializing the public service, for senior executives were seen to be too preoccupied with advising the minister and insufficiently attentive to managing their organizations. It was also affected generally by chief executives who wished to either bypass or at least undermine the capacity and role of the public service.

Despite these reforms, the policy advisory function has survived in the public service – although more so in some than others – and has been consolidated through structural changes in specific cases. The advantages of retaining a significant public service capacity are powerful and will ensure its continuance.

The public service has, however, been substantially changed. Senior public servants must now pay greater attention to a much wider range of influences and sources of policy knowledge and expertise. They must contend with the wider range of political, nongovernmental, and international actors who are now contributing to policy processes. The response to the new challenges has taken the form of experiments with the organization, process, and performance involved in the provision of policy advice. It is clear, however, that in each of the countries under review, there has been no final settlement of the role of the senior public service and its operating conditions. They are continuing to be subject to scrutiny, review, and change.

NOTES

1 The permanent secretaries still tend to reflect the traditional backgrounds of public schools and Oxbridge ("Reassuring Sir Humphrey" 1994:67).
2 For the 1993 election, the Opposition developed, with the assistance of these former Treasury consultants, the most sophisticated election manifesto ever seen in Australia and launched it around eighteen months before the election.
3 A more general estimate is that policy work and the activities of departmental headquarters account for about 10 percent of the civil service in the u.k. (British Government 1994:7).

BIBLIOGRAPHY

Aberbach, J., and B. Rockman. 1989. On the rise, transformation, and decline of analysis in the u.s. government. *Governance* 2, 3 (July):293-314.

Adler, Emanuel, and Peter M. Haas. 1992. Conclusion: epistemic communities, world order, and the creation of a reflective research program. *International Organization* 46, 2:367-90.

Aucoin, Peter. 1988. Organizational change in the Canadian machinery of government: from rational management to brokerage politics. In *Organizing Governance, Governing Organizations*, ed. Colin Campbell and B. Guy Peters, 283-308. Pittsburgh: University of Pittsburgh Press.

———1990. Administrative reform in public management: paradigms, principles, paradoxes and pendulums. *Governance* 3, 2 (April):115-37.

Aucoin, Peter, and Herman Bakvis. 1993. Consolidating cabinet portfolios: Australian lessons for Canada. *Canadian Public Administration* 36, 3:392-420.

Auditor-General, Project Audit Department of the Treasury. 1992. *Procedures for Managing the Economic Policy Program.* Audit Report No. 36 1991-92. Canberra: Australian Government Publishing Service.

Barker, Anthony, and B. Guy Peters. 1992. *The Politics of Expert Advice: Creating, Using and Manipulating Scientific Knowledge for Public Policy.* Edinburgh: Edinburgh University Press.

Bennett, Colin J. 1991. What is policy convergence and what causes it? *British Journal of Political Science* 21:215-33.

Boston, Jonathan. 1991. Reorganizing the machinery of government: objectives and outcomes. In *Reshaping the State: New Zealand's Bureaucratic Revolution,* ed. Boston et al., 233-67. Oxford: Oxford University Press

_____1994. Purchasing policy advice: the limits to contracting out. *Governance* 7, 1 (January):1-30.

Bourgault, Jacques, and Stéphane Dion. 1989. Governments come and go, but what of senior civil servants? Canadian deputy ministers and transitions in power (1867-1987). *Governance* 2, 2:124-51.

Bulmer, Martin. 1993. The royal commission and departmental committee in the British policy-making process. In Peters and Barker. 1993b.

Campbell, Colin. 1983. *Governments under Stress: Political Executives and Key Bureaucrats in Washington, London, and Ottawa.* Toronto: University of Toronto Press.

Campbell, Colin, and John Halligan. 1992. *Political Leadership in an Age of Constraint: The Experience of Australia.* Pittsburgh: University of Pittsburgh Press.

Craswell, Emma, and Glyn Davis. 1993. Does the amalgamation of government agencies produce better policy coordination. In *Reforming the Public Service: Lessons from Recent Experience,* ed. Patrick Weller, John Foster, and Glyn Davis. Melbourne: Macmillan.

_____ Forthcoming. The search for policy coordination: ministerial and bureaucratic perceptions of agency amalgamations in a federal parliamentary system. *Policy Studies Journal.*

Department of Finance. N.d. Organization structure and managing for results: separation of policy and operations. Canberra.

Dingwall, John. 1993. Special operating agencies: the experience so far. Canadian Centre for Management Development.

Doern, G. Bruce. 1992. *Implementing the U.K. Citizen's Charter.* Ottawa: Canadian Centre for Management Development.

Dynes, Michael. 1993. Whitehall reformers step up pressure on mandarin's power. *The Times*, 1 February.

Edwards, Meredith. 1992. Evaluating policy advice: a comment. *Australian Journal of Public Administration* 51, 4 (December):447-9.

Ferman, Barbara. 1989. Sloughing towards anarchy: the policy-making implementation gap revisited. *Governance* 2, 2 (April):198-212

Gore, Albert J. 1993. *From Red Tape to Results: Creating a Government that Works Better and Costs Less*. Report of the National Performance Review. Washington, DC: Government Printing Office.

Gray, Andrew and Bill Jenkins. 1992. The civil service and the financial management initiative. In *Handbook of Public Services Management*, ed. Christopher Pollitt and Stephen Harrison, 168-78. Oxford: Blackwell.

Haas, Peter M. 1992. Introduction: epistemic communities and international policy coordination. *International Organization* 46, 2:1-35.

Halligan, J. Forthcoming. The diffusion of civil service reform. In *Civil Services in Comparative Perspective*, ed. Hans Bekke, James L. Perry and Theo A. J. Toonen. Bloomington: Indiana University Press.

Halligan, John, and John Power. 1992. *Political Management in the 1990s*. Melbourne: Oxford University Press.

Hawke, G.R. 1993. *Improving Policy Advice*. Wellington: Institute of Policy Studies.

Hennessy, Peter. 1988. Demystifying Whitehall: the great British civil service debate, 1980s style. In *Organizing Governance, Governing Organizations*, ed. Colin Campbell and B. Guy Peters, 183-208. Pittsburgh: University of Pittsburgh Press.

_____ 1989. *Whitehall*. London: Secker and Warburg.

Kettl, Donald F. 1993. *Sharing Power: Public Governance and Private Markets*. Washington, DC: The Brookings Institution.

_____ 1994. Managing on the frontiers of knowledge: the learning organization. In *New Paradigms for Government: Issues for the Changing Public Service*, ed. Patricia W. Ingraham and Barbara S. Romzek. San Francisco: Jossey-Bass.

Levine, Charles H. 1988. Human resource erosion and the uncertain future of the U.S. civil service: from policy gridlock to structural fragmentation. *Governance* 1, 2 (April):115-43.

Lindquist, Evert A. 1991. *Public Managers and Policy Communities: Learning to Meet New Challenges*. Ottawa: Canadian Centre for Management Development.

Marsh, I. 1990. Globalisation, governance and think tanks. Paper presented to Third International Workshop on Governance in the Asia-Pacific Region, Canadian Institute for Research on Public Policy, Kuala Lumpur.

Mascarenhas, Reggie. 1990. Public sector reform in Australia and New Zealand: a framework for the analysis of policy development. In *Dynamics in Australian Public Management: Selected Essays*, ed. A. Kouzmin and N. Scott. Melbourne: Macmillan.

Massé, Marcel. 1993. Partners in the management of Canada: the changing roles of government and the public service. The 1993 John L. Manion Lecture. Ottawa: Canadian Centre for Management Development.

Nicholson, John. 1994. Monitoring the efficiency, quality and effectiveness of policy advice to government. Working Group on Program Evaluation, International Institute of Administrative Sciences.

Organization for Economic Cooperation and Development. 1990. *Aspects of Managing the Centre of Government*. Paris: OECD.

———— PUMA. 1993. *Market-Type Mechanisms Series No. 6: Internal Markets*. Paris: OECD.

Osborne, David, and Ted Gaebler. 1992. *Reinventing Government: How the Entrepreneurial Spirit is Transforming the Public Sector*. New York: Plume/Penguin.

Performance assessment of policy work. 1992. Report of the Working Group. Canberra: Australian Government.

Peters, B. Guy. 1986. *American Public Policy: Promise and Performance*, 2d ed. Chatham, NJ: Chatham House.

Peters, B. Guy, and Anthony Barker. 1993a. Governments, information, advice and policy-making. In Peters and Barker 1993b, 1-19.

———— 1993b. Eds. *Advising West European Governments: Inquiries, Expertise and Public Policy*. Edinburgh: Edinburgh University Press.

Plowden, William. 1991. Providing countervailing analysis and advice in a career-dominated bureaucratic system: the British experience, 1916-1988. In *Executive Leadership in Anglo-American Systems*, ed. Colin Campbell and Margaret Jane Wyskomirski, 219-47. Pittsburgh: University of Pittsburgh Press.

Pollitt, Christopher. 1994. Making policies: if agencies are the answer what is the question? Discussion paper prepared for LSE Seminar, 16 February.

Prince, Michael J. 1979. Policy advisory groups in government departments. In *Public Policy in Canada: Organization, Process and Management*, ed. Bruce Doern and Peter Aucoin. Toronto: Macmillan.

———1983. *Policy Advice and Organizational Survival: Policy Planning and Research Units in British Government*. Aldershot, Hampshire: Gower.

Pusey, M. 1991. *Economic Rationalism in Canberra: A National State Changes its Mind*. Cambridge: Cambridge University Press.

Reassuring Sir Humphrey. 1994. *The Economist*, 19 March, 65-7.

Rhodes, R.A.W., and David Marsh. 1992. 'Thatcherism': an implementation perspective. In *Implementing Thatcherite Policies: Audit of an Era*, ed. David Marsh and R.A.W. Rhodes. Buckingham: Open University Press.

Rourke, Francis E. 1992. American exceptionalism: government without bureaucracy. In *The State of Public Bureaucracy*, ed. Larry B. Hill, 223-29. Armonk, NY: M.E. Sharpe.

——— 1993. Professionals, politics and policymaking. Paper for the Annual Meeting of American Political Science Association, 2-5 September, Washington Hilton.

Savoie, Donald J. 1994. *Thatcher, Reagan, Mulroney: In Search of a New Bureaucracy*. Pittsburgh: University of Pittsburgh Press.

Self, Peter. 1993. *Government by the Market? The Politics of Public Choice*. Basingstoke: Macmillan.

Seymour-Ure, Colin. 1987. Institutionalization and informality in advisory Systems. In *Advising the Rulers*, ed. William Plowden, 175-84. Oxford: Basil Blackwell.

Singleton, Gwynneth. Forthcoming. Trial by Westminster: the fate of economic advisory councils in the United Kingdom, Canada and Australia. *Journal of Commonwealth and Comparative Politics*.

Smith, Bruce L.R. 1992. *The Advisers: Scientists in the Policy Process*. Washington, DC: The Brookings Institution.

Smith, James Allen. 1991. *The Idea Brokers: Think Tanks and the Rise of the New Policy Elite*. New York: Free Press.

State Services Commission. 1991. *Review of the Purchase of Policy Advice from Government Departments*. Wellington: SSC.

Sutherland, S. L. 1993. The public service and policy development. In *Governing Canada: Institutions and Public Policy*, ed. Michael M. Atkinson. Toronto: Harcourt Brace and Jovanovich Canada.

United Kingdom Government. 1994. *The Civil Service: Continuity and Change.* London: HMSO.

U.S. General Accounting Office. 1991. *Government Contractors: Are Service Contractors Performing Inherently Governmental Functions?* Washington, DC: U.S. Government Printing Office.

Waller, Mike. 1992. Evaluating Policy Advice. *Australian Journal of Public Administration* 51, 4 (December):440-9.

Weiss, Carol H. 1992. Helping government think: functions and consequences of policy analysis organizations. In *Organizations for Policy Analysis: Helping Government Think,* ed. Carol H. Weiss. Newbury Park: Sage.

Wilenski, Peter. 1986. *Public Power and Public Administration.* Sydney: Hale and Iremonger.

Williams, Walter. 1990. *Mismanaging America: The Rise of the Anti-Analytical Presidency.* Lawrence: University of Kansas Press.

Wiltshire, Kenneth. 1993. Other government-funded advisors. *Canberra Bulletin of Public Administration* 75 (December):121-7.

Accountability and Administrative Reform: Toward Convergence and Beyond

PHILLIP J. COOPER

In the report on progress attached to the first annual report on the implementation of Public Service 2000, the Clerk of the Privy Council, writing of accountability, insisted that "the principles are clear" (Tellier 1992:79). On the very next page, however, he noted:

To put it more simply, Public Service 2000 involves the increased delegation of decision-making authority from headquarters to points of service delivery. Only by pushing authority down and out to the regions can federal departments and agencies provide services with the quality and efficiency that Canadians are demanding. At the same time, departments must assure Ministers, Parliament, and a host of other interested parties ranging from the Auditor General to the national media that the authority that has been given to officials is being exercised responsibly (ibid., 80).

He added, "The accountability of Deputies is a particularly complex matter" (ibid.).

Like Mr. Tellier, many in public administration regard accountability as a familiar concept. There is an intuitive sense in which public managers feel as though everyone understands, or ought to understand, what accountability means in public service and how it functions. After all, accountability is one of the first responses given when the question is posed as to what makes public administration different from the management of private sector organizations or not-for-profits.

At the same time, it is increasingly apparent that, like most other facets of the profession, accountability is changing. While it continues to be a core concern in public administration, it is not all that clear precisely what accountability will look like in the new world of public service toward which we are moving or how it will operate. Beyond that, some of the older tools of accountability are precisely the "problems" targeted by reformers. Tellier announced: "The old 'command and control' model is not dead yet, but it is rapidly being replaced by a new kind of institutional culture ... " In Washington, the publication of the National Performance Review (Report of the National Performance Review 1993) and the launching of the effort led by Vice President Gore to reinvent government[1] was staged on the White House lawn between two forklifts bearing stacks of regulations that were presumably on their way to the trash heap. As the Clerk of the Privy Council's remarks suggest, accountability may look very different in a system that attacks rules, flattens hierarchies, and empowers officials at lower levels of ministries and departments.

Let us think for a time about what the forces are that are reshaping administrative accountability, where they seem to be taking the discussion, and what some of the implications of that new direction might be. Such a consideration suggests that, for a variety of reasons, parliamentary systems that have traditionally relied upon political mechanisms of accountability in the form of ministerial responsibility have been moving away from the classic formulation of that idea and more in the direction of legal and individual accountability. Ironically, other systems, like the United States for example, that have traditionally relied upon legal mechanisms of accountability have reacted against what appear to be legal excesses and toward more political accountability. However, while this convergence was in progress, the more recent efforts to fashion a new public service in a reinvented government have interposed, in both kinds of systems, what can be termed market mechanisms of accountability, a performance-based accountability in which the effort is to be responsible for service to clients. These changes raise a variety of important issues.

THE MOVE FROM PARLIAMENTARY POLITICS TOWARD
INDIVIDUAL LEGAL RESPONSIBILITY

The principle that ministers are individually responsible for the operation of their departments and the officials who manage them and collectively responsible for the policies of the government is as pristine a statement of political accountability as can be found. "The concentration of responsibility in the hands of Ministers reflects the fundamental democratic principle that the power of the state be exercised under the authority of elected officials accountable to the representatives of the electorate" (Tellier 1992:94-9). It is an approach to accountability common to the Westminster system followed by governments around the globe.

Yet in Canada, and other parliamentary systems, ministerial accountability has been changing. Indeed, there has been movement away from the classical formulation of the concept and toward accountability that is increasingly legal in character and targeted more toward the individual official. That trend has been in progress for the past decade or so in various countries. Several forces have been driving the shift, including outright legal challenges to the premises of ministerial responsibility, increasing tendencies for subjects to regard themselves as citizens who view government from a rights-based perspective, discomfort with enforcement of ministerial responsibility in large and complex governments, and a movement to require individual responsibility for officials as the price for increased stature and autonomy.

Legal Challenges to Ministerial Responsibility
and Parliamentary Privilege

Tate and Vallinder (forthcoming) have recently assembled studies done by scholars in a variety of countries where legal challenges and court rulings have come to play an increasingly important role in systems in which political institutions had previously been more important guarantors of official responsibility. Several factors have been influential in these countries, including increased demands for openness and rejection of broad-based claims of cabinet and parliamentary privilege, pressure for constitutional courts to play more significant roles in ensuring accountability, expectations that there should be enforcement of legal standards beyond the ministerial responsibility based in contemporary political majorities, and insistence upon a more individualistic, as compared to a collective, concept of accountability. It is one thing for these forces to play out in nations with a strong tradition of separation of powers, a coequal and independent judiciary, and a written constitution, but quite another in countries that have not shared these characteristics.

In Australia, for example, courts have rejected claims to cabinet privilege (Galligan and Slater, in Tate and Vallinder, forthcoming). In 1978 and again in 1991, the federal courts denied government assertions that such documents as minute papers of the Executive Council, communications between senior officials and their ministers, communications between ministers, and cabinet notebooks are immune from disclosure (*Sankey v. Whitlam* 1978; *Commonwealth v. Northern Land Council* 1991). In *Sankey v. Whitlam*, A.C.J. Gibbs wrote:

The fundamental principle is that documents may be withheld from disclosure only if, and to the extent that, the public interest renders it necessary. That principle in my opinion must also apply to state papers. It is impossible to accept that the public interest requires that all state papers should be kept secret forever, or until they are only of historical interest ... In other words state papers do not form a homogeneous class, all the members of which must be treated alike. The subject matter with which the papers deal will be of great importance, but all the circumstances have to be considered in deciding whether the papers in question are entitled to be withheld from production, no matter what they individually contain (*Sankey v. Whitlam* 1978, para 42).

Gibbs went on to observe that: "The fact that members of the Executive Council are required to take a binding oath of secrecy does not assist the argument that the production of state papers cannot be compelled" (ibid., para 44).

The Federal Court in *Commonwealth v. Northern Land Council* (1991) followed the lead of the High Court in the earlier *Sankey* case:

> It follows from Sankey v. Whitlam that in the case of Cabinet papers their membership in that class is no longer to be regarded as affording absolute protection against disclosure. Indeed membership of any class of official documents is no longer a basis for otherwise unqualified immunity from production.

The Australian courts took the same approach adopted by the United States Supreme Court in the infamous Watergate tapes case, *United States v. Nixon* (1974), an authority cited to the High Court during the *Sankey* litigation. But the u.s. does not have a concept of ministerial responsibility and it does have a very different conception of the relationship between executive and legislative functions.

These rulings are but examples of a wider phenomenon. The creation of constitutional courts in a variety of countries with a parliamentary tradition and the expanding role of those courts in the governments of several Western nations have been of considerable significance to both policy making and administration over the past decade. In England, for example, courts have taken a more expansive view of the doctrines of judicial review of administrative decisions.[2] In France, the Constitutional Court has been involved in a number of controversial political discussions, most recently in striking down a proposed school finance plan permitting parental choice in a wide variety of schools. In Germany, there have been a number of critical battles, including the much publicized abortion case.

Rights Charters and Changing Self-Image

In a number of cases, including several brought before the Canadian Supreme Court (Bogart, Russell, in Tate and Vallinder, forthcoming) and some provincial tribunals,[3] these challenges to government action have been based upon various kinds of human rights charters or bills of rights. The Canadian Charter, and the Supreme Court's role under it, have been matters of controversy for some time. Few would argue that the Charter has resulted in waves of major rulings striking down government policy. On the other hand, the Charter, the debate about its import, and changing self-perceptions have encouraged more people to think in terms of their individual rights as the touchstone for accountability. While formally Canadians, and for that matter many in other countries, are subjects, this focus on individual rights reinforces a growing tendency to think of one's self as a citizen, as that concept is used in, for example, the United States. When the language of accountability shifts from ministerial responsibility to individual rights, the implications can be significant.

In addition to the obvious fact that these discussions of accountability are inherently more legalistic in character than ministerial in accountability, they have two other important characteristics. First, they suggest, albeit informally and perhaps even indirectly, by virtue of the focus on the concept of rights, that officials govern in the name and for the sake of the people, rather than in the name of the Crown. It is not coincidental that some members of Parliament have felt increased pressure to provide constituent casework services and other direct representation.

Second, and of more direct and significant import, is the fact that a legal claim is a much more individualistic mode of accountability than ministerial responsibility. The former seeks recompense and protection for the individual, while the latter focuses upon correcting deficiencies in departmental operations in order to serve the entire community better. Even where litigants bring suit in an attempt to affect policy, it is a very different enterprise than when a minister works through his or her deputy to conduct a review, explain the problem, and indicate corrective or disciplinary action.

Discomfort with Enforcement of Ministerial Responsibility in Large and Complex Governments

Sutherland has noted that there are two other types of arguments that have been used in the move away from ministerial responsibility (Sutherland 1992:573-603). First, there is the contention that it is not a form of accountability well adapted to governing with large complex organizations. Second, such incidents as the al-Mashat affair, suggest that ministerial accountability simply is not working very well.

As to the latter, Sutherland blasted the process by which two officials were brought to answer in a committee process for the al-Mashat case.

> In a moral sense, it is not too strong to say that the dynamic of the staged inquiry was both foolish and awful . . .
>
> In a more practical sense, the managerialist philosophy appears to be deeply unworkable, at least when its propositions are incrementally superimposed on a system of responsible government. It apparently seals ministers off from the democratic pressure points and safety valves that are built into the system. In this sense, managerialism is both closed-minded and ideological at the same time, because it refuses to let the minister hear the signals from the opposition and the public. The use of the political forum to punish officials is profoundly anti-democratic in a broad sense, because it is an attempt to manipulate public opinion using the symbolism of personal accountability without the substance of policy accountability. The bottom line of such managerialism may be the individual accountability of officials for their efficient discharge of narrow duties but the bottom line of responsible government is ideally something closer to government with the educated consent of Parliament (ibid., 602-3).

Quite apart from the continuing controversy over the al-Mashat matter, there have been a variety of questions raised about the efficacy of ministerial responsibility in its classical formulation in the contemporary setting. It is, of course, not the practice to seek resignations of ministers for maladministration. Increasingly, though, the question is whether ministers can be held responsible at all for events in their departments about which they were not aware. And as organizations and their functions are becoming more complex, the range of activity of which ministers may be unaware is substantial. If that explanation is employed to shift more accountability from the minister to subordinate officials, two problems arise. The first is how to maintain the clear connection of administrative accountability through the minister to Parliament and thus ensure political accountability in the most basic form. The second is that if ministers have a general responsibility to ensure the proper functioning of their ministries and provide prompt examination, explanation, and correction of mistakes and ministers have a collective cabinet responsibility for the actions of the government, how broadly can the direct knowledge defence be used by ministers without undermining the larger concept of ministerial responsibility?

Quite apart from conceptual difficulties, there are practical political dimensions that undermine ministerial responsibility. The contemporary need of ministers and members of Parliament to play to public opinion is not always compatible with the best traditions of ministerial accountability. Sutherland points out that since question period is televised, the opposition can take advantage of the opportunity to add criticism to the present government in any difficult situation (Sutherland 1992:586). Peter Aucoin has noted several contemporary political trends that have implications for the operation of government, including issues of accountability.[4] They include the weakness of parties, separation of many interest groups from the parties, the breakdown of party discipline, the increasing personalization of the prime minister, and the character and uses of public opinion polls. Aucoin also suggests that there are some accountability traps for public servants in this environment. They can be caught: between established formal policies and temporary political manoeuvres to address public opinion demands; between accountability constraints on discretion and demands for more flexible performance based on behaviour in response to consumer demand; between expert knowledge and experience and a rising and often ill-informed populism; between demands for rapid responses and expectations of expanded consultation and participation; and between demands for earlier and more open dissemination of critical information and punishment by the press of unrefined policy and management proposals that find their way into the public light.

The Movement to Require Individual Accountability for Officials as the Price for Increased Stature and Autonomy

Finally, there is the argument that if officials wish greater respect for their knowledge and experience in important issues in government and management, then they must be prepared to give up traditional anonymity (Sutherland 1992:583). The evidence is that this has happened. The Privy Council Office has noted a trend that "Parliament has increasingly accepted that officials answer" for administrative actions. "The development is best observed in the practices that have grown up in Parliament's standing and legislative committees, and the widening scope of these practices in recent years has reduced the traditional anonymity of public servants" (Tellier 1992:98; Management Advisory Board and Management Improvement Advisory Committee 1993:6-7).

These are some of the forces that have tended to move a number of countries, including Canada, away from traditional concepts of ministerial responsibility and toward a more legalistic and individualized approach to accountability. They have not altered the formal declarations of policy and principle in Canada or, for example, in Australia (Management Advisory Board and the Management Improvement Advisory Committee 1993:6), but they have clearly affected the practice.

THE REACTION AGAINST LAW AND
THE MOVE TOWARD POLITICS

It is perhaps ironic that at the very same time that some parliamentary regimes have moved away from classical political responsibility and toward more legalistic and individualized accountability, other governments, like the United States, with a strong tradition of legal and individualized responsibility have reacted against that approach and have moved in precisely the opposite direction. In the American case, several factors have played a role in this movement, including the assault on "judicial activism," the attack on administrative rule-making, the development of alternative tools to fashion and operate policy, and a call for administration that is not rule-based.

The Reaction Against "Judicial Activism"

Early in American national history, Alexis de Tocqueville correctly observed that sooner or later every significant policy in America finds its way into court. To that, many contemporary observers add a corollary: that sooner or later every significant administrative decision finds its way into court. While this may be somewhat of an overstatement, the point is clear. At the same time, Americans have not been willing to give up their opportunity to get their day in court on virtually any matter of significance.

There are a number of fascinating contradictions involved in attacks on judicial responses to agencies, and common perceptions in this area are often very wide of the mark. In the first place, administrative agencies win the overwhelming number of judicial review challenges to their decisions. It is true that there are more challenges in recent decades than in years past, but there are also more statutes and administrative agencies to enforce them. There have indeed been a host of cases in which courts have issued complex remedial orders requiring reforms in such institutions as prisons and mental health facilities, but it is also true that administrators have sometimes cooperated in these cases because they needed the resources, which public opinion would not support, to run facilities the public would just as soon ignore. Court orders bring resources. Many of these cases involved negotiated settlements, resulting in consent decrees rather than judicial opinions and orders mandating action. Even where adjudication was required, the orders produced were often recommended or crafted by the parties, including the administrative agencies involved (Cooper 1988). When critics became increasingly vociferous about these cases during the past two decades, the Supreme Court issued a series of rulings in which it admonished lower courts about intrusion into the operations of administrative agencies. In one such case, the Court suggested that injured citizens should cease attempting to use injunctions to change policy and simply sue the specific officials responsible for the damages the individual claimant felt had been suffered (*Rizzo v. Goode* 1976). That was not a move calculated to make administrators happy. In any case, a suit against a police officer does not ensure a change in a policy, albeit often an informal one, that was the cause of the officer's behaviour in the first place. A suit for money damages against an employee of an underfunded mental hospital accomplishes nothing.

Even the Supreme Court has had an ongoing internal debate about the proper balance between the need to ensure appropriate review of administrative agencies under the statutes and doctrines of administrative law while simultaneously avoiding inappropriate "Monday morning quarterbacking" (*Vermont Yankee Nuclear Power Corp. v. Nuclear Regulatory Commission* 1978, 547) of administrative decisions. On the other hand, the Court has resolved that issue with a trend toward increasing deference to administrative action, including statutory interpretation, a subject that has traditionally been regarded as a matter at the heart of the judicial function (*Vermont Yankee* 1978; *Chevron U.S.A. v. Natural Resources Defense Council* 1984). The Court has also moved, in the controversial abortion gag rule case (*Rust v. Sullivan* 1991), to grant considerable room for political change that rejects long-standing administrative practice, even when there was no significant basis for that departure.

Despite all of this, and many other contradictions, there continues to be substantial political and administrative capital associated with attacks on the courts. Indeed, that has been a continuing theme for more than a quarter century. Whatever the level of hyperbole, it is still true that many managers feel frustrated, angry, and, to one degree or another, fearful about the threat of suit. Even if they win, they say, the amount of time and energy that is involved in avoiding litigation, preparing for it if it should occur, and responding to formal legal challenges even if the matter never gets to a courtroom, is enormous and unacceptable in a period of declining resources.

The Attack on Administrative Rule-making

Long before *Reinventing Government* and the National Performance Review were even contemplated, large numbers of people from both parties and various interest groups made the attack on regulations and the rule-making process a central issue in politics. Once again there was a considerable irony in all that, in light of the fact that one of the continuing criticisms of American administrative agencies throughout the 1950s and 1960s was arbitrary behaviour. That criticism was based in substantial part upon the fact that regulators and even service providers were making up the rules in the middle of the game rather than promulgating regulations at the outset that would permit those who must deal with agencies to know the standards with sufficient time and clarity to bring themselves into compliance (Davis 1969).

The most recent attack has been targeted not only against the number of regulations and the level of their detail but also at the manner in which they were made. In a series of rulings in the late 1960s and early 1970s, the United States Court of Appeals for the District of Columbia Circuit (the principal administrative law court in the u.s.) insisted that agencies had to obey the requirements of the Administrative Procedure Act for open, orderly, and participative rule-making in substance as well as in form (*Natural Resources Defense Council v. u.s. Nuclear Regulatory Commission* 1976). The result was a process that came to be known as hybrid rule-making; more formal than simple notice and comment process and less complex than a full blown judicial-type proceeding. The court was attacked for mandating additional rule-making procedures beyond those required by statute and that line of rulings was rejected by a unanimous Supreme Court in 1978 (*Vermont Yankee* 1978).

Even before the Supreme Court decision, however, both the Congress and the President had accepted the utility of the kinds of procedures the courts had mandated. The Congress incorporated hybrid procedures in virtually every major piece of legislation where rule-making authority was granted during the 1970s and 1980s. President Carter mandated hybrid rule-making and, indeed, an expanded form of the process for every executive branch department through Executive Order 12044.

At the beginning of the Reagan administration, the White House issued Executive Order 12291 which added major burdens to rule-making processes and gave the Office of Management and Budget a mechanism by which to veto or at least delay proposed rules developed by agencies. When Congress reacted against the White House move and threatened to cut funding, the administration responded by using the review processes available under the Paperwork Reduction Act to accomplish the same kind of veto as before. In the meantime, the Reagan White House used executive means to get deregulation where it knew that Congress would be unwilling to cooperate, as in environmental and health and safety regulation. Moreover, the tension between these two branches was serious and continued throughout the Reagan and Bush years. That, in turn, prompted the Congress, using its reauthorization process (under the so-called "sunset" provisions of various statutes) to adopt revised legislation in several fields that mandated more rule-making, more detailed rules, and shorter deadlines for the issuance of the new regulations.

Not surprisingly, all of these factors exacerbated existing frustrations with rules and rule-making.

Development of Alternative Tools to Fashion and Operate Policy

The deregulatory fervour of the late 1970s and 1980s, plus the tensions over rule-making led to efforts that can be characterized in two quite different ways. One approach is to recognize that some agencies simply tried to get around rule-making requirements by terming their action guidelines, interpretive rules, or policy statements. Second, efforts were made to find innovative techniques that sought to deregulate or at least to avoid the need for the issuance of new regulations.

The Carter administration was responsible for more deregulation legislation than either of its Republican successors. Beyond that, Carter instituted what he termed the Innovative Techniques of Regulation program, which sought to find ways to avoid command and control techniques and obtained legislation known as the Paperwork Reduction Act to reduce excessive documentation and compliance requirements. He also achieved passage of the Civil Service Reform Act, which attempted to provide greater flexibility and performance-based techniques for supervision, control, and pay of civil servants.

At the same time, administration officials, frustrated by the host of accountability restrictions from pay caps to accounting requirements, searched for new organizational forms that might be more efficient and flexible and would have a culture more like a private sector firm. Thus was born the expanded use of government corporations that could be chartered in such a way as to avoid most accountability requirements and the civil service restrictions otherwise applicable to government agencies. It was also a hospitable environment for increased privatization. There ensued debates, not about whether some degree of privatization was a positive development, but whether there should be some kind of boundaries, both theoretical and practical, concerned with the selection or structure of organizations and programs. Responding to Bozeman's *All Organizations Are Public* (1987), Moe warned that there are, or should be, limits to privatization, and the failure to recognize the critical public law foundations for administering public policy carries serious risks (Moe 1987:453-60; Sullivan 1987:461-7). He pointed to what he termed "quasi-crypto-pseudo" governmental organizations like the Federal Assets Disposition Association (FADA) and expressed concern about the dangers involved in placing some types of government functions in the hands of organizations that lack properly crafted legal foundations and mechanisms of accountability. (It turned out that many of Moe's warnings about the organizations involved in the bank bailout debacle of the 1980s and 1990s were uncannily accurate.)

Bozeman replied that Moe and other critics who anchored their arguments in public law were engaged in the effort to maintain a "Maginot Line" (Bozeman 1988:672-4). Moe answered that he was not opposed to privatization, but was very concerned about excessive pragmatism that simply considered anything that seemed "to work" as acceptable. What appears to work in the short term may carry grave risks for the future, Moe argued. He concluded: "The objective standard I argue for is the 'law.' The objective standard Bozeman advocates is 'performance'" (Moe 1988:675).

Reinvented Administration: Governance Based on Performance, Not Rules

Indeed, there were many would-be reformers who have taken performance as the primary criterion and the proper focus for accountability. One of their principal targets has been "command and control" administration. The term itself has several meanings and uses, but the common characteristic is criticism of what are regarded as excessive regulations and legal constraints. Indeed, that was the central theme of the National Performance Review (known as REGO) and *Reinventing Government.*

The REGO report charged that "Thousands upon thousands of outdated, overlapping regulations remain in place. These regulations affect the people inside government and those who deal with it from the outside" (Report of the National Performance Review 1993:32). Although the report admits that "we have no precise measurement of how much regulation costs or how much time it steals from productive work" (ibid., 32), it recommended that the President should require all agencies to move toward a three-year "goal of eliminating 50 percent of those regulations"(ibid., 33).

That is interesting political rhetoric, but hardly helpful. There is no recognition that a very large percentage of rules are mandated by statutes – dozens of them. It does not come to terms with the forces that led to increased rule-making or changes in the process. It also does not discuss the fact that a substantial amount of the burden of the rule-making process and many agency internal operating rules stem from White House mandates. For example, Presidents Reagan and Bush imposed more than a half-dozen executive orders governing rule-making by all executive branch agencies: these could have been eliminated with the stroke of a pen by President Clinton. They were all retained and, indeed, the first thing the President did after his inauguration was to sign a new executive order on ethics.

The point is that legal restrictions have become an important political target. It is no accident that the REGO report is entitled *From Red Tape to Results*. Of course, it is an old line that one person's red tape is another person's accountability. On the other hand, it is also not surprising that in recent decades the same administrations which have made cutting red tape a rallying cry have often had difficulty giving up top-down control. The point is that most have favoured moving away from legal accountability toward greater political accountability.

CONVERGENCE BUT THEN A NEW DIRECTION: TOWARD MARKET ACCOUNTABILITY

What we have seen from all of this is a kind of convergence in which parliamentary governments have, by degrees, moved away from the purest form of political accountability, the classical formulation of ministerial responsibility and others at the other end of the spectrum have moved from the legal foundation toward political accountability. In the midst of that process, however, waves of management reform have taken governments in a third direction, toward market accountability. It is different from either the legal or the political variety and in fact may conflict with them. On the other hand, it is unlikely that most regimes will be willing to give up the political and legal values in favour of the market approach.

At the heart of market accountability is an economic efficiency premise. That value takes several forms. First, there is simple cost. That which costs less is better. In truth, that is an economy judgment rather than what is normally considered efficiency (see Mintzberg 1982), but the distinctions are often lost in the political arena and particularly in a period of fiscal austerity when deficit reduction is a national priority.

Second, there is a cost/benefit form. A government action meets the test of market accountability if, and only if, it has a positive cost/benefit calculation. Unfortunately, such assessments often use relatively simplistic measures, tending systematically to over-count costs (since they are easier to calculate) and underestimate benefits (which may be extremely difficult to determine). The cost/benefit approach may vary from a simple admonition to show that the real impacts of government action have been carefully considered in advance of implementation to a far more draconian calculus. Consider, for example, the requirements of President Reagan's Executive Order 12291 issued in 1981.

Regulatory action shall not be undertaken unless the potential benefits to society for the regulation outweigh the potential costs to society;

Regulatory objectives shall be chosen to maximize the next benefits to society;

Among alternative approaches to any given regulatory objective, the alternative involving the least net cost to society shall be chosen; and

Agencies shall set regulatory priorities with the aim of maximizing the aggregate net benefits to society, taking into account the condition of the particular industries affected by regulations, the condition of the national economy, and other regulatory actions contemplated for the future.

Among the difficulties with such mandates for agencies, of course, is the fact that they are faced by civil servants who are mandated by legislation to act but must do so within these kinds of constraints. It is that sort of tension that encourages some degree of cynicism about the way such cost/benefit calculations are done.

Third, there are performance standards, often anchored in a kind of input/output efficiency model, with the emphasis on outputs. The focus, indeed, is most often on measurable outputs. The measurement of results is valued over control by rules or by hierarchical authority. This approach takes on a wide variety of forms from the descriptions in Public Service 2000 to *Reinventing Government* and from management by objective (MBO)to total quality management (TQM). There is a kind of irony in this approach, however, because in operation performance standards work a good deal like regulations. They set behavioural boundaries, the violation of which may carry relatively stiff sanctions.

Fourth, there is a definition of market accountability based upon client satisfaction. It assumes that if customers receive adequate levels of quality service at a good price, then accountability is achieved. This approach views citizens or subjects as consumers or customers.

Another variant on the client satisfaction model is the market choice perspective typified by voucher programs. Again, the assumptions of the marketplace concerning knowledge and competition are applied. If given choices, consumers will select the better services and those organizations, whether public or private, that win those customers will prosper by virtue of their performance.

There is also an important premise in this approach that assumes that public policies should function as fee-for-service operations. If the direct customers of an organization's services are satisfied, then presumably the organization is properly accountable. Moreover, this approach combines issues of just what it is for which public officials are responsible and the processes according to which they are to be held accountable for their actions. The market assumptions set both ends and means.

One of the difficulties here is the failure to distinguish between clients and constituents. The Australian Management Advisory Board observed: "Officials have the responsibility, on behalf of government, to deal equitably, justly and responsively with all individuals or groups whose interests they may affect, even when the relevant program may not be designed to confer a benefit on those affected" (Management Advisory Board and Management Improvement Advisory Committee 1993:11). There may be many who are affected by a policy and its administration, though they may not be the clients directly targeted. Social welfare programs, medical care policies, and public safety services provide examples.

One is reminded of the fact that in some American communities, people look back nostalgically to the days of the political machine and swear that services were more personal and more responsive in the good old days. Of course, they overlook the corruption and the manifold inequities that were the hallmarks of machine politics. It is interesting that in the one page that Osborne and Gaebler devoted to "a new accountability system," the question was asked: "If it costs far more to eliminate corruption than we save by doing so, is it worth the expense?" (Osborne and Gaebler 1993:137). Clearly, many would answer, yes.

In the regulatory arena, it is one thing for the government to reach an agreement with a polluter about the level and financing of a toxic waste cleanup operation, but quite another to satisfy wider community expectations. Put differently, it is not all that simple to determine precisely who are the consumers of a given policy or service.

The other issue that arises here is the fact that the assumption of measuring performance against customer satisfaction and choice, quite apart from debates concerning assumptions about knowledge and competition, disregards the fact that the citizen or subject is more than a consumer of discrete services. They have rights, legal and political, which are defined in the fundamental character of the nation. Whether they stem from a constitution, a charter, a bill of human rights, statute, or custom, taken together, they constitute membership in the political community. That membership entails a legitimate expectation of accountability to the community itself rather than to discrete interests within it.

In sum, it is possible to think of a set of characteristics for political, legal, and market accountability in order to compare their natures. They are matters of degree, not hard, fixed, and exclusive categories, but they do reveal a number of relatively substantial differences. Political accountability is concerned with the collective values, legal with norms found in law, and the market with the market process. Political accountability tends to operate at the macro level, while the legal focuses on the micro level, and the market process is diffuse. Political accountability tends to emphasize substantive values, the legal often highlights procedural rules, and the market mechanism emphasizes transactions. The political accountability is based in political consensus, the legal approach is often rights-based, and the market emphasizes individual choice as a foundation. Political accountability is democratically oriented, the legal is fairness oriented, and the market is efficiency focused. The political approach is parliament (or its counterpart) directed, the legal is court directed, and the market is, of course, market directed. Political accountability emphasizes consensus building, the legal is concerned with conflict, and the market prefers negotiated processes. Political accountability is public centred, the legal uses public power to protect private claims, and the market emphasizes a private sector orientation. Political accountability has a policy emphasis, legal mechanisms highlight statutes, charters, regulations, or constitutions, and the market approach focuses upon contracts. Political accountability often takes an incremental and medium-term perspective, legal approaches emphasize continuity and predictability over the longer term, and the market often assesses action on a short-term basis. In political accountability elected officials lead, while in the legal case advocates lead, and in the market firms lead. In the political context the citizen or subject is fundamental, in the legal setting the client is primary, and in the market, the market actor is fundamental. Political accountability often carries a transitional character, as an existing political consensus gives way to the next one, legal accountability supports a relatively stable and conservative view, and the market, at least in a deregulated condition, may be open to greater volatility. Political conceptions of accountability are often cooperative in character, the market competitive, and the legal coercive. Although there are areas of overlap and compatibility, these are some of the ways in which these three approaches are quite different in character and operation.

ACCOUNTABILITY AND THE GLOBALIZATION OF PUBLIC MANAGEMENT

It is an unfortunate fact that most discussions of accountability emphasize domestic matters. However, the globalization of public management discussed earlier by Donald Savoie plainly has important implications for accountability. In the first place, international and regional agreements have significant consequences for domestic administration. Thus, we have seen business persons in Britain and the Netherlands who have brought law suits on the basis of the European Charter of Human Rights to defeat local and national regulations. Legal attacks have already been contemplated under GATT that would challenge domestic health, safety, and environment regulations as anti-competitive barriers to trade. Debates over the North American Free Trade Agreement (NAFTA) emphasized future enforcement of environmental and labour standards. Indeed, the mere presence of NAFTA brought uncharacteristic responses from the Salinas government in the wake of an uprising by indigenous people in the Mexican state of Chiapas.

To some extent the discussions of management reform have ignored accountability as an issue in the Third World, even as institutions like the IMF and World Bank have pressed them to adopt the market mechanisms. Debt rescheduling and restructuring have been premised in many instances on privatization, deregulation, and other market-oriented changes. Yet there is virtually no literature that addresses the meaning of all those changes in terms of accountability.

One reason for the dearth of study on accountability in developing nations is that it can be difficult to conceptualize the idea in the very different context of the Third World. For one thing, political and legal accountability have been difficult to address when so many nations were governed by authoritarian regimes or accepted corruption as normal, though plainly not desirable. There are difficulties, too, for contemplating market models of accountability, so popular now. There are really two very different kinds of markets or settings from which to draw accountability values. The developed countries tend (with exceptions) to be larger, wealthier, and less densely populated (relative to available suitable space). They tend to have a larger middle class, more capital, more competing firms, a more diverse economy, less institutional power differential, more adaptive capacity, and less dependence on external players than the developing countries. (Then there is the set of nations sometimes called transitional countries that present unique circumstances for which generalizations are even more difficult.)

In fact, even when one asks regional specialists on Latin America, Africa, or Asia about the concept of accountability, the reaction is often puzzlement. There are, however, some interesting events that have taken place recently that suggest that it may be time to look more closely at the concept in the third world, beyond the fact that these nations and cultures can no longer be written off as though they were isolated from the rest of the global community. Consider that both Brazil and Venezuela have removed presidents by political and constitutional processes in the past two years without intervention by the military. Indeed, a number of Brazilian legislators appear about to be held to account for their own behaviour. It is worth noting, too, that the High Court of South Africa ruled against the authority of the state to try a member of the African National Congress (ANC) who had been kidnapped while outside its borders. Finally, there have been efforts by international groups to develop mechanisms of accountability for abuses within individual countries (Africa Watch 1992). Accountability is coming to have more meaning in those parts of the world than our literature recognizes.

ACCOUNTABILITY IN THE HYBRID STATE: NEW CHALLENGES FOR THE NEW PUBLIC SERVICE

We have arrived today at the problem of public management in the hybrid state. Old concepts of politics, law, and culture have been dramatically altered by technology, market forces, and globalization. It is useful as we contemplate the new challenges to consider some of the premises of reform, a few of the problems posed by the rise of market accountability, and the kind of unanswered questions that need to be addressed as we move beyond arguments about whether to change and on to discussions about how to operate in the changed world we already face.

Assumptions About Change

Unfortunately, it is too often the case that there is a kind of bandwagon effect at work. If one does not accept completely and without reservation proposed reforms in their purest form, there is the risk of being charged with mindless conservatism and an unwillingness to change. That is unfortunate.

While it is true that large public organizations resist change, the same is true of private sector firms and large financial institutions. Moreover, the public sector, contrary to common criticism, is constantly changing. In fact, given history, some governments can be said to have adapted more rapidly and dramatically than many private sector organizations.

The argument, particularly as posed by some economists, seems to be that public administration is unwilling to be informed by lessons from the private sector and the marketplace. That is simply untrue, and has been since at least the early decades of the twentieth century. In fact, public administration is, and always has been, a borrower profession. It has appropriated large quantities of knowledge and technique from many fields, ranging from organization theory to finance.

The problem seems to be that instead of learning lessons and determining how best to integrate them into public administration, what we see is a relatively dramatic attack on the enterprise of public administration. Much of the reinventing literature appears to be based on the assumption that the public sector has failed in virtually all significant respects.

That attitude is certainly characteristic of the market-oriented, efficiency-based critics. Perhaps it is not surprising that they posit the premise that only decisions taken by individuals as market actors are efficacious and efficient. However, that is somewhat ironic in light of the fact that markets, at least sophisticated markets, cannot operate effectively in the absence of the considerable infrastructure that government is expected to provide and maintain.

Related to this market choice demand is the assumption that what government can and should do is to establish or develop systems and processes but not manage them. There is a sense in which policy design in what has become primary and public management is either unnecessary or actually destructive. To the degree that political accountability becomes an issue for some of these critics, it is in the realm of policy failure rather than responsibility to political values.

Finally, some of the market advocates "view their role as advocacy of a cause and thus feel little need to consider the possible limitations to their arguments" (Moe 1987:458). Nowhere is this more true than in the area of accountability. Little attention is paid to the idea, even though the concepts, processes, and techniques proposed by that model present crucial accountability concerns.

The Downside of the Market

Recognizing that there is much to learn that is useful from the private sector and the marketplace, then, it is still important to contemplate some of the problems presented by the market model of accountability. It is necessary to see that it is essential to integrate market concepts with political and legal accountability, rather than attempting to have the market model displace the others. Related to that is the fact that there are problems with market accountability.

The pressure for the market concepts grounded in efficiency to predominate has been clear in many places around the world. Even someone as pragmatic as Bozeman agrees with Moe that "policy decisions about allocation of responsibilities are too often made on the basis of a narrow conception of economic efficiency" (Bozeman 1988:672). In fact, criticism of that tendency surfaced in relatively high relief in Russia with the elections of 1993. The resignation of Finance Minister Boris Fyodorov came because the Yeltsin government had to recognize that other values could simply not be completely subordinated to economic "shock therapy." Similarly, some of the criticism that surfaced in the wake of the Chiapas uprising in Mexico argued that the Salinas government bore responsibility because it had focused on market reforms to the exclusion of critical political and legal questions of social equity and human rights.

Market mechanisms represent one set of devices for accountability, but only one. The issues of accountability today are more, not less, complex. The simple reference to performance standards and market choice will not change the fact that public policies emerge from a political process and are constrained by a host of legal norms. For example, the effort to decentralize and flatten organizations in order to reduce overhead control, lower middle management costs, and increase consumer responsiveness presents new accountability issues. The public and, perhaps as importantly, the media will not give up the legal and political mechanisms. They want to know who is responsible and within what limits. Ministerial responsibility may not be what it once was, but it is still a critical link between public managers and the democratic source of legitimacy. Osborne and Gaebler may be willing to accept some degree of corruption on efficiency grounds, but the citizens of Atlanta, Georgia who recently sat on juries in cases concerning alleged corruption at Hartsfield airport were not. It is an important challenge to consider how we will reconcile devolution, decentralization, and deconcentration with political and legal demands for overhead accountability.

There are also issues of the client and constituent, raised earlier. Although some degree of choice may be popular in certain programs, there remains a considerable difference between individual market-based decisions and concerted policy judgments. Jon Pierre has referred to this elsewhere in this volume as the distinction between policy and consumption. Citizens and subjects will continue to demand accountability for policy whether they are direct consumers of the services or not.

It is important as well to contemplate the relationships between legal accountability and claims by advocates of the market approach. While it may be true that there are many unnecessary rules and that rule-making procedures are unduly cumbersome, the unsophisticated attack on rules is far too easy and very unhelpful. Indeed, it can undermine efficiency. After all, one of the reasons why rules developed was because of continued complaints about a lack of orderliness and predictability in government. Business people do not wish to have to address dozens of different health and safety rules promulgated by every regional and municipal government. They have sought uniform national standards that permit ease of manufacture and shipment. Moreover, the ability to know and predict the behaviour of other agencies makes it possible within government to plan and order one's decisions more efficiently and effectively.

Additionally, the increased use of new market devices does not necessarily eliminate the need for political or legal accountability. They may indeed create new ones. For example, contracts, permit systems, fees, incentive systems, and various kinds of special-purpose enterprise funds do not manage themselves. Yes, procurement practices can be streamlined, but they also create burdens as the sheer amount of contracting increases. For example, discussions of contracting processes emphasize the process from the RFP through the bids to the letting of the contract. However, studies of contracting, in the U.S. at least, suggest that the most difficult problems arise in contract administration and accountability actions in the event of substandard performance. Thus, the need is to re-examine contracting processes, particularly those involving service contracts, to develop effective mechanisms of management and accountability, including the professional development of contract administrators.

Finally, as government changes roles and becomes more involved in different kinds of relationships with a wide range of organizations in the private and not-for-profit sectors, the issues of political and legal accountability must be revisited. For example, much of the legal and political structure was designed to evaluate government as regulator or infrastructure builder. As governments at all levels become market participants as well as market regulators, a variety of questions arise that have not yet received clear answers. For example, to what degree should government units which purchase, vend, or compete for services develop favoured relationships, as compared to open and equal interactions, with all firms or government units within a given sector? How are local government units which vend services to another community, for example ambulance operations, to be held accountable to the residents of the community served? What liability, if any, attaches to higher level units which authorize the purchase of emergency services in the event of malpractice?

CONCLUSION

In the end, the challenge of accountability in the contemporary environment is to understand the movement away from the dominance of one form and the need to integrate a variety of frameworks to meet changing needs. It is critical to move beyond the unhelpful attacks on legal and political accountability and to incorporate market tools carefully and with serious attention not merely to the opportunities they pose but to the new challenges they present. The other critical task is to consider how best to equip public service professionals to operate with this multifaceted perspective on a day-to-day basis.

NOTES

1 For the foundations, see Osborne and Gaebler 1993.
2 See Sunkin in Tate and Vallinder. Forthcoming. Sunkin considers *R. v. Hull Prison Board of Visitors, Ex Parte St. Germain (1979); R. v. Panel on Take-overs and Mergers, Ex Parte Datafin Plc. (1987); Council for Civil Service Unions v. Government Central Communication Headquarters (1984).*
3 Consider, for example, the celebrated case of Xe Thi Ngunyen in which the Quebec Human Rights Commission struck down the welfare compliance enforcement operation put in place in 1986 by the provincial minister because it violated the Quebec Charter of Human Rights (see Torczyner 1991).
4 This material was taken from his presentation at the c.c.m.d. in September 1993.

BIBLIOGRAPHY

Africa Watch. 1992. *Accountability in Namibia: Human Rights and the Transition to Democracy.* New York: Human Rights Watch.
Bogart, William A. Forthcoming. Judicialization and social progress: the case of Canada. In Tate and Vallinder.
Bozeman, Barry. 1987. *All Organizations Are Public.* San Francisco: Jossey-Bass.
———— 1988. Exploring the limits of public and private sectors: sector boundaries as Maginot Line. *Public Administration Review* 48 (March/April):672-4.
Chevron U.S.A. v. Natural Resources Defense Council. 1984. 467 u.s. 837.
Commonwealth v. Northern Land Council. 1991. 30 FCR 1.
Cooper, Phillip J. 1988. *Hard Judicial Choices.* New York: Oxford University Press.
Council for Civil Service Unions v. Government Central Communication Headquarters. 1984. 3 All E.R. 935.
Davis, Kenneth Culp. 1969. *Discretionary Justice: A Preliminary Inquiry.* Baton Rouge: Louisiana State University.
Management Advisory Board and Management Improvement Advisory Committee. 1993. *Accountability in the Public Sector.* Canberra: Australian Government Publishing Service.
Mintzberg, Henry. 1982. A Note on that dirty word 'efficiency.' *Interfaces* 5 (October):101-5.

Moe, Ron. 1987. Exploring the limits of privatization. *Public Administration Review* 47 (November/December):453-60.

_____ 1988. 'Law' versus 'performance' as objective standard. *Public Administration Review* 48 (March/April):675.

Natural Resources Defense Council v. u.s. Nuclear Regulatory Commission. 1976. 547 F.2d 633 (D.C.Cir.).

Osborne, David, and Ted Gaebler. 1993. *Reinventing Government.* New York: Plume/Penguin.

Report of the National Performance Review. 1993. *From Red Tape to Results: Creating A Government That Works Better & Costs Less.* Washington, D.C.: Government Printing Office.

Rizzo v. Goode. 1976. 423 U.S. 362.

Russell, Peter H. Forthcoming. Canadian constraints on judicialization from without. In Tate and Vallinder.

Rust v. Sullivan. 1991. 114 L.Ed 2d 233.

R. v. Hull Prison Board of Visitors, Ex Parte St. Germain. 1979. All E.R. 701.

R. v. Panel on Take-overs and Mergers, Ex Parte Datafin Plc. 1987. QB 815.

Sankey v. Whitlam. 1978. 142 CLR 1.

Sullivan, Harold J. 1987. Privatization of public services: a growing threat to constitutional rights. *Public Administration Review* 47 (November/December):461-7.

Sunkin, Maurice. Forthcoming. Judicialization of politics in the United Kingdom. In Tate and Vallinder.

Sutherland, S.L. 1992. The al-Mashat affair. *Canadian Public Administration* 34 (Winter):573-603.

Tate, C. Neal, and Torbjorn Vallinder. Forthcoming. *The Judicialization of Politics: Essays on the Worldwide Expansion of Judicial Power and Legal Procedures.* Westport, CT: Greenwood Press.

Tellier, Paul M. 1992. *Public Service 2000: A Report on Progress.* Ottawa: Minister of Supply and Services.

Torczyner, Jim. 1991. Discretion, judgment, and informed consent: ethical and practice issue in social action. *Social Work* 36 (March):122-7.

United States v. Nixon. 1974. 418 U.S. 683.

Vermont Yankee Nuclear Power Corp. v. Nuclear Regulatory Commission. 1978. 435 U.S. 519.

PART FOUR

PUBLIC MANAGEMENT
AND THE REFORM
OF GOVERNANCE

Management Techniques for the Public Sector: Pulpit and Practice

CHRISTOPHER POLLITT

INTRODUCTION

There is a suspicious similarity to the sermons of many Western governments concerning the progress of the "new public management" (Hood 1991). Responsibility is to be decentralized, targets – not procedures – are to become the key focus for public officials, costs will be cut, bureaucracy eliminated, standards raised, and service to the citizen-customer thrust to the foreground of concern (see, e.g., Auditor General of Canada 1993; National Performance Review 1993; Prime Minister 1991). What is more, all these actions will be continuously monitored and evaluated (see, e.g., Duran and Monnier 1992; H.M.Treasury 1988). Taken together they will constitute a fundamental cultural shift in the public sector. Through these programs the state will re-emerge as a leaner, more flexible and swiftly responding creature than it had become during the decades of easy growth that followed 1945.

The application of certain *techniques* has been widely seen as central to the promotion of this cultural shift. In particular heavy political emphasis has been given to:

- Various decentralized budgeting techniques
- Performance indicators
- Performance-related pay (especially in the u.s. and in "Westminster" systems)

- Techniques for setting standards and thereby raising the quality of public services (again, especially in the U.S. and "Westminster" systems, although "quality" is now beginning to become a more prominent term in continental European states)
- The contractualization of relationships that were previously hierarchical (and, frequently but not always, the opening up of the contracting process to private sector for-profit firms and/or private voluntary agencies)
- Evaluation, to ensure systematic learning about "what works and what doesn't" and value for money.

This is a noticeably programmatic approach, and it is accompanied by periodic "preaching from the pulpit." One senses an "official line" advanced, with local inflexions, by most national government leaders. Of course, such leaders operate under extremely difficult circumstances. They lead countries that appear to be losing competitiveness relative to the burgeoning economies of the Pacific rim. They face uncomfortable scissor movements between politically feasible revenues and continuing increases in the demand for public services. The state apparatuses of which they are in nominal charge have been leaking legitimacy for two decades or more. Doubts about the appropriateness of national institutions abound, some of them actively fostered by political leaders themselves (Pollitt 1992). Understandably, leading politicians are anxious to be seen to be dealing with the concerns of their publics (or, at least, the most powerful and vociferous sections of them). They are, therefore, anything but neutral witnesses; neither are the senior civil servants who shape and operationalize the reform programs, nor the management consultants who have profited extensively from being brought in to assist NPM reforms. In 1992/93 British central government had apparently spent £565 million on consultants but could only identify £10 million of savings that could be directly attributed to their advice (Jones and Hibbs 1994).

Hence, there is a clear need for considerable caution in interpreting claims from political pulpits about the "reinvention" of government. It would be sensible to ask, for example, how widely the new techniques are being put in place? It would also seem wise to enquire whether, once in operation, the techniques are producing the desired effects – and whether they seem to carry "side effects" as well? Do rank and file public officials support the reforms? Do citizens notice any difference? In short, are there any "implementation gaps" between the promise and the performance and, if so, what is their nature?

The remainder of this chapter will be devoted to an exploration of the questions raised at the end of the previous section. Unfortunately, not all the questions posed there can be covered equally. So as best to complement the other chapters this section focuses on the implications of these widely applied management techniques for:

- Changes in the distribution of power and authority within public sector institutions
- Changes to the cultures and subcultures of public sector institutions.

A number of preliminary caveats are required. First, the account is inevitably biased towards the author's own particular zones of knowledge and interest – health care, education, and personal social services, together with the civil/federal services in the U.K. and the U.S. Other countries and agencies are mentioned less frequently – and conceivably might have afforded a different picture had they been given deeper treatment.

Second, the main focus will be on applications of individual techniques rather than upon whole systems or cultures. Again, this is bound to impart a certain slant to the analysis, and it may result in the neglect of phenomena that only emerge at the national or global system levels, where many of these techniques interact with each other.

Third, it has to be confessed that we are still very short of independent, systematic, and reliable evidence concerning much of the impact of the NPM. Thus much of what follows is illuminative rather than synoptic.

Finally, it must be acknowledged that many important questions concerning the impact of NPM techniques will be left unanswered. We will say only a little about the overall cost-effectiveness of the new techniques and virtually nothing about their interactions with developing information and communication technologies (but see Bellamy and Taylor 1994). It is also too soon to know whether citizens have either noticed or appreciated the NPM changes.

TERMS AND CONCEPTS

There are some terms and concepts that crop up repeatedly in the debates about the NPM, and they are used in a bewildering variety of ways. These include:

- Decentralization, devolution, and deconcentration
- Quality and standards
- Organizational culture
- Citizens, customers, clients, users.

Many volumes have been written on each, so all that will be attempted here is a brief statement of how these key concepts are going to be defined for the particular purposes of this chapter.

Decentralization will be used as a generic term covering at least three different types of shift of authority and power. First, there are two types of vertical decentralization. *Hierarchical decentralization* involves the pushing of specific decisional authority down to lower levels of an administrative hierarchy. Thus, a decision to spend more than $1 million but less than $10 million may previously have had to be cleared by a grade 1 senior official, but now this authority is given to a less senior grade 2. A second type of vertical decentralization, here termed *devolution*, is more radical in that it entails passing a specific decisional authority *across an organizational boundary*, that is, giving it to a separate and previously subordinate or independent agency. Thus, in the U.K. civil service, certain departmental spending and personnel authorities have now been devolved to the Next Steps executive agencies, which have their own accounting officers, responsible to Parliament (Chancellor of the Duchy of Lancaster 1993). Finally there is *horizontal decentralization*, defined by Mintzberg (1979:186) as "the extent to which nonmanagers control decision processes." The nonmanagers could be professionals, craftspeople, clerks, or even customers.

A *standard* is a description of a desired state, which may be qualitative or quantitative or both. A minimum waiting time of fifteen minutes or a claim assessing accuracy rate of 98 percent are both quantified standards. A health care protocol of "each patient's discharge is planned in accordance with his/her wishes and needs" is an unquantified standard (Sale 1990:15).

Quality is a much more difficult and complex notion. One recent definition is:

The degree to which agreed standards are achieved, and to which those standards are related to the highest priority requirements or needs of the users of the service (Centre for the Evaluation of Public Policy and Practice 1992:6).

Even this formulation leaves several issues open. Who are the relevant users? Should not standards be dynamic – moving upwards to reflect a process of continuous improvement? What about public services supplied to certain "users" against their will, such as child protection, and antipollution or correctional programs? These could be thought of more as activities of "social ordering" (Stewart 1992) than as "services" in the conventional sense. Nevertheless, this will serve as an opening definition of quality and stresses the central role of user's rather than provider's requirements.

During the 1980s the notion of organizational *culture* became extremely popular in both business and academic circles. There was – and still is – much talk of "cultural change." However, there is also a good deal of confusion about "culture" and it is apparent that the term is used in a variety of significantly different ways. One dividing line is between those commentators who see culture as encompassing attitudes, behaviours, and social/organizational interactions and those who define the concept less inclusively, using it to denote the set of beliefs and ideas that give meaning to, but are conceptually distinct from, the actual behaviours and structures of a particular society or organization. In this second view, which is the one adopted in this chapter, culture is seen as "an ordered system of meaning" (Geertz 1973). One problem with the first view is that it is very broad indeed and appears to lose the power to discriminate clearly between beliefs and actions. It can lead to facile suggestions that by changing this or that procedure one is changing the culture, whereas the truth may be that while staff can be forced to change their behaviours they may still retain, perhaps resentfully, their original beliefs and attitudes.

In the definition used here, therefore, a culture is less something that an organization "has" and more something an organization "is." It is its way of thinking about itself and, as such, probably cannot be redesigned overnight merely by some top-down initiative of newsletters, seminars, and new logos. The extent to which "management" has either the knowledge or the tools deliberately to redesign the organization's culture has probably been extensively overestimated, as anyone who has researched in the middle and lower ranks of public service organizations will know (see Lynn Meek 1988 and, as a recent case study, Colville et al. 1993).

Finally we come to the nomenclature surrounding those who use or are affected by the goods and services produced within the public sector. The choice of term is often a significant indicator of the underlying model or ideology. For example:

We have customers. The American people (Vice President Al Gore 1993).

In the U.K. Citizen's Charter, similarly, there are many references to customers – rather more than there are to citizens (unlike the more state-centred traditions reflected in the French Charte des Services Publics or the Belgian Charte de l'Utilisateur des Services Publics). Yet the words are not interchangeable. To be a *customer* is to perform a role within a system of market relations, a role to do with the satisfaction of individual wants and needs under certain conditions of supply and demand. A *citizen*, however, is, as the French and Belgians recognize to a greater extent than the British, a concentration of rights and duties situated within a framework of constitutional law and regulation. In so far as there is a direct relationship between the roles of the citizen and the customer for public services the latter is subordinate, contained within the former. To characterize the principal relationships between the citizen and state as those of customer and supplier is, it could be argued, to impoverish our concept of democratic citizenship.

To be a *client* is different again. The most common use of the term is to denote one pole of a dyadic relationship of professional trust. There is the professional (doctor, solicitor, etc.) and his or her client. Clients therefore exist within principal-agent relationships in which the professional agent is supposed always to act *in the client's (principal's) interests*, something a customer would be naive to expect the supplier to do in a market transaction.

Throughout most of this chapter we will refer to people who avail themselves of public services (or have them thrust upon them) as *users*. Not everyone is happy with this term, but it seems marginally less loaded than "customer," considerably more general than "client" and more specific/less all-encompassing than "citizen." Of course, users are not the only *stakeholders* in the public service sector. Taxpayers, the families of users, employers, civil servants, and other public agency staff are all stakeholders, and this has implications for, inter alia, the design of performance indicator systems and the setting of quality standards (Cave et al. 1994). One of the difficulties with importing the market language of customers into public sector transactions is that it tends to overlook the more complex play of interests that so often lie behind public programs.

DECENTRALIZED BUDGETARY TECHNIQUES

Having indicated some of the conceptual and terminological complexities surrounding our topic we can now turn to a direct examination of the management techniques that lie at the heart of much recent and prospective public sector change.

Decentralized budgeting may involve all or any of our three species of decentralization. Increased financial authority may be given to lower hierarchical levels within a bureaucracy, or it may be accorded to separate organizations or agencies (the Local Management of Schools initiative in the U.K., for example). It may involve horizontal decentralization, as when a finance division transfers certain decisions over money to a consultant (medical doctor) who acts as clinical director for a particular service within a hospital (general surgery, pathology, etc.). These various forms of budgetary decentralization have been attempted in virtually all OECD countries (OECD 1990:11-12).

Budgetary decentralization is supposed to generate a wide range of benefits. It is said to increase cost-consciousness and inculcate a heightened sense of personal responsibility among those staff who are recipients of enhanced financial authority. It may simultaneously increase efficiency and cost-effectiveness, since quick decisions, informed by detailed local knowledge, may now be made. Previously there would have had to be time-consuming referrals to a more distant location in the organization – or even to another organization (in the case of devolution). The actual mechanisms of budgetary decentralization are given different titles in different settings (the Financial Management Initiative, Local Management of Schools, Resource Management, performance budgeting, etc.) but the above benefits are sought in virtually every case.

What is more it is not hard to find evidence of managers in decentralized units who are eager for greater financial freedom (Packwood et al. 1991; Pollitt et al. 1994; Le Grand and Bartlett 1993:135-6). In the u.k. this enthusiasm has been deliberately heightened by hints and promises from central government that schools and hospitals which "opted out" of local authority/health authority control would receive favourable budgetary allocations and/or wider borrowing powers.

At least four kinds of qualification need to be made to this rosy picture. First, there have been some cases where financial decentralization does not appear to have yielded the predicted benefits (or not yet) because the model of budgeting failed to take account of salient features of the local situation. For example, there have been cases where hospital doctors lacked timely and accurate clinical information that should be integrated with data about financial flows (e.g., Packwood et al. 1991; Pollitt et al. 1988). Also, even where decentralization has achieved its predicted benefits, there may be other, additional effects of the process, which are deemed undesirable; for example, schools shedding long-serving, experienced teachers and replacing them with inexperienced newcomers because the latter are cheaper.

Second, there have been cases where inadequate financial management information systems have handicapped managers wishing to use delegated freedoms rationally, or where such managers have received little or no training for their new responsibilities. The probability of under-educated financial management may be particularly high where horizontal decentralization takes place, so that professional specialists with little previous management experience are thrust into "money roles." Such cases have occurred in (at least) health care, education, and the personal social services. In the U.K. both the Audit Commission and the National Audit Office have expressed concern over dangers of this type.

Conflicts of interest are also possible, especially where local units with delegated financial authority let contracts to companies in which their own staff or employees who have recently left the company have a stake. Organizational fragmentation and "downsizing" increase the probability that such situations will occur. Early in 1994 the Public Accounts Committee of the House of Commons hit the headlines with a report cataloguing a series of failures in financial management (Committee of Public Accounts 1994). These included waste, mismanagement, and improper expenditures. Among the Committee's admonishments were:

failure to ensure that delegation of responsibility is accompanied by clear lines of control and accountability, leading to the waste of large sums of public money (ibid. vii), and;

care should be taken to provide staff with the financial skills required and to ensure that staff responsible for securing major changes in accounting systems are suitably experienced (ibid. vi).

In the U.S. parallel concerns have been voiced by the General Accounting Office in its first comments on the National Performance Review (General Accounting Office 1993:3).

Third, it is quite clear that budgetary decentralization is not in everyone's perceived interest, and that some opposition to it may be expected. The two most likely sources are first – and at a high level – central treasuries or finance departments and, second, at a lower level some professional service providers, who are averse to the high opportunity costs they incur when they have to take on more "administration." Treasuries may fear the loss of their own supervisory powers and/or the development of injudicious or inflationary behaviour by expansionist delegated agencies. The British Treasury displayed elaborate caution over delegated pay arrangements and delegated running costs for departments and executive agencies in the restructured U.K. civil service (see e.g., Kessler 1993; Thain and Wright 1990). Equally, at the "receiving end," enthusiasm may be limited. University professors frequently prefer their research to reading budget printouts and trying to reconcile them with a pile of invoices, a task also disliked by many lawyers, head teachers, and medical doctors. They are content for someone else to look after the money and, indeed, may wish to preserve a traditional budgeting system so that the true costs of some of their activities do not become public property. "Transparency" is favoured by economists, but its popularity is less than universal among other disciplines.

Fourth, much may depend on the circumstances in which financial decentralization takes place. To become the manager of a devolved budget where unit resourcing is increasing, or even level, is one thing. To assume that same role at a time when sharp cuts in unit resources are being made may seem more like being passed a buck than a benefit. As a budget-holding National Health Service clinical director said to us recently:

The worst restrictions on us aren't to do with rules, they are to do with limited resources (quoted in Pollitt et al. 1994:9).

It is worth noting, en passant, that these four types of problem are generic implementation problems and will recur in the consideration of other management techniques. They correspond to underlying issues of inadequate causal knowledge or modelling (where the predicted results of a technique are, therefore, inaccurate or seriously incomplete); inadequate implementation (where the model is correct but the putting-into-practice is faulty); conflicting interests (where changes meet successful or partly successful resistance); and instances where the impact of a technique is nullified by the contrary effects of some other system-wide factor(s) or policy.

What, then, can be said about the effects of decentralized budgeting techniques on the distribution of power within the public sector and on its organizational cultures? The impact on the balance of power appears far from straightforward. Central treasuries and finance departments have been ingenious in minimizing the loss of their control, sometimes paradoxically devising elaborate rules to govern the exercise of devolved financial freedoms. Treasuries may be mistaken in thus regarding decentralization as a zero-sum game, but it is their perception that determines their behaviour, not the non-zero sum possibilities that theoretically may be present.

Some agencies and groups within agencies have taken readily to increased financial autonomy but others have resisted it, regarding greater financial transparency as a threat rather than an advantage. Willingness to embrace increased financial decentralization may vary with the nature of the service and its relationship with its users. In some services professional providers interact frequently and directly with individual members of the public, such as in health care, community care, and education. In these circumstances professionals may find their jobs made more difficult if the users know that the professional with whom they interact is also having to think about which resource to allocate to their case. This may seem to impart an unwelcome calculative dimension to what has hitherto been regarded (by both parties) as a professional/client relationship, in which the agent holds unwaveringly to the interests of the principal, not to his or her own budgetary concerns. At this point, financial decentralization may begin to take on the guise of an unwelcome cultural shift. Yet in other types of service (street cleansing, the issue of licenses for vehicles) such considerations play little or no part, and financial decentralization may be welcomed in a relatively uncomplicated way.

Politicians are, of course, a key group, yet their attitudes to financial decentralization appear highly ambiguous. On the one hand, they might be thought to welcome developments that would allow them to disperse responsibility for service cuts and reductions, leaving them in charge of general policy but not answering on a day-to-day basis for the adequacy of the service in this or that locality or agency. On the other, however, they may calculate that the public is likely to remain insensitive to the niceties of such reorganizations, and still to hold them, the politicians, responsible, for local service provision. In personal social services, for example:

managers [with devolved authority] start to expose service shortfalls more precisely and publicly and this increases political nervousness.

Some politicians consider they are being asked to be accountable publicly for a myriad of resource decisions over which they have little control (Warner 1992:192).

Indeed, while many of the academic discussions of cultural change have focused on middle managers who are losing their monitoring roles (and often their jobs), or on professional service providers who are now being required to take on new financial responsibilities, it could be argued that the most fascinating cultural change is the one that beckons for politicians. Do they really want to leave managers to manage, so that elected representatives can concentrate on policy and strategy? Are politicians mentally prepared for *their* role in the "hands-off" culture for which their own rhetoric has prepared us? Evidence from the financial management reforms in the U.K. and Australia during the 1980s suggests otherwise (Zifcak 1992:168-72). Not unreasonably, politicians wish to be able to disown organizationally distant administrative failures, but they also wish to be able to claim credit when things go right and to intervene wherever the volatile spotlight of media interest may fall. By and large they are not trained for the role of strategic managers, and, more prosaically, their re-election is unlikely to depend on their success in this particular role.

PERFORMANCE INDICATORS

In the U.K. during the 1980s performance indicators (PIs) were a major growth industry (Pollitt 1990). Almost every U.K. public service acquired an impressive array of such measures – the civil service, the police, the NHS, the probation service, the universities, local authority Social Services Departments – even the national museums and galleries. The vigilant citizen, turning to the government's annual white paper on public expenditure, or to the reports on the Next Steps program of civil service reform (Chancellor of the Duchy of Lancaster 1993) could review literally thousands of such indicators. Was this not a remarkable improvement in public domain information, a formidable enhancement of the bureaucracy's accountability to Parliament and public?

Certainly it would be hard to deny that the volume of regularly published performance-related information has increased. Furthermore, with increasing devolution PIs have moved towards the centre of operational management. Whereas in their early years PIs were sometimes seen as a "bolt-on" extra, they are now built into the contracts and quasi contracts within which many devolved public service providing agencies operate. The promiscuity of the early and mid-1980s, when some public service organizations seemingly took any old statistics out of their filing cabinets and made PIs of them, has been slowly superseded by a parsimonious approach in which smaller numbers of key indicators are defined and used more as "dials" than as "tin openers" (Carter et al. 1992; Carter and Greer 1993). Facilitated by ever-improving computer systems, PIs have become firmly rooted in the culture of most public sector organizations, at least at the upper levels.

Yet it would be naive to assume that time alone will see to the perfection of transparent sets of key PIs. Despite real progress, significant problems continue to surround the use of PIs as a central technique for controlling and holding devolved agencies accountable, not only in the U.K. but throughout the developed world (OECD 1994). As in the case of financial decentralization, these problems may be classified into those of poor modelling, inadequate implementation, conflicts of interest, and larger system effects.

As has often been observed, strong PI systems encourage teachers to "teach the test" and civil servants to "play the game." However, if the PIs describe only part of the game, then the other part is liable to be neglected. The efforts of public servants are increasingly focused on "scoring well" against the prescribed targets. In the British Inland Revenue, tax inspectors, when set targets in terms of numbers of inspections per unit time, tended to pass over large, complex cases and select for quantity rather than quality (National Audit Office 1994:18). If, as has often happened, the PIs concentrate on what is more easily measurable, then the intangibles of a service may suffer. For example, money spent can usually be measured much more easily than can the quality of care provided. For a decade now public sector PI systems have tended to contain far more programs to measure efficiency and process than effectiveness or user-satisfaction . In the u.k. this is changing, but slowly and incompletely (Carter and Greer 1993; Pollitt 1990). In the u.s., even in six performance measurement programs selected for their advanced nature, "gauges of outcome are relatively rare" (Congressional Budget Office, 1993:xii). For some services, especially health care, education, personal social services, and correctional programs, there may be little consensus as to what the objectives (and therefore the targets and therefore the PIs) *should* be. Cure or care? Punishment or rehabilitation? Passing tests or unlocking creativity and individuality? Where agencies have such multiple (and even mutually contradictory) objectives, the fashioning of a set of key indicators is anything but straightforward.

Inadequate implementation is the second problem. Staff will need training to understand the indicators and their significance. It is not unusual to find that the top two layers of management understand the role of PIs and the technical and tactical details of how to score well, but professionals and lower tier managers do not. Front-line staff may not have access to PI data or may have no incentive to utilize it.

Conflicting interests are obviously present. Devolved agencies will wish to be measured against variables that are within their control and targets that are readily attainable. They may favour aggregate measures which leave them with plenty of room for internal manoeuvre. They will tend to avoid, wherever possible, PIs that compare them with rivals or competitors. Parent departments and supervisory or regulatory agencies will, by contrast, seek disaggregation, tough targets, and data that can be compared with that from other, similar service providers. The moves in this game are now well known. Redefine categories so as to undermine time series and obscure comparisons. Set initial targets low to leave room for improvement. Invent new ratios on which one's agency appears to be performing well. Add new services, merge or split organizations – anything that will allow a claim that there is now a new situation and old measures are irrelevant.

If we take as an example the mass of information put out by the Next Steps executive agencies (Chancellor of the Duchy of Lancaster 1993), one can see how misleading the appearance of intensive performance measurement can be. Whilst acknowledging improvements, one set of expert commentators reached the following conclusions:

The form and contents of the annual accounts are diverse in many respects. This suggests that the ability to compare one agency with another, or even with the private sector, is not a high priority . . . From a technical point of view it is difficult to see how [these reports] can be used by Members of Parliament to hold the agencies accountable (Pendlebury et al. 1994:44-5).

Finally there is once more the problem of wider system changes that may undermine what would otherwise have been the positive effects of the specific management technique. Carter and Greer (1993:414) note that:

Departments are required to make efficiency gains of at least 1.5% annually and cumulatively on the whole of their running costs provision. Agencies are expected to achieve a higher saving . . . In this climate, the more successful agencies are in achieving targets, the more likely it is that targets will become increasingly stringent.

In sum, the Thatcher and Major administrations in the u.k. have been successful in implanting a more performance-oriented culture throughout many parts of the public service. However, the exact nature of this culture may not be quite as they had hoped. Among service providers there remains a widespread scepticism about the validity of many of the pis and the pi researcher will meet as many weary and cynical game-players as true pi believers. pis have become a significant new focus for beliefs, aspirations, and even myths, but the new culture is often composed of "espoused values" rather than "values-in-use" (Argyris and Schon 1978).

As far as the distribution of power is concerned, senior civil servants in central departments and top managers in decentralized agencies continue to argue over which pis are fair and meaningful and how far they should be "home grown" or centrally and uniformly prescribed. These struggles are probably indeterminate, in the sense that no one partner always "wins" or holds the upper hand. Meanwhile, there are few signs that elected representatives are particularly interested in mastering the technical details of performance measurement, so the great outflow of new information has been largely ignored by parliamentarians (Carter et al. 1992:182-3).

Finally, while PIs can and do serve many purposes, it is hard to resist the conclusion that the overall net effect of their spread has been an enhancement of the power of senior managers relative to the autonomy of other groups such as professionals, clericals or even middle managers. However crudely or unfairly, PIs have been used to establish a higher degree of "remote control" by senior management over the activities of other groups within public sector organizations. Recently there has been talk of using PIs to inform and empower service users (especially in the context of citizens' charters, of which more later) but little has come of this as yet (Pollitt 1990; 1994).

PERFORMANCE-RELATED PAY

Performance-related pay (PRP) is an extension of the same target-setting model of behavioural management from which PIs spring. Since the late 1970s PRP, in various forms, has become much more widely used in the public sectors of North America and the U.K. More recently Denmark, the Netherlands, Sweden, and New Zealand have introduced schemes (OECD 1993). The underlying theory is a fairly simple one: staff will work harder or more effectively if they can see that meeting and exceeding targets set by their employers will bring them a higher wage. By contrast, it is said that uniform national pay rates, where everyone on a particular grade receives the same remuneration irrespective of the effort they put in or the successes they achieve, act as a disincentive to high performers.

Here the experience of both public and private sectors shows that the model itself contains some serious weaknesses (Thompson 1993). Its individualistic and mechanistic assumptions underestimate at least two difficulties. First, the majority who do *not* achieve "merit bonuses" are demotivated. Second, even the minority who may win increased remuneration are motivated by many other factors – including *intrinsic* elements – than just pay. Pay may, therefore, be rather an indirect and inefficient means of motivating higher performance. It is ironic that British central government is redoubling its efforts to spread the merit pay gospel just at the time when leading private sector corporations appear to be distancing themselves from PRP.

In addition to its theoretical failings, PRP has suffered from a number of weaknesses in implementation. Some of the early schemes were centrally imposed, against the wishes of many of those in line departments (OECD 1993:11). The appraisal, which necessarily undergirds merit pay decisions, is very often perceived as unfair and poorly executed (Thompson 1993). A number of public sector PRP schemes "were introduced in the face of union opposition and partly as a consequence in a half-baked way" (Kessler 1993:327). Considerable evidence has accumulated to indicate the widespread unpopularity of PRP schemes (ibid.:329-30). In the U.S. civil service similar serious problems have been encountered (Perry et al. 1989). Surveys show that a majority of public sector managers support the principle of linking performance and at least some element of pay, but the practical means for doing so in an acceptable way remain elusive (OECD 1993).

As for clashes of interest, these are fairly obvious. On the whole unions are against PRP because it is seen as divisive. Even group schemes are suspect because they are usually financed by top-slicing total pay budgets, thus reducing the baseline increase for all staff. Less obviously, in the U.K. case, the Treasury, though supportive in principle, has been cautious about PRP in practice. It has taken a close interest in the design of individual schemes and has laid down fairly strict rules as to how they are to be financed. Some of the continental European systems have, however, allowed greater local freedom than the U.K. or the U.S. federal service.

Finally, the same systemic factor that has taken the gloss off budgetary decentralization in the U.K. has also reduced the potency of PRP. Tight general expenditure curbs have meant that the actual merit bonuses frequently represent an exceedingly modest after-tax sum that is very unlikely to trigger major motivational change among staff. For example, the author, as a Head of Department, gets to allocate four or five merit bonuses per annum, each to the princely sum of about £375 after standard rate income tax (see also Carter and Greer 1993:414). The suggestion that rewards of this magnitude are likely significantly to alter the behaviour of tenured academic staff is simply ludicrous.

It is therefore difficult to see that PRP has had much impact on either power relationships or organizational cultures. Few managers themselves appear to believe in it. Unions are intensely suspicious. A majority of employees see it in practice as unfair, demotivating or both. Only for a handful of very senior managers are the after-tax sums involved more than trivial. The continuing spread of PRP in some public sectors is more a tribute to the overweening power of central government than to any evidence of benefit. Evaluations to see whether performance has improved (and whether it has been worth the cost) have been rare, in both public and private sectors (OECD 1993:9).

STANDARDS AND QUALITY

It is in respect of standards and quality that governments most often claim to have achieved a "cultural shift." The preoccupation with these issues came later than the first wave of concern for economy and efficiency and was, to some extent, intended to ameliorate some of the less pleasant consequences of the incessant economy drives and staff cuts of the 1980s. In "quality" politicians found a rallying cry that both appealed to the electorate and took the edge off the antipublic sector rhetoric of Reagan and Thatcher, a rhetoric that had seemingly contributed to a serious slump in the morale of many vital public services (Pollitt 1992). It is probably not coincidental that political endorsement for Total Quality Management (TQM) peaked under the milder successors to "Ronnie and Maggie," George Bush and John Major.

In thus espousing "quality," however, it is questionable whether the governments of the early 1990s fully realized what a Trojan horse they were admitting within the walls of the residual (postprivatization) public sector. For the leading private sector models thus imported, especially TQM, laid considerable stress on being "customer-driven." At first sight this may have seemed just another way of breaking down bureaucracy and setting a counterweight to excessive professional autonomy. As the implementation of schemes proceeded, however, a new tension began to become apparent. What if the customers exhibited different preferences from those held by political leaders? How will those leaders deal with new alliances forged between local professionals, service managers, and service users, demanding increased expenditure and higher standards? What, therefore, are to be the limits of customer influence?

These tensions are only now beginning to surface. The majority of quality schemes thus far have remained firmly within the grip of managers, with service users being allocated a very limited role (for the u.k. see Pollitt 1990; 1993b; for the u.s. see Ingraham, in this volume). Frequently they have been treated as add-ons, just another element of managerial reform, rather than being accorded the dominant, strategic role ascribed to them in the TQM texts. Some public service agencies have adopted a range of different quality techniques and have failed either to integrate them, one with another, or to invest in them on the scale felt necessary by commercial companies (Centre for the Evaluation of Public Policy and Practice 1993).

Quality improvement schemes can certainly involve clashes of interest. In the British NHS quality concepts, labels, procedures, and data have all been contested by doctors, managers, and nurses (Pollitt 1993b). Until recently doctors had been successful in creating medical audit as their own, private, and confidential form of quality assurance, totally free of any "customer" influence. Now this medical bastion is under attack, not so much from patients as from both managers and other health professionals. These groups question the logic and cost of monoprofessional quality procedures in circumstances where most health care is delivered by multiprofessional teams.

The concept of *standards* is a crucial one in most contemporary quality improvement techniques. Prime Minister Major made it the heart of his Citizen's Charter (Prime Minister 1991). It was central to the adoption of TQM in the u.s. federal bureaucracy in the early 1990s. However, it is often overlooked that standards come in a number of fundamentally different forms. *Minimum* standards are those which a service promises to reach every time – in effect they become a user entitlement. *Average* standards are quite different as many as half the users of a service may expect to receive something less than its average standard. *Best practice* standards, long a familiar concept in professions such as teaching or medicine, are different again. By definition they will be attained by only a minority of practitioners – for the majority they are aspirational rather than immediately attainable. Inspection of the reports, brochures, and charters of a wide range of public agencies reveals that these differences are frequently obscured or unrecognized (Pollitt 1994). Yet each type of standard has somewhat different implications in terms of power and culture within service delivery organizations. For example, it may be that in some public services, dwindling unit resourcing means that *average* standards are falling at the same time that management efforts are being devoted to raising and publicizing *minimum* standards. Improvement-oriented professionals may be most concerned with average or best-practice standards, whereas politicians and managers, keen to avoid scandals and adverse publicity, may prefer to focus on always delivering minimum entitlements.

As quality issues are being dealt with at greater length in the chapter by Ingraham it is unnecessary to delve deeper at this point. Suffice it to say that quality improvement schemes currently constitute a fascinating battleground between groups with very different visions of public service. Some managers approach such schemes as though they were principally opportunities for increasing control over the detailed performance of staff, or licences to demand not only compliance with managerial authority but also commitment to and enthusiasm for stated organizational objectives (Storey 1989). By contrast, some public service professionals see quality improvement as a way of generating systematic data to support claims for higher levels of resourcing. A few (professionals, user activists, and even managers) emphasize the possibilities for using the quality motif significantly to increase user participation in service design and delivery.

Behind all this, however, lie two inevitable and uncomfortable trade-offs. First, higher standards or lower expenditure? Who is to make this judgment? Are standards really to be "user-driven," as TQM enthusiasts would have us suppose? Second, given limited resources, which dimensions or aspects of service quality are to take priority, and which are to be left (for the time being) unimproved? Neither question has a simple, technical solution.

H.M.Treasury has no doubt of the appropriate response to the first of these dilemmas. They see it as a decision for ministers, not users:

One of the most important aspects of target-setting is to ensure that the targets for standards and quality on the one hand and those for efficiency on the other reflect an explicit decision by Ministers on the desired balance between these two aspects of performance (H.M.Treasury 1992:3).

Again, however, we need to ask how far political leaders are prepared for the world of NPM (albeit one largely of their own making). Can politicians be persuaded to make clear, public decisions to strike this or that balance between service quality and expenditure restraint? Or will they persist in their more usual stance of simultaneously insisting on quality improvements and efficiency savings?

The second issue is perhaps more subtle. Given that service quality is multifaceted, how can decisions be arrived at to enhance one service characteristic (say, speed) at the expense of another (say, accuracy). Few public sector schemes have yet addressed this question; most are still coming to terms with straightforward user satisfaction surveys. In the commercial sector, however, techniques have been developed that enable service providers to identify which characteristics are most salient for users, and how the latter would trade these off, one against another. It would appear that stated preference approaches to such choices may have fewer drawbacks than the application of willingness-to-pay criteria, but examples of the implementation of either technique in the public services sector are few and far between (Cave et al. 1994). As service providers become more sophisticated, however, contingent quality valuation could become one way in which user preferences begin to displace, or at least influence, managerial and professional judgment.

CONTRACTUALIZATION

Contracts and quasi contracts ("service agreements," "framework agreements") have become a ubiquitous feature of the NPM. In many instances they have enabled the replacement of hierarchical relationships within a unified bureaucracy by "arms length"relationships between a public purchasing authority and a devolved provider agency. Some commentators are so enthusiastic about the advantages of the contractual format that they advocate extending their application so that it embraces even the function of giving policy advice to political leaders (Kemp 1993). In New Zealand there has been a major attempt to put this notion into practice (State Services Commission 1992).

In theory such contracts provide for greater clarity about objectives, available resources, and performance criteria. They hold out the promise of more precise accountability and of regular reappraisals of both the quality and cost of the services provided, as contracts come up for renewal.

Against this there is a growing understanding that the benefits of contracts are contingent upon the satisfaction of certain prerequisites. Where these prerequisites are absent, hierarchical or other forms of relationship may be more appropriate (Boston 1994; Williamson 1975). Some of the major public services appear to be provided in circumstances where the requirements for efficient contracting are particularly hard to meet. Notoriously, services such as health care and education, which possess multiple, conflicting, and vague objectives, are prone to local monopolies or oligopolies and harbour considerable asset-specific sunk costs (Le Grand and Bartlett 1993). In addition, the "production function" may be very imperfectly understood and quality hard to specify. One consequence is that contracts are bound to be technically incomplete and the providers of educational or health care services, faced with cost pressures, may be tempted to make covert reductions in quality that are not detectable by purchasers. Another conclusion would be that a complete shift from traditional input controls to control through the specification of outputs in a contract simply may not be feasible for certain services, so that certain input or process (behavioural) controls must be retained (Mol 1989).

The emerging quasi markets in the U.K. for health and community care already provide practical examples of precisely these difficulties. Transaction costs have soared as purchasers and providers wrestle with the difficulties of specifying the required service (including quality standards) and costing it. The administrative overhead appears to be *increasing* as accountants, IT experts and contract specialists are brought in to perform functions that were unnecessary when the same services were subject to internal bureaucratic planning rather than quasi-market competition. It is entirely possible that this growth in transaction costs will equal or outweigh any efficiency gains that result from competition (Le Grand and Bartlett 1993).

Nor are these drawbacks exclusive to the particular forms of contractualization adopted in the U.K. Reviewing the U.S. experience with public service contracting Wise comments that:

Government investigators as well as academic researchers have also documented significant problems arising from contractor-government relationships including goldplating, overspecification, overregulation, inability to shift contractors, conflicts of interest, reduced services, low-ball introductory offers followed by large cost increases, and ambiguous definition of contractor performance (Wise 1990:147).

Thus, while contracting is an entirely appropriate approach for some services, it may offer no obvious advantage for others and for others again it will prove positively detrimental. As with decentralized budgeting, the danger is that a blanket approach will ride roughshod over significant differences in the cultures and administrative technologies of different services. Like the installation of PIs (which it often accompanies), contractualization tends to strengthen certain occupational groups at the expense of others. Within the NHS it is clear that the contracting process has sometimes been used by managers to tighten their control of the medical and nursing staffs ("we have to do this because of the contract"). The initial effect is usually one of horizontal and vertical centralization within the provider unit, even if, subsequently, participation in the contracting process is decentralized again (Pollitt et al. 1994). Shortages of skilled contracting and accountancy staff may strengthen the tendency to concentrate control of such dangerous new processes near the top of the organization.

Contractualization may also have significant implications for accountability. In terms of the discussion in Phillip Cooper's chapter, it usually represents a shift from political accountability to market accountability. Yet the framework of law can be slow to register this shift, leaving worrying gaps and ambiguities during the interim (Harden 1992). For example, when what was previously an in-house public service is contracted out to a private organization, can the relevant national or local audit body still pursue the use of public money across the contractual interface? Culturally a customer focus, which is deliberately encouraged by contractualization, appears to be very different from the traditional public service orientation upwards to a politically appointed (or, indeed, elected) leadership.

EVALUATION

The treatment of this final technique will be on two distinct levels. First, as with the previous techniques, something will be said of the ways in which evaluation has been implemented, and what effects it appears to be having on power relationships and public service cultures. Second, attention will be given to the substantive findings of such evaluations as have taken place. This is done in the expectation that these "results" may offer some clues as to the success or otherwise of NPM techniques.

In theory the multifarious changes wrought by the introduction of NPM techniques should have been subjected to rigorous evaluation. "Value for money" and "cost-effectiveness" have been among the leading slogans of the managerialists (see, e.g., H.M.Treasury 1988). The virtuous cycle of (1) forming objectives, (2) setting operational targets, (3) implementing plans to achieve those targets, (4) evaluating results and then, (5) reconsidering the objectives has been repeated in hundreds of textbooks and guideline documents and preached at thousands of seminars. Without evaluation, the feedback loop is not complete. And undoubtedly there has been a good deal of evaluatory activity going on – so much, in fact, that some commentators have been led to write of the "rise of the evaluative state" (Neave 1988).

Yet while "evaluation" – together with allied processes of assessment, inspection, monitoring, and review – has burgeoned (especially in the U.K., Australasia, and North America) there has also been an almost theological aspect to much of the management reform that has taken place. Faith and commitment, rather than clinical evaluation, have often been dominant. On a number of occasions reformers have explicitly rejected evaluation of the broad outline of their reforms, so sure were they that their private sector-inspired, market-oriented solutions were along the right lines. Thus we are sometimes confronted with a paradox: managerial reforms that incorporate a powerful imperative to evaluate yet have not themselves been much evaluated. As noted above, for example, the superiority of performance-related pay has for the most part been advanced as a self-evident truth.

The paradox can be somewhat disentangled by giving closer attention to the types and levels of evaluation that have been carried out. Many specific activities or individual services have been subjected to new or intensified forms of performance measurement. As noted above (section on performance indicators), these measures have most commonly comprised indicators of efficiency or throughput, with money as an input and numbers of units or procedures as an output. Thus, evaluation as practised within NPM has tended to be narrow, positivistic, and economistic. In terms of power relationships and culture, influence has flowed towards accountants, economists, and management consultants. It has flowed away from the traditional professions (education, medicine) with their "softer," formative, and peer review-based conceptions of evaluation. It has also flowed away from middle managers, the former day-to-day regulators of "street level" bureaucrats, who are no longer necessary in the era of top management information systems and performance indicators (an example of the general tendency discussed earlier in the present volume by Aucoin). In this climate, multistakeholder evaluations and more qualitative/pluralistic approaches (see, e.g., Guba and Lincoln 1981) have been the exceptions rather than the rule (for the U.K. see Pollitt 1993a; for France see Duran and Monnier 1992).

However, since the late 1980s user satisfaction ratings or other measures of user quality have also begun to appear, first in the U.K. and North America, and more recently in some parts of continental Europe. Typically these have been collected by essentially mechanical and "distant" means, especially the survey questionnaire. From management's viewpoint these are cheaper and more manipulable than more discursive and participatory methods for collecting opinions. It remains to be seen how such measures will be combined with the more long-standing and "harder" indicators of efficiency. In so far as the visible engagement of citizen opinion is becoming an important part of political legitimation processes (Aucoin, this volume) there may be a growing tension between managerial measures of efficiency and citizens' ratings of quality.

While narrow-scope, managerialist indicators have proliferated, broader evaluations of whole programs or restructuring efforts have been much rarer (Pollitt 1993a). Sweden has attempted a heroic assessment of public sector productivity as a whole, but the findings are open to considerable interpretation. Interestingly, the Swedish study suggests that the rate of productivity-increase during the 1980s varied with the type of service and the degree of overall budgetary constraint. Routinized, large-scale central government services, such as social benefits, and certain "softer" services in education and community care recorded the greatest improvements, and there was a general tendency for the more tightly budgeted central government services to show more rapid change than the less hard-pressed local government activities (Expertgruppen för Studier i Offentlig Ekonomi 1994).

The Swedish study also points to a conundrum that has been posed in many countries but convincingly answered in none. What proportion of recorded public service productivity gain can be attributed to the implementation of NPM techniques such as those discussed in this paper, and what proportion has occurred simply because of crude budgetary pressures? In other words the imposition of arbitrary percentage budget cuts on public services may itself constitute the major spur to managerial and professional creativity, rather than the application of particular techniques.

To a considerable extent the relative scarcity of broad evaluations of the NPM can be connected with the sheer methodological difficulty of mounting assessments of this kind. There are often problems of establishing a "before" benchmark against which to compare what happens "afterwards" (appropriate performance data frequently were not collected "before"). The establishment of control groups may also be fraught with difficulty. Those organizational units first volunteering (or being thrust forward) for NPM-style techniques may well be an unrepresentative elite (i.e., they were already unusually efficient or quality-conscious, even before reform). The restructuring of the British NHS as a "provider market" with most hospitals reconfigured as autonomous trusts is a clear example of both kinds of evaluatory difficulty (Robinson and Le Grand 1994). Ministers have proudly pointed to indicators of improved productivity since the market-type mechanisms were introduced on 1 April, 1991. However, definitions and categories have shifted during the crucial time period, productivity was in any case increasing before the reforms (in some cases more rapidly), and the whole situation has probably been influenced by the government's large injections of extra funds precisely so as to make sure that the reforms did not crash.

A further methodological problem has been attribution (more often than not a given service will undergo several different change processes at the same time), new IT, contractualization, TQM, decentralized budgeting, and so on. In such a situation, it may well be impossible to say what has worked and what has not, since the streams of cause and effect (or action and reaction) become so entangled and complex.

There are more profound difficulties also. The appropriate criteria for more ambitious types of evaluation are seldom as obvious as for the narrower genre. As several commentators have remarked, "value for money" sounds like a straightforward and sensible criterion whilst one is concentrating on measuring the money, but when it comes to assessing value(s) complexity soon sets in. How should the divergent values of service users and taxpayers, the young and the elderly, social democrats and conservatives, the unemployed and entrepreneurs, etc. be determined and then aggregated? How should, say, high ethical standards be weighed against efficiency? How much additional corruption is it worth to stimulate how much innovation and entrepreneurialism? How many mistakes and inaccuracies are tolerable as services gear up to provide speedier responses? How much inequity is acceptable in the name of local flexibility? The different modes of accountability (political, legal, market) discussed by Cooper tend to incubate different answers to these awkward but crucial questions.

In short, broad yet rigorous evaluations of the impact of the new techniques have been few and far between. Narrower, economistic tests of the performances of particular services or processes have abounded, but these can never by themselves answer the "big questions" concerning the overall effectiveness of the reforms, the singular impact of a given technique or the incidence of other types of "costs" (equity, ethical standards, etc.), which may have been incurred.

There are, however, other kinds of "softer" evidence, which we have not yet considered. There are, for example, local reforms that are generally regarded as a "success" by those who work with them. An example is the performance measurement system in Sunnyvale, California, which allegedly inspired the United States 1993 Government Performance and Results Act. There are units and agencies that apply for management prizes and competitions, such as those discussed in the chapter in this volume by Sandford Borins, or those in the u.k. which enter the annual competition for the Prime Minister's "Chartermark" (see Prime Minister 1991:6).

It is hard to know quite what to make of this kind of relatively unsystematic evidence. Four points may be in order. First, there is certainly a great deal of innovation taking place, in many countries, and much of it appears to be solidly beneficial, at least against most normal criteria. Bureaucrats, it seems, are not as bereft of creativity as certain theories suggest. Second, a proportion of the writing and speechmaking about these "successes" is unhelpfully evangelical. Critical questions are not infrequently left unasked, not least about the particular local circumstances – political, financial, demographic, managerial – that have been conducive to progress in a particular case but which may not be reproducible elsewhere. Third, therefore, there is a need for careful and preferably independent analysis of a wide portfolio of "success" stories to see what sound general lessons can be drawn (see Borins, in this volume). Interestingly, early work of this kind has highlighted the importance, not of technique but of "faith," and of the need for organizational "slack" rather than relentless pressure (Light 1994). Fourth, and finally, there remains a need to situate local success stories within a wider assessment of the structural changes and broad trends. Public sectors are very large and variegated systems. One Sunnyvale or Chartermark winner may be inspirational, but should not lead observers to forget, for example, evidence of widespread low morale in both the u.s. and u.k. public services, of continuing staff cuts, falling real-term budgets and so on.

CONCLUDING COMMENTS

In this chapter I set out to question the new orthodoxies of public sector management. I have endeavoured to show that currently fashionable techniques still contain a high faith-to-fact ratio, and that the faith itself could usefully be confronted with some persistent doubts.

Some of the lessons to emerge are obvious: that effective implementation of organizational change takes time and resources; that an over-emphasis on particular measures may result in a diversion of effort from improving organizational performance to improving the score on the measures; that selective experiments may sometimes be a wiser first move than blanket, system-wide restructurings. Other implications are more subtle or ambiguous. Just three will be addressed in this final section.

First, there is the impact of the NPM on political (rather than managerial) roles and structures. What if politicians are not willing to confine themselves (as much of the NPM seems to imply they should) to strategic policy making? What if, by contrast, many of them still wish to be involved with the detail of specific agencies and their activities? How can this desire best be accommodated? Does the fragmentation of institutional structures and the devolution of financial and other authority open up the possibility of new types of local political role to complement the new local manager (Hoggett 1991:254)? Or will local political legitimacy be provided by service users, registering their opinions of services both through user surveys (voice) and through the exercise of choice within the new public market-type mechanisms (exit)?

We may, therefore, be on the verge of a reconsideration of which roles in our public institutions should be appointed and which elected, and of how political representation and user empowerment can best be combined. If so, what principles could be used to guide such a debate? These questions clearly take us well beyond the adoption of particular management techniques, but the answers to them will provide the framework within which questions of technique will have to be resolved. The present discussion perhaps hints at a rank-ordering similar to that proposed by Aucoin: continental European democracies have been least susceptible to faith in "technique" (and most devoted to the idea of a career public service); Westminster systems have been more enthusiastic; and the United States, with its fragmented governmental system and deep suspicion of "bureaucracy," has been the most deeply seduced by apparently "technical" solutions to what may, at root, be fundamental problems of political accountability and governmental effectiveness.

Second, one message that emerges strongly from much of the evidence we have examined – from systems of performance indicators, from attempts to set quality standards, from contractualization, and from the Swedish calculations of public sector productivity – is that different public services really are different. Their varying characteristics make it more or less likely that a particular technique will "fit" the local context. This observation leads to the question of whether a formula be found for matching techniques to contexts, tools to purposes? Several authors have already made promising suggestions, but more work remains to be done. For example, Stewart (1992) identified the following as salient organizational characteristics that influence how an activity can be most successfully managed:

- The degree to which an organization interacts directly (face-to-face) with its citizen/users
- Whether an organization is principally concerned with providing a service (e.g., education) or "ordering society" (e.g., a pollution inspectorate)
- To what degree and how a service is rationed
- The time span of the relationship with users (continuous, episodic, etc.)
- The urgency of the service (routine, emergency, etc.).

To which we might add:

- The "technicity" of a service (how far it is dependent upon particular equipment, and what the characteristics of that equipment are)
- The degree of understanding of the "production function" (how well understood are the relationships between what an agency does and the effects its activities create)
- The degree of social and political consensus that exists concerning the proper objectives of the agency.

A list such as this, further refined, could form one axis of a matrix in which the other axis showed the behavioural characteristics of specific management techniques. For example, letting a short-term performance contract is probably inappropriate for a service (e.g., monitoring pollutants in the environment) concerned with medium-term social ordering, or for one which needs to maintain continuous, long-term relationships with its users (e.g., caring for the mentally ill). Similarly, heavy emphasis on a few key output PIs may be damaging where there is wide disagreement over the proper objectives of an activity (e.g., social work with "problem families") or where its production function is only poorly understood (Mol 1989).

In general, it may be said that some of the most resource-intensive parts of the public sector (health services, education) are the least well suited to narrow-scope managerialist techniques or formulaic treatments. They comprise services where intensive face-to-face interaction is a central feature and there is a noticeable degree of coproduction (i.e., the users themselves play an important part in determining service outcomes). Where these service characteristics predominate, participative and multistakeholder approaches to provision and evaluation may be more appropriate than the managerialist battery of PIs, PRP and contractualization. On the other hand the latter may have much to offer when applied to large volume, standardized services that are not face-to-face, such as processing routine types of tax return, issuing patents, paying public service salaries or state pensions, testing vehicles for roadworthiness, printing and retailing government publications, registering changes of land ownership, or carrying out weights and measures inspections.

The validity and reliability of the relationships suggested by the matrix could be tested by research and evaluation. In this way the dangers of the crude general application of specific techniques would be reduced and notions of organizational balance and individuality be somewhat restored.

Finally, it follows from the above that we should expect and encourage a variety of organizational cultures within the public sector. These will vary with the nature of an agency's relationship with its users (ordering or service; episodic contact or continuous, etc.). There "is no such thing as a single 'public service ethos'" and there probably never was (Kemp 1993:33). Single, universalistic prescriptions for the culture of the future ("We must create a culture of public entrepreneurship") must also be suspect. In so far as managers can create new values-in-use (and it may not be very far), these should be chosen with the specific and salient characteristics of the activity in mind. I do not want an entrepreneur looking after my state pension (or my aged grandparent), but neither do I want a cautious bureaucrat driving the fire engine or giving pump-priming grants to inventors. The problem is not one of how to apply a magic set of management techniques right across the public sector, it is much more a question of seeking, in each separate case, a match of function, form, and culture. A less rousing sermon, no doubt, but perhaps a more useful one.

BIBLIOGRAPHY

Argyris, C., and D. Schon. 1978. *Organizational Learning: A Theory of Action Perspective*. Reading, MA: Addison-Wesley.

Auditor General of Canada. 1993. Canada's public service reform and lessons learned from selected jurisdictions. *Report*, chap. 6. Ottawa.

Bellamy, C., and A. Taylor. 1994. Eds. Towards the information polity? Public administration in the information age. Theme issue of *Public Administration* 71, 1 (Spring).

Boston, J. 1994. Purchasing policy advice: the limits to contracting out. *Governance* 7, 1 (January):1-30.

Carter, N., R. Klein, and P. Day. 1992. *How Organizations Measure Success: the Use of Performance Indicators in Government*. London: Routledge.

Carter, N, and P. Greer. 1993. Evaluating agencies: Next Steps and performance indicators. *Public Administration* 71, 3 (Autumn):407-16.

Cave, M., et al. 1994. *The Valuation of Changes in Quality in the Public Services.* Report prepared for H.M.Treasury by Brunel University, London: HMSO.

Centre for the Evaluation of Public Policy and Practice. 1992. *Considering Quality: an Analytical Guide to the Literature on Quality and Standards in the Public Services.* Uxbridge: CEPPP, Brunel University.

_____ 1993. *Evaluation of Total Quality Management Projects in the National Health Service: Fourth Interim Report to the Department of Health.* Uxbridge: CEPPP, Brunel University.

Chancellor of the Duchy of Lancaster. 1993. *Next Steps Review.* Cm 2430. London: HMSO.

Colville, I., K. Dalton, and C. Tomkins. 1993. Developing and understanding cultural change in H.M. Customs and Excise: there is more to dancing than knowing the steps. *Public Administration* 71, 4 (Winter):549-66.

Committee of Public Accounts. 1994. *Eighth Report: the Proper Conduct of Public Business.* London: HMSO.

Congressional Budget Office. 1993. *Using Performance Measures in the Federal Budget Process.* Washington, DC: CBO.

Duran, P., and E. Monnier. 1992. Le développement de l'évaluation en France: necessités, techniques et exigences politiques. *Revue Française de Science Politique* 42, 2 (April):235-62.

Expertgruppen för Studier i Offentlig Ekonomi. 1994. *Den offentliga sektorns produktivetsutveckling 1980-1992.* Stockholm: Finansdepartmentet.

Geertz, C. 1973. *The Interpretation of Culture.* London: Hutchinson.

General Accounting Office. 1993. *Management Reform: GAO's Comments on the National Performance Review's Recommendations.* GAO / OCG-94-1 (December) Washington, DC

Gore, Albert J. 1993. Speech to a Town Meeting, Department of Housing and Urban Development 26 March, quoted in the *Report of the National Performance Review, Executive Summary* 8.

Guba, E., and Y. Lincoln. 1981. *Effective Evaluation: Improving the Usefulness of Evaluation Results through Responsive and Naturalistic Approaches.* San Francisco: Jossey-Bass.

Harden, I. 1992. *The Contracting State*. Buckingham: Open University Press.

H.M.Treasury. 1988. *Policy Evaluation: a Guide for Managers*. London: HMSO.

_____ 1992. *Executive Agencies: a Guide to Setting Targets and Measuring Performance*. London: HMSO.

Hoggett, P. 1991. A new management in the public sector? *Policy and Politics* 19, 4:243-56.

Hood, C. 1991. A public management for all seasons? *Public Administration* 69, 1 (Spring):3-19.

Jones, G., and J. Hibbs. 1994. Labour attacks £500M fees to save £10M. *The Independent*, 27 April 4.

Kemp, Sir Peter. 1993. *Beyond the Next Steps: A Civil Service for the 21st Century*. London: Social Market Foundation.

Kessler, I. 1993. Pay determination in the British civil service since 1979. *Public Administration* 71, 3 (Autumn):323-40.

Le Grand, J., and W. Bartlett. 1993. *Quasi Markets and Social Policy*. Basingstoke: Macmillan.

Light, P. 1994. Creating government that encourages innovation. In *New Paradigms for Government: Issues for the Changing Public Service*, ed. P. Ingraham and B. Rimzak. San Francisco: Jossey-Bass.

Lynn Meek, V. 1988. Organizational culture: origins and weaknesses. *Organization Studies* 9, 4:453-73.

Mintzberg, H. 1979. *The structuring of organizations*. Englewood Cliffs: Prentice Hall.

Mol, N. 1989. Contract-based management control in government organisations. *International Review of Administrative Sciences* 55:365-79.

National Audit Office. 1994. *Inland Revenue: Selective Examination of Accounts*. HC260. London: HMSO.

National Performance Review. 1993. *From Red Tape to Results: Creating a Government that Works Better and Costs Less. Report of the National Performance Review*, Vice President Al Gore. Washington, DC.

Neave, G. 1988. On the cultivation of quality and enterprise: an overview of recent trends in higher education in Western Europe, 1986-88. *European Journal of Education* 23:1-2.

Organization for Economic Cooperation and Development. 1990. *Public Management Developments: Survey 1990*. Paris: OECD.

_____ 1993. *Private Pay for Public Work: Performance-related Pay for Public Sector Managers.* Paris: OECD.

_____ 1994. *Performance Measurement.* Paris: OECD.

Packwood, T., J. Keen, and M. Buxton. 1991. *Hospitals in Transition: The Resource Management Experiment.* Buckingham: Open University Press.

Pendlebury, M., R. Jones, and Y. Karbhari. 1994. Developments in the accountability and financial reporting practices of executive agencies. *Financial Accountability and Management* 10, 1 (February):33-46.

Perry, J., B. Petrakis, and T. Miller. 1989. Federal merit pay, round 2: an analysis of the performance management and recognition system. *Public Administration Review* 49 (January/February):29-37.

Pollitt, C., S. Harrison, D.J. Hunter, and G. Marnoch. 1988. The reluctant managers: clinicians and budgets in the NHS. *Financial Accountability and Management* 4, 3 (Autumn):213-33.

Pollitt, C. 1990. Performance indicators: root and branch. In *Output and Performance Measurement in Government: the State of the Art,* ed. M. Cave, M. Kogan, and R. Smith, 167-78. London: Jessica Kingsley.

_____ 1992. *Managerialism and the Public Services: Cuts or Cultural Change?* 2d ed. Oxford: Blackwell.

_____ 1993a. Occasional excursions: a brief history of policy evaluation in the U.K. *Parliamentary Affairs* 46, 3 (July):353-62.

_____ 1993b. The struggle for quality: the case of the National Health Service. *Policy and Politics* 21,3:161-70.

_____ 1994. The Citizen's Charter: a preliminary analysis. *Public Money and Management* (April):1-5.

Pollitt, C., J. Birchall, and K. Putman. 1994. *The Self-Governing Hospital: Freedom and Responsiveness in NHS Trusts.* Paper presented in April to the European Consortium for Political Research conference, Madrid.

Robinson, R., and J. Le Grand. 1994. Ed. *Evaluating the NHS Reforms.* London: King's Fund.

Sale, D. 1990. *Essentials of Nursing Management: Quality Assurance.* Basingstoke: Macmillan.

State Services Commission. 1992. *The Policy Advice Initiatives: Opportunities for Management,* New Zealand: SSC.

Stewart, J. 1992. *Managing Difference: the Analysis of Service Characteristics.* Birmingham: Institute of Local Government Studies/Local Government Management Board.

Storey, J. 1989. Human resource management in the public sector. *Public Money and Management* 9, 3 (Autumn):19-24.

Thain, C., and M. Wright. 1990. Running costs control in U.K. central government. *Financial Accountability and Management* 6, 2:115-31.

Thompson, M. 1993. *Performance-related Pay: the Employee Experience.* Brighton: Institute of Manpower Studies, University of Sussex.

United Kingdom. 1991. *The Citizen's Charter: Raising the Standard.* London: HMSO.

Waldegrave, W. 1993. *The Reality of Reform and Accountability in Today's Public Service.* London: Public Finance Foundation.

Warner, N. 1992. Changes in resource management in the social services. In *Handbook of Public Services Management,* ed. C. Pollitt and S. Harrison, 179-93. Oxford: Blackwell.

Williamson, O. 1975. *Markets and Hierarchies: Analysis and Anti-trust Implications.* New York: Free Press.

Wise, C. 1990. Public service configurations and public organizations: public organization design in the post-privatization era. *Public Administration Review* 50, 2:141-55.

Zifcak, S. 1992. *Administrative Reform in Whitehall and Canberra in the 1980s: the FMI and FMIP Compared.* Ph.D. thesis. London School of Economics.

Quality Management in Public Organizations: Prospects and Dilemmas

PATRICIA W. INGRAHAM

INTRODUCTION

In the past two decades, two sets of organizational reforms have been introduced in both public and private organizations that have struggled to become smaller, more flexible, and more innovative. There are clear tensions between the intent and the processes of the two sets, but they have often been adopted simultaneously or in close sequence. One set of reforms is characterized by an emphasis on greater efficiency, improved responsiveness to elected officials and various forms of decentralization and/or privatization. Activities include pay for performance, better financial management, contracting out, and movement of public corporations and activities to the private sector (Pollitt 1990; Hood 1995). Economic constraints that forced a reconsideration of both the scope of government activity and the size of government provided the foundation for such efforts; ideological politics provided the mechanism. This set of reforms, frequently referred to as managerialist, are now widespread in Europe, Canada, the United States, Australia and New Zealand (Savoie 1994; Ingraham 1995).

At the same time, other reforms have also taken hold. In many ways, they implicitly reject key assumptions that underpin the managerialist reforms described above. Total quality management efforts focus on improved quality of service, improved service delivery, and greater customer satisfaction. They also emphasize

239

expanded employee participation in decision making and in com-munication within the organization. The emphasis on *organizational* resources is very different from that of most managerialist efforts. "High performance" relies upon improved use of existing resources and expertise; employees throughout the organization – not just those at the top – have a stake in achieving quality; the role of external di-rection – save that of the customer and customer satisfaction – is sig-nificantly diminished. This emphasis necessarily questions and attenuates the attention given to hierarchical direction and authority, which is central to the improved political responsiveness common to many managerialist efforts.

The widespread acceptance of quality principles is clearly demon-strated in the United States by Vice President Gore's National Per-formance Review. NPR is founded on four fundamental quality concepts: (1) Cutting red tape; (2) Putting customers first; (3) Empow-ering employees to get results; and (4) Cutting back to basics (Na-tional Performance Review 1993:6-7). In the United Kingdom, similar principles underpin the Citizen's Charter, which as Doern notes, is intended to "give more power to the citizen," while also releasing the "well-spring of talent, energy, care, and commitment in (the) public service" (Doern 1992:3). In the Canadian context, Kernaghan (1993) observes that TQM principles such as empowerment, flatter organiza-tions, improved communication, and a focus on customer service are becoming common at both the federal and provincial levels of gov-ernment. The federal government's Public Service 2000, for example, draws heavily on TQM principles. In Australia, the Continuous Im-provement effort, one of three major initiatives of the national Public Service Commission, is essentially a quality activity (Ives 1993).

In comparison to managerialist reforms generally, total quality re-forms and activities in public organizations have received relatively little attention. They are equally important, however, both for the changes they advocate for public organizations and employees and for the dramatically changed relationship they advocate between public institutions and the citizens they serve. Just as pay for perform-ance and related efforts were not, and could not be, merely technical improvements to civil service systems, Total Quality Management (TQM) is not simply a new management tool. TQM rejects most existing structures, procedures, and relationships in public management systems. As a result, it is as important for what it suggests about democratic governance as for what it intends for management.

Total Quality Management is based on the work of W. Edwards Deming (1986) and others. It has been popularized in work such as Osborne and Gaebler's *Reinventing Government* (1992) and Barzelay's *Breaking Through Bureaucracy* (1992). Although the principles of TQM have a compelling simplicity about them, a more analytic consideration of their content and application in a public setting quickly demonstrates the profound challenges they pose. A brief summary of the most important principles is a necessary starting point.

Move from a Focus on Procedure to Focus on the Product

In testimony before the National Performance Review staff in the United States, one federal employee observed that "process is our most important product" (NPR 1993). This fixation with procedure is one of the most frequently cited complaints about large bureaucratic organizations. While there were reasons for creating the procedural baggage now carried by public organizations and their employees, whatever rationale did exist has been overwhelmed by the stultifying, and frequently infuriating, presence of "red tape."

The rules and regulations that are now the target of reform were often the product of efforts to direct and control civil servants; when old rules failed, new ones were added. Rather than achieving the desired constraints, however, the reliance on rules and legal controls created public organizations that were more complex and difficult to understand and manage. Of equal significance, they created organizations whose focus was internal, on procedures and administrative guidelines. Effective action was defined as successfully following the rules. The focus on *product* sought by TQM was notably absent. Injecting it into the equation means not only rejecting and removing many existing rules and regulations; it also means an agreement from external directors that new ones will not be created.

Focus on the Customer, on Quality, and on Customer Satisfaction

For public organizations, this principle explicitly rejects the old adage "It's good enough for government work." Quality is to be built into every process of the organization. Processes are to be mutually supportive and reinforcing; consistent customer satisfaction – not following the rules – is to be the measure of effective performance.

Continuous improvement and continuous efforts to refine quality and its measurement become integral components of organizational activities. This necessarily implies careful definition of customer or customers. For public organizations, this is a complex and multidimensional activity. In addition, for many organizations it will imply destruction of existing processes, so that new, customer-focused ones may be created.

Topple the Pyramid; Empower Employees

Most previous reforms worked within the confines of traditional patterns of power and authority: hierarchy was the defining concept. TQM advocates devolution of both power and authority. Front-line workers are "empowered"; problem solving occurs throughout the organization, but is particularly important at the point of service delivery – the intersection between customer and organization. Group problem solving and team efforts are critical to the new decision-making patterns. Consensus, rather than orders, is the foundation for key decisions. The role of "top" management is redefined to resemble facilitation more accurately. The role of middle management is dramatically reduced, if not eliminated. At the very least, it is redefined.

Constantly Track Success and Progress

Again, a focus on *external* satisfaction and evaluation is emphasized. Achieving quality according to external standards necessitates much higher levels of discretion and flexibility for all employees, but again those who are at the boundaries of the organization are key. Recognizing mistakes early and correcting them quickly is critical. A corollary is that mistakes are tolerated and not punished; they are learning experiences and can serve to improve long-term performance.

Obviously, evaluation must be a critical organizational function. It must focus not only on external measures of effectiveness, but on their relationship to internal processes. Feedback and critical analysis replace rejection of bad news. The need to evaluate for results – and the ability to specify what those results should be – is high on the quality organization's agenda.

Because evaluating for results suggests different definitions of employee effectiveness and productivity, fundamental rethinking and restructuring of organizational incentives and rewards are also necessary. As later discussion will demonstrate, important questions about organizational commitment and accountability also become part of the quality equation.

THE QUALITY MOVEMENT:
BENEFITS AND SUCCESSES

The fundamental restructuring suggested by the above principles is daunting. Nonetheless, many public organizations have embraced Total Quality Management. The United States is probably the farthest along the quality road: most federal agencies, many state governments, and a substantial number of local governments have adopted total quality objectives and methods. At the federal level, a Federal Quality Institute oversees and provides guidance for individual agency efforts. A General Accounting Office study (1992) reported that 68 percent of the agencies surveyed had some TQM effort underway. Annual awards, similar to the Baldridge Awards in the private sector, are made to those organizations deemed to have the best records.

The Internal Revenue Service, the Navy, the Air Force, and the Patent Office, among others, have won such awards. One 1993 winner, the Naval Air Warfare Center, included the following achievements in its application:

- On time delivery rate for aircraft carrier products and systems improved from 85 percent to 99 percent.
- 120 process improvements.
- $22 million in savings. (Federal Quality Institute 1993:vii).

Other Quality Award winners, such as the Ogden Service Center of the Internal Revenue Service, have become prototypes for their organizations.

The Total Quality concept was formally endorsed by the entire Department of Defense in 1986; two years later the Comptroller General of the United States initiated organization-wide TQM at the General Accounting Office. The Department of Agriculture has created TQM processes and teams at all levels of the organization; training in TQM is a major organizational priority. The National Aeronautic and Space Administration credits TQM and employee involvement with much of its ability to recover as an organization from the Challenger tragedy; the EPA gives TQM equally high marks (Cohen and Brand 1990). The National Performance Review's strong endorsement of key TQM components further invigorated an already strong trend.

In the United Kingdom, the Major government has also formally endorsed the concept and institutionalized it in the Citizen's Charter. The Charter articulates seven principles of public service:

1 Standards – explicit, published standards at each point of service delivery;
2 Openness – disseminate information about services and end public employee anonymity;
3 Information – full and easy access to necessary information;
4 Choice – competition for service delivery when possible, but also citizen participation in service design and delivery;
5 Nondiscrimination; and
6 Responsiveness – full understanding of complaints procedures, but also remedy.

The Citizen's Charter applies to all public services (Doern 1992:5). An early analysis of the effectiveness of the Charter concludes, however, that "quality improvement through the medium of

Charters may be an idea whose time has come for managers and politicians, but it has only marginally entered the awareness of citizen-users" (Beale and Pollitt 1994:16).

The Canadian experience with quality management is well demonstrated by the Canadian Institute of Public Administration's annual award for innovative management. Provincial and municipal governments compete with federal organizations for the award. Kernaghan (1993) reports that empowerment and other total quality principles were a common management pattern in the sixty-eight submissions in 1991. The winning organization in that year, B.C. HYDRO, argued that empowerment allowed it to "unleash the talent" of its employees and to significantly restructure the organization (Kernaghan 1993:197).

A related development in the use of TQM in public organizations is that some are now using TQM techniques to redesign earlier reforms. In the United States, for example, the Internal Revenue Service recently began the "reinvention" of performance management. The first report noted, "The project arose from the widely held perception among IRS employees at all levels that the current systems are broken – not helping and, in fact, harming performance and quality of work life," and "We cannot effectively deliver Tax Systems Modernization and other future initiatives unless the agency begins reinventing itself as a Total Quality Organization and thereby empowering the workforce to meet these challenges."(IRS 1993:1-3).

The newly designed performance management system will reward contributions to organizational performance, teamwork, and quality of work life. The overall objective emphasized by the project team is the improvement of *organizational* quality and performance, not the rating of individual performance; individual performance appraisals and ratings will, if the team's recommendations are followed, be eliminated (IRS 1993:4).

THE BENEFITS OF TOTAL QUALITY EFFORTS

Clearly, Total Quality Management and related efforts have served an important function in many public organizations and have included a variety of real or perceived benefits.

Improved Communication, Decision Making, and Problem-solving Ability

It is not surprising that many large organizations, both public and private, have fallen into rigid and duplicative bureaucratic decision processes. The common problem of reducing size while also improving performance, however, demonstrated the serious weaknesses of the closed, retrospective systems. Most prevalent was the inability to understand fully the objectives and functions of the organization and its programs from any perspective other than existing systems and internal processes. The comprehensive total quality analysis of what the organization does, how it does it, and how it could do it better is a quantum leap from previous incremental analyses. Further, the necessary focus on external assessment of performance and quality introduced an entirely new dimension to the decision processes of many organizations.

Improved Employee Participation and Commitment

Total quality processes also challenge traditional hierarchies in another way. Inside the organization, all employees are involved in problem identification and solution; those who deliver the service are now part of determining what is wrong with the delivery system. The increased stake in the organization that more widespread participation creates – the "empowerment" of employees – not only improves the quality of decision making, but enhances the potential for effective implementation of new processes and systems. Recognition and reward systems that recognize teams and team effort further reinforce this potential. As Barzelay (1992) and others have noted, the increased involvement and participation of employees creates flexibilities within the organization that also translate into improved relations with the environment and with those the organization serves.

Improved Productivity

At least in part because employees from all levels of the organization are now involved in problem analysis, many organizations that utilize TQM techniques report decreases in duplication and other improvements in resource utilization.

It is important to note, however, that the majority of organizations able to report such improvements are those whose tasks are somewhat routine, or at least amenable to both routinization and simplification. Of seventeen Quality Award winners in the United States in the years 1989-1993, for example, only two had a function that was not service delivery (for example, IRS Service Centers and defense maintenance establishments) or contract management (Federal Quality Institute 1993). In Canada, Ingstrup observes that "some of the greatest apparent successes of Total Quality in the public sector have been at the municipal levels of government or in parts of government that are relatively well insulated from political and public policy debate" (Ingstrup 1993:6).

Other types of organizations, such as policy advising and research units, may not be so amenable to TQM improvements (or perhaps, in the presence of already more flexible internal arrangements, are not so amenable to easily measured improvements). Further, as Ingstrup implies, as political consensus about organizational mission declines, the ability to arrive at measures of quality and success that are widely accepted declines as well.

Improved Communication
Inside the Organization

The emphasis on improved – and different – channels of communication is a hallmark of Total Quality Management. The involvement of all levels of the organization in information gathering, problem identification, and solution proposals is a dramatic move away from the traditional hierarchical communication and decision-making patterns. Earlier reforms such as pay for performance were heralded for their improvement of communication between manager and subordinate (Ingraham 1993). TQM focuses on improved communication throughout the organization; patterns of communication and fundamental communication processes – as well as the technology that supports them – are significantly redefined.

Despite these successes, or perhaps because of them, it is important to examine other impacts and outcomes of Total Quality Management. Policy diffusion is common in public reform efforts. Perceived success in one setting consistently leads to duplication of reform initiatives in different and frequently dissimilar settings. Halligan, for example, observes that "borrowing is a normal and constant element in the policy maker's range of options" (Halligan 1995:4).

The implications of Total Quality Management in public organizations are far more daunting than a summary of its strong points would suggest. The public setting, the extent to which performance is subject to competing perspectives and values, and – perhaps most significantly – the casting of citizen as customer cause TQM in the public sector to be an unpredictable and rather iconoclastic endeavour. The following issues are a summary of some, but not all, of the most important problems.

The Citizen and the Client

Total Quality Management emphasizes customer service and customer satisfaction. In a public setting, this raises issues at two levels. Ingstrup summarizes the first eloquently:

What is lost and what is gained when public servants begin to think of those they serve as "customers" rather than "citizens"? The distinction is subtle but significant. The concept of "customer" is atomistic: the customer is sovereign. A citizen is not sovereign: a citizen is a citizen by virtue of something he or she shares with others. The satisfaction of individual "customers" may not add up to some kind of overarching public good that serves the best interests of the citizenry at large (Ingstrup 1993:9).

The second level of concern is equally complex. The benefits of moving from an internal focus on process to an external assessment of product are relatively straightforward and, for most governments, a new opportunity to emphasize productivity. For public organizations, however, the first step in this process – that of accurately identifying the customer or customers – is an extremely problematic endeavour. For most public programs and agencies, there are multiple customers. Some are internal to the organization; some are clearly the clients served by the program; some are political actors and interest groups. For some kinds of public organizations, such as those involved with policy analytic or advising activities, the concept of "customer" is even more nebulous.

DiIulio, Garvey, and Kettl identify four dimensions of the citizen/customer relationship: citizens can be service recipients, partners in service provision, overseers of performance, and, of course, taxpayers. The significance of these multiple dimensions is twofold. The simple identification of customer becomes much more complex and each of the dimensions or roles for the citizen implies a different value perspective from which the quality of the service or product will be evaluated. Responsiveness will be valued from the recipient perspective. Partners will value effectiveness, overseers will place heavier emphasis on accountability, and taxpayers will judge both quality and productivity on the basis of efficiency (1993:49). It is extremely likely, of course, that none of these perspectives will exist in isolation from the others. The blending or overlay that will occur further obfuscates both definition of customer and criteria which will serve as the basis for evaluation of quality.

None of the above discussion accounts for the role played by elected and appointed officials as both customers of public services and evaluators of quality. While some of the criteria and value perspectives may overlap – accountability and efficiency are likely to appear in the political constellation as well as in that of citizen – others will be quite different. Certainly the time frame for evaluation will not be the same. For politics and elected officials, windows for change and improved performance are limited and short term. For clients of services, the time frame will be longer; for the organization itself, the appropriate frame for assessment and evaluation will be even longer term.

Further, the resources provided by political actors to public agencies cause the political client to be the most immediate in important ways. Organizational constraints and political realities, however, essentially ensure that political expectations for, or definitions of, quality cannot be met. In this setting, the promise of Total Quality Management is aborted.

The juxtaposition of political direction and quality-management endeavours raises other issues as well. Most recent efforts at improved political direction of public organizations emphasize hierarchical models of direction and control (Ingraham and Peters 1987; Savoie 1994). This emphasis conflicts quite directly with the TQM principles of increased employee discretion and empowerment. At best, any potential fit requires political "space" or an agreement by political leaders that the organization and its leaders will be granted the flexibility and discretion to pursue quality initiatives without interference. At worst, a continued political emphasis on hierarchical responsiveness simply subverts critical TQM processes.

The Tension between TQM, Shrinking Government, and Organizational Survival

Donald Kettl asks an important question which underpins this issue. "If reinventing government is the answer," he asks, "what is the question?" Is it possible to reduce size, restructure processes and improve performance at one and the same time? Should governments try?

Common sense and hard lessons from the past suggest not. Common sense and past experience count for little, however. Many governments currently have little choice; they *must* try to cut back, reinvent, and improve quality at the same time. There are obvious tensions between the activities; the problems for quality management initiatives in this climate deserve consideration. Two principles of TQM merit special attention.

First, quality management emphasizes employee empowerment, discretion, and flexibility. It explicitly endorses risk taking and advocates rewarding risk and building probable occasional failures into organizational learning processes. Second, the emphasis on external assessment and evaluation dramatically increases the potential for failure. Evaluation measures move beyond bureaucratic control – or at least become less hierarchical; traditional process rationales, allowing for less than fully effective performance, become another indicator of failure. In competition for scarce resources, neither risk taking nor increased potential for negative evaluation is a positive attribute. Further, inside the organization the competition spurred by downsizing contradicts the need for trust, community, and fair play emphasized by TQM.

Do Public Organizations Possess Internal Culture and Values that Are Supportive of Change in General and Quality Initiatives in Particular?

Two issues are of special significance here: the structures of public management (civil service systems) and leadership in public organizations. To a significant extent, the success or failure of total quality initiatives in an organization depends upon the existence of an organizational culture and value set that supports change and can endure the inevitable tumult it will cause. The creation and maintenance of such a culture, in turn, is contingent upon the support of strong and creative leadership. Do the qualities and characteristics of large public organizations provide these foundations? By and large – but, of course, with exceptions – the answer is no.

One component of the problem was succinctly summarized by Harlan Cleveland, who observed that "Public administrators [tackle] twenty-year problems with five-year plans staffed with two-year personnel funded by one-year appropriations" (in Bushnell and Halus 1992:355). Another dimension is provided by the structures and processes of the civil service systems within whose constraints most public organizations operate. The emphasis is on stability, predictability, and standardization. All of these characteristics contrast starkly with those advocated by Total Quality Management: flexibility, risk, and individual discretion.

Further, the role TQM assigns to lower-level employees in the organization – active participation in problem solving and decision making – conflicts with traditional civil service hierarchy and authority. This is not an insurmountable problem; it does suggest, however, that substantial system changes are necessary if total quality processes are to be supported. In addition, organizational cultures will need to change rather dramatically, and new levels of organizational learning need to be developed.

In terms of leadership, the role of politics and the quality and impact of political leadership is critically important. Despite their redefined role in Total Quality Management, the commitment and energy of top leaders in the organization provide the foundation upon which employee empowerment and flexibilities can be built. Further, the commitment of leaders provides the space necessary for change correction and for risk taking and learning from mistakes. The ability to set an example that tolerates – much less encourages – risk and mistake is unusual in any circumstance; it is extremely unlikely in a political setting in which short-term success is the goal and full understanding of the organization is unlikely (Mintzberg 1987; Tichy and Devanna 1986; Heclo 1978).

The issue is further complicated by the combination of political leaders and members of the higher civil service. In the United States, it is notable that TQM initiatives have taken firmest hold in organizations with the lowest levels of political penetration – the IRS with one political appointee is the most prominent example. The quality movement in that agency is led by *career* executives. The same is true of most Defense agencies. Political executives are less likely to play such a role for two reasons: they frequently lack the long-term perspective necessary for successful implementation of TQM, and they are generally not selected for their leadership and/or management skills (Campbell 1988).

The role of political leaders and their relationship to the efforts of the executives in the higher civil service are not well documented in countries in which TQM efforts have not received as much attention as in the United States. Evidence about quality initiatives is beginning to emerge in Canada (Ingstrup 1993; Kernaghan 1993), the United Kingdom (Beale and Pollitt 1994) and Australia (Ives 1993). There is little discussion, however, of the role and activities of political leaders and appointees in those initiatives.

What Are the Mechanisms or Processes for Ensuring Accountability?

The above discussion skirts, but does not address, a fundamental issue. Accountability of public employees is a serious concern for all modern nations. Traditionally, this accountability has been addressed by rules, regulations, and laws (as in the u.s.), by political direction and control (as in recent cases in the u.s., the u.k., and Canada), and by reliance on the public service norms of the higher civil service (as in the u.k., Canada, France, and Australia). Addressing accountability for *results* has been notably absent in most cases, although the contract arrangements for senior executives in New Zealand and Australia have started to move in that direction.

Most of the mechanisms listed above are directed at the higher civil service or, at least, at management levels. Total Quality Management addresses different parts of the organization. It explicitly advocates the devolution of authority and discretion to all levels; those employees in most direct contact with the customer/citizen are targeted for dramatically increased flexibilities. This makes good sense for an improved understanding of citizen preference and satisfaction. The implications for accountability and external assessments of legitimate authority are less clear. Obviously, traditional mechanisms for direction and control are attenuated. But what replaces them?

The design of new accountability mechanisms that are acceptable and satisfactory for all concerned parties is a central task for Total Quality Management in the public sector. Elected officials are not likely to cede their direction and oversight responsibilities to the ideal flexibilities advocated by TQM. Mistakes, to be honest, are generally not viewed as learning experiences in a politicized environment.

While it is possible that professional and public service norms associated with the higher civil service in particular, and the public service in general, could play a new role in an environment of expanded discretion, the extent to which political officials would defer to them – or *should* defer to them – is a legitimate topic for debate. Because client opinions are likely to be both diverse and disparate, looking to them for legitimation and formal accountability is problematic.

Further, the new focus on external (but not necessarily political) criteria for effectiveness and success raises questions about both incentives and rewards. Again, civil service systems and the different incentives they provide must be considered. The tightly bounded and very clearly defined set of incentives and rewards inherent in civil service systems are not always satisfactory; they are, however, generally understood and are directly related to traditional patterns of hierarchy and control. Despite their problems, they are certain. For managers, employees, and citizens, the new patterns and systems are not. There are risks for all parties; for those most endangered – the boundary-level employees – the benefits are least clear. This leads directly to the next issue to be considered.

A focus on customer service and an emphasis on external accountability pose a serious dilemma for those organizations in all countries that now rely heavily on contracting out for service delivery and other functions. The space that contracting out and "hollow government" places between the public employee and the citizen who receives the service becomes a veritable chasm in the context of TQM. Neither monitoring for quality and satisfaction nor alternative mechanisms for accountability has been adequately considered in this context (Kettl 1988; Milward 1994). TQM empowers public employees to be more responsive to customer satisfaction for services delivered by a third party. What does this mean? Who is to be held accountable and how?

How is Equity Defined in this New Context?

To fall back one more time on the distinction between the old and the new, public service systems have traditionally tended to define equity as sameness – as standardization. (This is a bit of an oversimplification because fairness has obviously been a key part of the equation, but the emphasis on standardization is well documented.) The intrusive role of politics in the delivery and design of public services has led to a consistent fear of differentiation and discretion; the "boxes" of public service delivery systems are the obvious outcome.

Are services to be delivered and policies made for those with the most direct access to bureaucratic actors? In many respects, these are the customers of TQM. Is it possible to empower employees at all levels of the organization, in the context of what we know about bureaucratic politics and bureaucratic policy making, and not raise issues of legitimacy and equity? Further, the implications of empowering the bottom levels of the organization and the clients of the organization have not been explored. Nor, for that matter, have the issues been addressed in the case of the "involuntary client" – the service recipient who has no other source of service or assistance, or who, alternatively, does not wish to be associated with the organization but is required to be through law or regulatory procedures. Two very different groups of citizens would be involved in these scenarios: in the case of the monopoly provider of service, the clients would likely be disadvantaged, elderly, or ill. At least two of these groups are not in a strong position to assume the new role suggested for them. In the second scenario, that of regulation, the clients would likely be business or other groups with both a well-established capacity for political action and a history of using it. In this case, the new emphasis on external evaluation criteria and mutual equity could well work to the disadvantage of the organization in attempting to achieve broader social objectives.

A different kind of problem is posed by the question of whether the boundaries of public organizations can actually be opened to permit citizens the equitable access mandated by TQM. Exchange with citizen and client in bureaucratic terms is always in the language and processes of the bureaucracy. In TQM terms, it is in the language and evaluative criteria of the citizen. In organizations that have long been essentially immune from citizen satisfaction as a criterion for success, how does the transformation occur? Is it, given competing definitions of customer and client, even likely?

How Is the Success of Total Quality
Management to Be Determined?

If all of the problems outlined above were to be overcome, how would the effectiveness of Total Quality be evaluated? More to the point, is any effort at evaluation likely? Public sector management reforms have a long history of diffusing and recycling from one context to another (Ingraham and Peters 1987; Ingraham 1993; Halligan 1995). It is not unusual for a reform or "technique" to be adopted in a new setting without analysis of the initial experience. It is also not unusual for the expectations for the new reform to be unclear, multiple, and often conflicting. This lack of clarity can be exacerbated by the symbolic political rhetoric that accompanies reform advocacy and adoption. The National Performance Review in the United States is an excellent case in point.

Evaluation of Total Quality Management encompasses all of these problems and adds others: will the efforts be assessed for long-term or short-term outcomes and effects? What, in fact, is the appropriate span of analysis? Private sector experience with organizational change and restructuring suggests that a five- to seven-year time period is necessary for the change really to take hold (Hammer and Champy 1993). Will public organizations have the luxury of such a length of time?

Should the effort be judged according to internal or external criteria? The answer is, of course, by both, but the conundrum for public agencies is that internal and external criteria may conflict in important ways. The different criteria may also address different levels of change. Team formation, for example, is one sign of movement toward quality management and could be viewed as one measure of success. It is, however, only one step in a very long process which, if effective, would see those teams assume broad decision-making responsibility and authority. It is much more difficult to gauge the effectiveness of these later stages of development.

The difficulty with all of this is that the lack of initial clarity about what the reform is supposed to achieve effectively derails later efforts to determine whether or not the reform was a success. Learning from the past and from the experience of other governments is difficult because the lessons are not clear. We cannot learn *if* a reform was a success or failure, much less *why*. The reform cycle and the constant search for new solutions are reinforced.

CONCLUSION

In the case of Total Quality Management, as with the case of many management reforms which preceded it, discussion of utility for public organizations has proceeded with little attention to the broader impact on governance. It is increasingly clear, however, that no public management reform is or can be simply technical or managerial but must, inevitably and irretrievably, be about the quality of government and the relationship of government institutions to the citizens they serve.

The frequent cycling of new management trends tends to obscure this. Hart observes that "management fads come and go as the seasons; spring promises efficacy in one minute; the summer searches for excellence; the nirvana of fall lies hidden in total quality; and hard winter demands lean management." (Hart 1994:107). The emphasis on different values, different processes and different techniques, combined with a consistent lack of agreement on fundamental objectives, ensures that dissatisfaction with the operation of public organizations will endure (See Peters 1994, for a discussion of competing values).

In the final analysis, why reforms such as Total Quality Management rise is not as important as why they fall. Building quality into public organizations is about creating the capacity, the commitment, and the will to do the necessary jobs. It is also about creating the political space that allows positive change to occur. Total Quality Management and the redefined organizations it espouses can make an important contribution to creating better quality public organizations (Swiss 1994). It can only make a contribution, however; by itself it will not solve the problems confronting public organizations in virtually every modern nation. Creating national civil services with the capacity to "be creative, to seek out compromises, to educate, and to initiate and manage change" (Savoie 1994:2) requires political leadership, will, and support, as well as more effective organizational leadership and management. It requires both sets of leaders to be clear about the intent of reform and the expectations for the outcomes of reform. It requires learning, rather than duplication or simple transplanting; therefore, it requires attention to serious evaluation and analysis. This makes reform much more difficult; it will also cause it to be more significant.

BIBLIOGRAPHY

Barzelay, Michael, and B.J. Armajani. 1992. *Breaking Through Bureaucracy: A New Vision for Managing Government.* Berkeley: University of California Press.

Beale, Valerie, and Christopher Pollitt. 1994. Charters at the grass roots: a first report. *Local Government Studies* (Summer).

Bushnell, David, and Michael Halus. 1992. TQM in the public sector: strategies for quality service. *National Productivity Review* (Summer):355-70.

Campbell, Colin. 1988. The political roles of senior government officials in advanced democracies. *British Journal of Political Science* 18:242-72.

Cleveland, Harlan. 1985. The twilight of hierarchy: speculations on the global information society. *Public Administration Review* 45:185-95.

Cohen, Steven, and Ronald Brand. 1990. Total quality management in the U.S. Environmental Protection Agency. *Public Productivity and Management Review* 14 (Fall):99-114.

Deming, W. Edwards. 1986. *Out of the Crisis*. Cambridge, MA: MIT Press.

DiIulio, John, Gerald Garvey, and Donald Kettl. 1993. *Improving Government Performance: An Owners' Manual*. Washington, DC: The Brookings Institution.

Doern, G. Bruce. 1992. Implementing the U.K. Citizen's Charter. Ottawa: Canadian Centre for Management Development.

Halligan, John. 1995. The diffusion of civil service reform. In *Civil Services in Comparative Perspective*, ed. Hans Bekke, James L. Perry, and Theo A.J. Toonen. Bloomington, IN: Indiana University Press.

Hammer, Michael, and James Champy. 1993. *Re-engineering the Corporation: A Manifesto for Business Revolution*. New York: HarperCollins.

Hart, David K. 1994. Administration and the ethics of virtue: in all things, choose first for good character and then for technical expertise. In *Handbook of Administrative Ethics*, ed. Terry L. Cooper. New York: Marcel Dekker.

Heclo, Hugh. 1978. *A Government of Strangers*. Washington, DC: The Brookings Institution.

Hood, Christopher. 1995. Exploring variations in 1980s public management reform. In *Civil Services in Comparative Perspective*, ed. Hans Bekke, James L. Perry, and Theo A.J. Toonen. Bloomington, IN: Indiana University Press.

Ingraham, Patricia W. 1993. Of pigs in pokes and policy diffusion: another look at pay for performance. *Public Administration Review* 53 (July/August):348-57.

Ingraham, Patricia W. 1995. The comparative reform agenda. In *Civil Services in Comparative Perspective*, ed. Hans Bekke, James L. Perry, and Theo A.J. Toonen. Bloomington, IN: Indiana University Press.

Ingraham, Patricia W., and B. Guy Peters. 1987. The conundrum of reform. *Policy Studies Journal* (Fall).

Ingstrup, Ole. 1993. Total quality in the public sector. Ottawa: Canadian Centre for Management Development.

Ives, Denis. 1993. *Next Steps in Public Management*. Canberra: Public Service Commission.

Kernaghan, Kenneth. 1993. Empowerment and public administration: revolutionary advance or passing fancy? *Canadian Public Administration* 35 (Summer):194-214.

Kettl, Donald F. 1988. *Government by Proxy: (Mis)Managing Government*. Washington, DC: Congressional Quarterly Press.

Pollitt, Christopher. 1990. *Managerialism and the Public Service*. Oxford: Basil Blackwell.

Savoie, Donald. 1994. *Thatcher, Reagan, Mulroney: In Search of a New Bureaucracy*. Pittsburgh: University of Pittsburgh Press.

Swiss, James E. 1994. Adapting total quality management to government. In *Contemporary Public Administration*, eds. David Rosenbloom, Deborah Goldman, and Patricia W. Ingraham, 171-82. New York: McGraw-Hill.

Tichy, Noel, and Mary Anne Devanna. 1986. *The Transformational Leader*. New York: John Wiley.

GOVERNMENT DOCUMENTS

U.S. Federal Quality Institute. 1993. *Quality Improvement Prototype Award*. Washington, DC: Government Printing Office.

U.S. General Accounting Office. 1992. Total Quality Management Initiatives in the Federal Government. Washington, DC: Government Printing Office.

U.S. Internal Revenue Service. 1993. A Report on the Reinvention of IRS Performance Management. Draft Report, IRS Project Team, Washington, DC.

Public Sector Innovation: The Implications of New Forms of Organization and Work

SANDFORD F. BORINS

INTRODUCTION

The common objective of this volume is to assess the impact of a number of important trends in the socio-economic environment of government on the theory and practice of public management. This particular chapter will look at how three major trends – the revolution in information technology, the pressure of financial constraint, and the challenge of a diverse work force – are shattering the traditional bureaucratic paradigm of public management.[1] After exploring this point on a conceptual level, we will look at concrete evidence about how a number of leading-edge public sector organizations, identified among the winners of two major public management innovation competitions, are responding to these trends. We find that these organizations are changing their technology, their relationship with clients, and their ways of organizing work. The final part of the chapter returns to the conceptual level by sketching out the implications of these new forms of organization and work for the following topics: the relative standing of front-line workers, clerical workers, and middle managers; training within the public sector; the public sector's salary structure; the role of policy and planning units in government; the power of public sector unions; and the aggregate level of public sector employment.

THE BUREAUCRATIC PARADIGM

The bureaucratic paradigm of public management in North America is an amalgam of the ideas of Adam Smith, F.W. Taylor, Max Weber, and the Progressive reformers early in this century. Smith, writing at the dawn of the industrial revolution, developed the concept of the division of labour, whereby production processes would be divided into many discrete operations, and workers would specialize in performing the same operation repeatedly (Hammer and Champy 1993:11-17). F.W. Taylor drew out the implications of the division of labour for organizational structure and developed techniques for maximizing workers' productivity. His approach involved several steps: shifting the responsibility for organizing work (and, indeed, for all thinking) from workers to managers; using scientific time and motion studies to determine the most efficient way to perform any discrete task; and then selecting, training, and monitoring workers (Morgan 1986:19-38).

As the responsibilities of the state grew in the late nineteenth and early twentieth centuries, it was necessary to create organizational capability: armies and navies for mechanized warfare, an expanded postal system to deliver "penny postage" over an increased area, social security systems to calculate and pay the benefits of the welfare state, and tax collection agencies to implement the income tax. Mintzberg (1979:314-47) described these large public sector organizations doing repetitive tasks as "machine bureaucracies." In that Germany began doing many of these things earlier and on a larger scale than Canada and the United States, the sociologist Max Weber developed the ideal type of bureaucracy, inferring from what he observed there (Weber 1958:196-244). Weber characterized bureaucracy as being a hierarchy of officials who had expertise developed on the basis of specialized training and who received life tenure. The bureaucracy's records were kept in writing ("the files"), and decisions were made on the basis of applying general rules to specific cases. Weber (1958:214) cited as advantages of the bureaucratic form of organization, "Precision, speed, unambiguity, knowledge of the files, continuity, discretion, unity, strict subordination, reduction of friction and of material and personal costs – these are raised to the optimum point in the strictly bureaucratic administration, and especially in its monocratic form."

At the same time Weber was writing, the reform movement in North America was making activist government possible by replacing amateur and patronage-oriented regimes with professional bureaucracies. Barzelay (1992:3-12) has articulated the practices of the professional bureaucracies the reformers created as the "bureaucratic paradigm" in which

- an agency defines standard operating procedures and sticks to them
- an agency closely controls costs
- an agency separates thinking from doing; thinking (planning) is the responsibility of its leadership, doing (implementation) is the responsibility of its front-line workers
- an agency is hierarchical, with clear lines of accountability, and clear definitions of the roles and responsibilities of its component parts.

Thus, the public sector took the machine bureaucracy model developed by Taylor and reinforced it ideologically. The next section outlines the forces which are making the machine bureaucracy model an inappropriate and increasingly irrelevant one for public sector organizations.

THE FORCES OF CHANGE

This section cites three forces which are revolutionizing the way public sector organizations do their work. They are the availability of information technology, financial constraints (or what radical political economists presciently referred to some years ago as the "fiscal crisis of the state"), and the changing composition and preferences of the work force.

Information technology has a number of impacts. First, there is inevitably a component of capital-labour substitution, such as the replacement of human receptionists with voice-mail systems. A more far-reaching impact is the ready availability of information throughout an organization. If an organization has established a computer network and keeps its files electronically, employees simultaneously can access its memory (Hammer and Champy 1993:83-101). An electronic mail system permits them to understand and participate in the organization's thinking. Finally, information technology has an impact on the expectations of citizens, as recipients of public services, concerning the quality of public service. If private sector organizations are using information technology to improve service quality, why can't the public sector do the same? For example, if one can perform banking transactions with an automated teller machine (ATM), why can't similar public service transactions, such as renewing a driver's licence, also be performed that way? Similarly, if most businesses have voice-mail systems that make unanswered phone calls and busy signals anachronisms, why can't the public sector do likewise?

Financial constraint refers to the relationship between the cost of providing public services and the fiscal capacity of government. Citizens, in their role as taxpayers, want to see the cost of government kept low. The United States has seen numerous taxpayers' revolts, starting with California's Proposition 13 in 1978. Canada's taxpayers have been more accepting of high levels of taxation than has been the case in the United States, but it appears that the limits of their tolerance have also been reached. Furthermore, the international capital markets have become concerned about the ability of Canadian governments, whether at the federal or provincial levels, to service high debt levels, and have registered this concern by frequently downgrading Canadian debt ratings.

In a global economy in which capital is the most mobile factor of production, all nations have become concerned about their ability to attract and retain firms that provide high-quality jobs for their citizens. Any government has an important role to play in achieving competitiveness, both in terms of the overall level of taxation it imposes in comparison to those of competitor governments and in terms of the cost and quality of the public sector inputs it provides to the rest of its economy.

The third factor overthrowing public sector machine bureaucracy is the changing nature of the work force. Part of this change is demographic, in that the work force has much more gender, racial, and ethnic diversity than in the past. The complexity and diversity of the new work force means that the "one size fits all" human resource policies of the past must give way to policies that deal more sensitively with a wide variety of circumstances. Just as citizens compare the quality of public and private sector service, and businesses compare tax levels across jurisdictions, workers compare wages and working conditions between the public and private sectors. The most skilled workers, having the widest set of opportunities, compare the public sector to the leading-edge private sector corporations. The challenge to the public sector will be to attract and retain a skilled and motivated work force. One consequence of the weakening of the nation state and the widespread disrepute of the public service is an attenuation of simple patriotism. It is increasingly doubtful that public sector employers will be able to staff positions with appeals to patriotic sentiment if the package of pay and working conditions is not competitive and the work itself is not meaningful. To the extent that the public sector pay tends to be less generous than that of the private sector, the burden falls even more on the public sector to maintain competitiveness through working conditions and the intrinsic meaningfulness of the work.

These, then, are the forces that are breaking down the bureaucratic paradigm. The challenge for public managers is not to resist these forces, for they are truly irresistible.[2] It is, rather, to master them and, by doing so, to place their organizations in the forefront.

INNOVATIVE PUBLIC SECTOR ORGANIZATIONS

How can one study the most innovative public sector organizations, the organizations that have responded most creatively to the forces of change? In recent years, there have been a number of public management quality or innovation competitions throughout the world. The organizers publicize their competitions widely; managers who think their organizations are performing well or are innovative enter these competitions in the hope of seeking recognition or of networking with managers of other well-performing and innovative organizations. A possible research strategy is to use their applications as a source of information about the best practices or innovations in the public sector.

For the last few years I have been using applications to two public management innovation competitions to build a data base for the systematic study of leading-edge public sector organizations. I began with the Institute of Public Administration of Canada's (IPAC) innovative public management competition, which was initiated in 1990 and for the last three years has received over a hundred applications per year (Borins 1991; 1993b). Recently, I have extended my research to the Ford Foundation-Kennedy School of Government state and local government innovations program, which has been in operation since 1986 and now receives over fifteen hundred applications per year. In the case of the latter, I have analyzed the seventy-five semifinalists in the 1993 competition.

One might ask whether it is possible to know with any certainty that these applications represent organizations that are truly innovative or perform well. In both competitions, entrants are required not only to describe their innovation but also to discuss its results. Two dimensions of results are impact and replication. Impact measures would include the effects of an innovation on program cost and/or output measured, if possible, with reference to a control group. A third possible dimension would be sustainability, or impact and replication over time. An innovation would be considered more significant if the program continues to operate and to deliver beneficial results and if it is widely replicated. Judges of innovation competitions look for all these three factors in making their awards. The innovations presented in this chapter are those that have received high marks from the judges, such as the Ford Foundation-Kennedy School of Government's seventy-five semifinalists. The discussion of each innovation includes impact and/or replication measures. Strong performance in terms of impact and replication in the short term are the best predictors of sustainability in the future.

While these innovations may be "points of light," they are not isolated points of light. If these really are best practices, then other organizations will emulate them. Indeed, governments will attempt to mandate such practices. Thus, one can see in these state and local government innovations the inspiration for the United States federal government's Gore Report. If one thinks of the diffusion of public sector innovations as being described by a logistic, or S-curve, then the innovations described in these competitions are at the base of the curve, and government-wide initiatives are intended to bring the diffusion process onto the steeply rising segment of the curve.

Although the objective of this chapter is not to undertake a comprehensive study of these innovations, it will provide examples of five types of public sector innovation that are representative of new trends in public sector management, and that illustrate the impact these trends will have on organizational form and on certain human resource management issues. The five types of innovation are: the application of information technology, initiatives to accommodate diversity and worker preferences, decentralization of operations, case management, and organizational re-engineering.

Information technology has been used for a number of purposes, such as improving service to an agency's customers, improving the enforcement of negative sanctions, and empowering certain groups of citizens. The beneficiaries of the technology may be the general public or more narrow target groups, such as actual or prospective government contractors, the homeless, children in public housing, and custodial parents.

Two examples of service to the general public are InfoCalifornia and Santa Monica's Public Electronic Network. InfoCalifornia (InfoCalifornia 1993), one of the ten winners of the 1993 Ford Foundation-Kennedy School awards, is a system of electronic kiosks (similar to ATMs) that allows citizens expanded access to a wide range of information about government services and facilitates performing some transactions, such as obtaining a birth certificate or vehicle registration, electronically. Like ATMs, the kiosks are accessible twenty-four hours a day. Information about services is organized by issues (e.g., employment issues, children's issues) rather than by department or program. A measure of InfoCalifornia's impact is that electronic transactions are an order of magnitude less expensive than manual transactions; for example, a birth certificate can be produced for $1, rather than $10 (Simon 1993). In addition, waiting time and transportation cost for the customer is sharply reduced. InfoCalifornia was introduced as a pilot project in 1991 and is now being replicated on a state-wide basis.

Santa Monica, California's Public Electronic Network (PEN) surpasses InfoCalifornia. It provides E-mail access to municipal government for anyone living or working in Santa Monica (Public

Electronic Network 1993). Currently, 5300 citizens, or 7% of Santa Monica's population participates. Besides providing information about services and the ability to perform online transactions, it also accesses the public library system and enables users to participate in "electronic town hall meetings" about public issues. PEN's semifinalist application to the 1993 Ford Foundation-Kennedy School innovation program describes how an electronic dialogue about the problems of the homeless developed the idea for Shwashlock, a program providing showers, washers, and lockers for the homeless.

The Gore Report (Gore 1993:112-15) proposes similar initiatives for the U.S. government, such as the electronic transfer of government benefits and electronic income tax filing. In addition, the White House is now available on Internet at the address "President@Whitehouse.gov," and receives a thousand E-mail messages daily (Patton 1993).

Two North American examples of service to business are the State of Oregon's Vendor Information Program, one of the ten winners of the 1993 Ford Foundation-Kennedy School Innovation awards, and Supply and Services Canada's Open Bidding System, a finalist in the 1993 IPAC Innovative Public Management Competition. In 1992, the Purchasing Division of Oregon's Department of General Services established a computerized vendor information system that allows any vendor with a personal computer and modem to access, from their office, general information about bidding, historical bidding information, and requests for proposals (Vendor Information Program 1993). Vendors without personal computers can access this information at 120 procurement centres throughout the state. The initial startup funding for the program came from the State's Productivity Improvement Commission, which provided a loan of $235,000 for computer hardware that was repaid from savings generated in the program's first year of operation. After a year of operation, twenty-four thousand vendors in Oregon and elsewhere were accessing the Vendor Information Program and the number of bidders for Oregon contracts increased by 50%. This program realized annual cost savings including $60,000 in paper and postage, $500,000 in personnel, and, most importantly, more than $10 million in products purchased.

The next major step in developing this program will be the electronic submission of bids.

Supply and Services Canada's Open Bidding Service (Supply and Services Canada 1993) provides information about $4 billion-worth of federal government procurement opportunities electronically. American government opportunities available to Canadian firms as a result of the Free Trade Agreement are also provided, and provincial government opportunities are being added. As in Oregon, plans are afoot for electronic bid submission. The Open Bidding Service has been privatized; a private sector contractor runs the service at no cost to the government, because it covers its costs through user charges. The system began operation in June 1992 and, after six months, had over ten thousand subscribers. Identified benefits for the government include $1 million in annual savings on staff and documents and $1 million in setup costs, which were paid by the contractor. Unlike the Oregon system, no attempt was made to identify savings on procurement as a result of increased competition. The Gore Report (1993:29-30) recommends a similar approach to procurement, namely that the United States government establish an "electronic marketplace" for procurement, in which suppliers would list prices and products electronically and departments would order the lowest-priced product that meets their needs.

The benefits to business of increased efficiency in the flow of goods and services are even greater in newly industrialized countries or the third world. Jenkins (1992) discusses how the government of Singapore put into place the world's most efficient communications system for processing imports and exports. It decreased the turnaround time for processing trade documents from two to three days in 1987 to fifteen minutes in 1990. The direct cost of establishing the system was $12 million u.s.; its *annual* benefits are $588 million u.s.

Two examples of the use of information technology to improve law enforcement are the State of Massachusetts' Automated Child Support Enforcement Program, a finalist in the 1993 Ford Foundation-Kennedy School competition, and the City of Chicago's Parking Enforcement Program, a finalist in the 1991 Ford Foundation-Kennedy School competition.

The impetus for establishing the Massachusetts Automated Child Support Enforcement System was dissatisfaction with the previous manual approach, due to the low rate of child support collected (less than 50%) and the substantial cost of improving this outcome by hiring additional case workers (Automated Child Support Enforcement System 1993). Responsibility for the enforcement of child support was transferred from the courts to the Department of Revenue. The Department of Revenue began by building a data base of child support cases. In cases where people are not meeting their obligations to pay child support, the department attaches administrative liens to any asset or income stream it can access, including wages, bank accounts, unemployment or workers' compensation benefits, and lottery winnings. Cost savings have come from doing this automatically, without human intervention.

Equipment and retraining costs for the automated enforcement system were covered by productivity increases. During the first two years of the program (1992 and 1993), despite the severe recession child support collections grew by an average of 10% per annum. During this period, child support enforcement staff were cut by over 10%. Finally, this program is clearly the leading edge in child support enforcement, and is now being replicated within the United States. The federal government is requiring all states to create centralized child support databases by 1995, thereby laying the groundwork for a national automated system. This will deal with the current problem of Americans moving from one state to another to escape their child support obligations.

In the late 1980s the City of Chicago identified the need for a turnaround in its enforcement of parking rules (City of Chicago Parking Enforcement Program 1991). Fewer than 10% of tickets were paid in the year they were issued, and illegally parked cars slowed traffic flow. In 1990 the city undertook a total redesign of its parking enforcement system. Key information technology components of the redesign included automated ticket writing, a computerized inventory of parking meters, and imaging technology that enabled citizens to contest tickets by mail or in person at administrative hearings. The administrative hearings replaced the old system of court hearings that required the presence of both plaintiff and police officer and resulted in long delays. In the program's first six months, there were three impacts: a dramatic increase in the rate of ticket collection from 10% in the year issued to 40% in the first six months issued; an annual saving of $5 million in clerical, court and police costs, and a 15% increase in travel speed through the Loop.

Finally, two examples of the use of information technology to empower the disadvantaged are the City of Seattle's Community Voice Mail for the Homeless and the Computer Learning Centers established by the Housing Commission in Lansing, Michigan – both among the ten winners of the 1993 Ford Foundation-Kennedy School innovation awards. Seattle's system of voice mail for the homeless (Community Voice Mail 1993) has evolved from a pilot program over the last three years and now provides voice mail boxes, in English or Spanish, free of charge for two hundred thirty homeless people. The voice mail boxes make it easier for these individuals to look for employment and housing and to keep in touch with government agencies and case workers. In addition, they mask the stigma of homelessness and improve self-esteem. Voice mail users were able to find housing and work in four to eight weeks, rather than the average of six months for those who did not have voice mail. This program, the first of its kind, has received a great deal of media attention, and has already been replicated thirty or forty times.

The Lansing Housing Commission has established three Computer Learning Centers (1993) to provide children living in public housing a socially constructive way to spend after-school hours. The centres have instructional games designed to assist with academic subjects and skills. The program was recently expanded to provide an opportunity for adults to earn credits at Lansing Community College. The project costs approximately $100,000, financed by the Housing Commission and the City. The children's participation rate is 80% and their performance at school is better than is normally the case for public housing children. In addition, there has been a dramatic reduction in illegal and/or drug activity in the public housing projects.

Innovative programs are also being designed to *accommodate the diversity and changing preferences of the new labour force*. The County of Los Angeles Telecommuting Program (1993) enables twenty-six hundred, or 3% of the county's seventy-eight thousand employees, to work all or part of the week at home. Because the county is experiencing a budget deficit, it could not pay for equipment. Nevertheless, in most cases, employees felt sufficiently strongly that telecommuting would benefit them that they provided their own equipment. Of the participating employees, 17 % are managerial, 65 % professional, and 17 % clerical. The program has had three impacts: significant productivity increases for participating employees, substantial improvements in morale, and a reduction in travel time and expense. Questionnaires of employees and supervisors indicated nearunanimity about productivity and morale improvements. Even if the county had paid for the equipment, the cost would have been covered by the savings resulting from productivity increases.

The Franchise Tax Board is the major tax collection agency for the State of California (Barzelay and Dickert 1993). In the last twenty years it has had to adapt to an increasingly heterogeneous work force, both ethnically and racially. In addition, in 1983 the board was required by law to give priority for its temporary positions to people on welfare. In trying to fulfil this mandate, the managers of the Franchise Tax Board discovered that people on welfare had low literacy and numeracy skills and poor work habits. The strategy the Franchise Tax Board adopted was to become the model of a caring employer by improving the skills and meeting the needs of its employees. This involved such initiatives as: instituting training courses for basic (reading, writing) and life (financial planning, stress management) skills; establishing a partnership with a community college to give more advanced courses; setting up a day care centre, instituting flexible hours and a telecommuting program; and working with the Sacramento public transit system to extend service directly to the FTB's head office. All this was done at no additional cost through budget reallocation; two outcomes of this program are significant reductions in the rates of employee grievances and turnover. Similarly, the Gore Report (Gore 1993:84-5) is recommending that the United States government institute greater work-time flexibility and telecommuting for its employees.

The California Franchise Tax Board's recognition that delivering high-quality service depends on meeting the needs of the work force, as well as those of the customer, is consistent with best practice in the private sector. To quote Heskett's (1987) well-known *Harvard Business Review* article, "High-performance service companies have gained their status in large measure by turning the strategic service vision inward: by targeting important groups of employees as well as customers . . . [they] invariably have operating strategies designed to maximize differences between operating costs and value perceived by employees in relations with the company. And delivery systems designed with the operating strategy in mind can form the foundation for remarkable gains in productivity."

A third area of innovation is *decentralization of operational decision making*, thus pushing responsibility closer to the front-line workers. The recent history of the Correctional Service of Canada (csc), the United States Air Force Tactical Air Command, and the Ontario Development Corporation all provide examples of this.

Starting in 1988, the Correctional Service of Canada undertook a major turnaround that began with the development of a statement of the organization's mission and core values (Borins 1993a; Vantour 1991:31-50). This launched the csc on a process of comprehensive organizational change. One part of this was decentralization, known in that context as unit management. At each prison, the inmate population was divided into units of between eighty and one hundred twenty prisoners. Staff members were also assigned to those units. The objective of unit management was to integrate case management, programming, and security so that there would be meaningful human interaction between inmates and staff and within teams of staff members. In addition decisions were delegated to the unit level rather than made centrally. Units are small enough that staff and inmates interact with one another more humanely. Similarly, case management teams now include any staff member, including guards, who interacts with an inmate. The involvement of guards in case management is a major change from the past, when they were simply required to maintain physical security. The overall reform program, of which unit management is a part, has substantially improved the performance of the federal prison system. Between 1988 and 1991, the parole population increased by 50%, but the number of crimes committed by parolees diminished by 25%. No new prisons were needed in the last six years. Surveys have also indicated that staff morale has improved.

The Tactical Air Command (TAC) of the United States Air Force was in a sorry state in the late 1970s, with only 58% of its planes able to fly on any given day, seven plane crashes (often due to faulty maintenance) every 100,000 hours flown, and pilots unable to fly enough hours to maintain combat readiness. Bill Creech, an experienced Air Force general, led an organizational turnaround in which decentralization played a key role (Finegan 1987; Creech 1994:114-57). Prior to this, at each base squadrons (or teams of twenty-four pilots) were flying aircraft from a central pool serviced by a central pool of mechanics.

Creech decided that the squadron should become the key organizational unit of TAC. He assigned both planes and mechanics to squadrons. Then he decentralized supply operations to give the squadrons many more spare parts and improved the computer system so that squadron mechanics could know quickly which parts were available centrally. Finally, he gave squadron commanders autonomy in planning their own sorties. This decentralization was reflected at the symbolic level by giving mechanics the same squadron insignia as pilots, painting squadron insignia on aircraft, and painting pilots' and mechanics' names side-by-side on aircraft. Creech also improved working conditions for mechanics by upgrading their living quarters and investing in training. Creech set clear and measurable goals for squadrons, encouraging them to compete with one another in terms of performance and gave recognition to the best-performing squadrons.

By 1984 when Creech retired, the performance of the TAC had improved dramatically. Aircraft availability had risen from 58% to 85%, pilots were flying an average of twenty-nine hours per month as opposed to seventeen, and the crash rate had fallen to one-fourth its previous level. The re-enlistment rate for first-time mechanics had nearly doubled from 35% to 66%. All this was achieved without any increase in budget or staff. In addition, Creech's doctrine of radical decentralization has been replicated by other commands in the Air Force, as well as by the Army. The Air Force leadership identified Creech's reforms as contributing significantly to their success during the Gulf War (Creech 1994:121-3). Creech's innovations achieved results on all three dimensions discussed above: impact on performance, replication, and sustainability.

The Ontario Development Corporation (ODC) was established as a Crown corporation in 1966 to provide loans to small manufacturers, tourism operators, and other businesses that could not find conventional funding (Borins 1993a). By the mid-1980s it was badly in need of major reform. While the ODC's fiscal responsibilities and loan portfolio had grown, its technology and management practices were woefully out-of-date. In 1985, David MacKinnon, an M.B.A. with experience in both government and business, was brought in from the Bank of Montreal to lead a turnaround. This involved a number of changes, including redefining the role of the board of directors and computerizing the corporation's lending and information systems.

Decentralization was also an important part of the turnaround process. Lending officers were moved from the head office in Toronto to fourteen regional offices, and regional managers were given a higher threshold for lending and loan guarantees. ODC had previously been organized on functional lines, with different units responsible for loan applications, disbursements, administration, etc. As a result, borrowers dealt with several staff members during the life of their loans and a great deal of intraorganizational negotiation was required among the different units responsible for any loan. This was changed to a "one window" approach, in which a staff member was given responsibility for all phases of a loan. The objective of both these changes was to improve customer service by pushing decision-making authority closer to the customer and simplifying communication between the customer and the ODC. Conversely, this increased accountability for staff, who were required to live with the consequences of their initial decisions. To prepare front-line staff for their new responsibilities, the ODC expanded its management education program. The set of changes MacKinnon introduced resulted in substantial productivity gains at the ODC, as evidenced by a doubling of its loan portfolio between 1986 and 1993, with a very small increase in staff. In addition, ODC's default rate has been reduced to 4%, only slightly higher than the chartered banks' rate of 3%.

A fourth type of innovation is *case management*. In many public management processes, complicated sequences of interactions with the client (whether an individual, a family, or a business) are required. If the public sector agency responsible for the process is organized on functional lines, the client must deal with a number of functional specialists;

similarly, if the process requires the cooperation of several different agencies, the client may be required to interact with representatives of each agency. This type of interaction has several consequences: clients become frustrated because they do not know whom they are to deal with and when; time is wasted by frequent transfers of the case or file from one unit or organization to another; and clients, frustrated by the process, often contact any of the units they are dealing with to find out about how their case is progressing, and the time spent providing such status reports increases overall delays.

In such circumstances, both public and private sector organizations have developed case management as a way of improving client service (Davenport and Nohria 1994). Case management involves reorganizing a service along process lines and appointing case managers who are responsible for seeing the process through from beginning to end. Case managers do not themselves develop the entire set of skills required to deliver all the services in the process; rather, they have learned enough about the skills involved that they can coordinate the process. Client confusion is eliminated because the primary contact is the case manager. Also, the case manager can easily update the client about how the case is progressing.

The following are a number of examples of public sector case management. They are primarily in the social services area, where government programs are designed to deal with difficult and multidimensional personal problems. As part of a turnaround, the Alberta Workers Compensation Board (WCB) initiated a case management approach for its most difficult rehabilitation cases (Borins 1991; 1993a). Previously, injured workers were required to deal with one part of the organization while their employers dealt with another. WCB reorganized to create a new Operations Division with responsibility for all client contact. Cases are now assigned to case managers, who are responsible for all contact, whether with workers, employers, or health care professionals.

One of the most difficult social problems in the United States is substance abuse by pregnant women. It is a major reason the infant mortality rate in the core areas of many cities in the United States is at Third World levels. Two projects using a case management approach to improve birth and development outcomes are the San Francisco Department of Health's Child and Mothers Parenting Project (1993) and the Baltimore City Health Department's Baltimore Project (1993). The former was a semifinalist and the latter a finalist in the 1993 Ford Foundation-Kennedy School of Government innovation awards. In the San Francisco project (CHAMP), public health nurses were the case managers, while the Baltimore Project trained and employed neighbourhood residents to play that role. In both, case managers work with the entire family, and attempt to coordinate treatment of many health and wellness issues, including drug addiction, family planning, education, and poverty. Thus, not only do these programs provide addiction treatment, but they also refer clients to other programs in the areas of health, general education, and housing assistance. In addition, the staff of CHAMP and the Baltimore Project now realize that the problems of clients are both serious and interrelated; as a consequence their mandate has been extended beyond the pregnancy period into infancy.

In both programs, the medical outcomes of participants (infant mortality rate, birth weight, frequency of infant hospitalization) have improved to approximate more closely those of the middle class. The Baltimore Project reports that it achieved a high enrolment rate of 85% of the pregnant women in its target neighbourhood and a two-year retention rate of over 90%. The Baltimore Project also sees the use of neighbourhood residents as an effective outreach mechanism, a way of bringing income into the neighbourhood, and a step in community transformation. While the CHAMP project costs $2000 per family, residential care for perinatal clients ($15,000 per year) and foster home placement for substance-exposed infants ($1500 per month) are much more expensive.

The fifth and final type of innovation is *organizational re-engineering*. This involves analyzing, and then reorganizing, the operations of a business or public sector organization on a process basis (Hammer and Champy 1993:31-82). This approach attempts to achieve fundamental change, rather than simply make marginal improvements on existing processes. Re-engineering is often a combination of many of the innovations discussed above, since it requires improved information technology and restructures processes so as to increase the autonomy of front-line workers, who are often operating as case managers. The following are three examples of total process reorganization in the public sector.

The Swedish National Student Aid Board (Kelman 1992) in 1978 and 1979 re-engineered its process for approving loans to university students by using a powerful computer system, decentralizing authority to staff in its local offices, and making staff case managers for the entire loan application process. Loan repayment servicing was improved by giving telephone service representatives computers that could access any student's account. The Board was so effective that the Swedish Finance Ministry gave it a mandate for high school student loans as well; the Board was soon able to do with twenty-nine people the work previously done by two hundred employed by local governments. In 1991 it was chosen by the Swedish government's executive development agency as one of the four best-performing Swedish government agencies. Given that the original innovation took place in the late 1970s, this innovation clearly demonstrates sustainability.

In addition to establishing a case management system for injured workers, the Alberta Workers' Compensation Board also re-engineered its rehabilitation centre (Alberta Workers' Compensation Board 1993). It redefined the focus of its multidisciplinary rehabilitation teams from a concentration on particular types of injuries (e.g., back, lower extremities) to dealing with the injuries incurred in different occupations. In this procedure, known as "work hardening," the teams study the types of injuries occurring in their industry and then develop real or simulated work activities that would be introduced as early as possible into the treatment. This approach led to an 86% productivity gain in 1991 and a reduction of the average length of stay at the rehabilitation centre from fifty-nine to forty-five days. This re-engineering of the rehabilitation process won second prize in the 1993 IPAC innovative management competition.

The City of Cleveland won a 1993 Ford Foundation-Kennedy School of Government innovation award for re-engineering its process of handling property tax delinquency to facilitate the process of urban redevelopment (Government Action on Urban Land 1993). Many properties in central Cleveland had been abandoned, leaving the city with over $30 million in uncollectible taxes and serious social problems, such as the use of those properties as crack houses. The city developed a streamlined, but constitutionally sound, procedure for foreclosing on those properties and then offering them at a sheriff's sale. The offer price covered the delinquent taxes, so as to discourage land speculation. Unsold properties are stripped of their tax obligation and put into the city's land bank. The land bank has now assembled large parcels of land that are being sold to developers. In some instances low interest mortgages are being made available. The city has also introduced a form of case management, assigning one community development staff member to each developer to help them with procedures for assembling land, securing financing, and getting building permits. The outcome is a dramatic increase in development in the central city: in 1986, there were 183 properties foreclosed and 89 new units of housing built; while in 1992, there were 1764 properties foreclosed and 653 new units of housing built.

The assumption people usually make about innovation is that it is most likely to happen in small organizations. However, the examples presented in this section include organizations of all sizes, as shown in Table 1, which presents three different measures of organizational size – annual budget, staff in person-years, and number of clients. This supports the argument that change is occurring in public sector organizations that have always been regarded as machine bureaucracies. It is also interesting to note that in two of the three largest organizations (U.S. Tactical Air Command and Correctional Services of Canada) the innovation involved decentralization.

IMPLICATIONS FOR ORGANIZATIONAL STRUCTURE AND HUMAN RESOURCE MANAGEMENT ISSUES

The previous section has presented numerous examples of innovative public sector organizations that are doing their work differently. If one thinks systemically, it is clear that the widespread adoption of these practices will have dramatic implications for organizational structure, and for many human resource management issues such as job content, working conditions, pay and benefits, and labour-management relations. The purpose of this final section is to begin to trace out at least some of these implications.

Hammer and Champy (1993:65) draw a very vivid picture of "the new world of work" in re-engineered organizations where

TABLE 1
Measures of Organizational Scale

Organization	Annual Budget	Staff(PYs)*	Number of Clients
InfoCalifornia	$ 1 million u.s.	4	pilot project, 15 kiosks 20,000 clients/month
Public Electronic Network	$ 130,000 u.s.		5300 citizens
Vendor Info Program			24,000 bidders
Open Bidding System			10,000 bidders
Automated Child Support Enforcement System	$36 million u.s.	53	220,000 cases
City of Chicago Parking Enforcement	$11 million u.s.	215	
Seattle Community Voice Mail	$66,000 u.s.	1	230 clients
Computer Learning Center	$98,000 u.s.		250 children
L.A. Telecommuting		78,000	2600 participants
Franchise Tax Board		5,000	
Correctional Services	$1 billion CDN.	10,000	13,000 inmates
Tactical Air Cmnd.	$40 billion u.s.	115,000	
Ont. Dev. Corp.		200	$1 billion CDN. in loans
CHAMP	$230,000 u.s.	3	55 families
Baltimore Project	$650,000 u.s.		265 pregnant women
Nat'l. Student Aid Bd.		200	500,000 students
Alberta WCB		160	1000 injured workers
City of Cleveland Land Bank	$1.4 million u.s.		

*PYs = person years

"jobs evolve from narrow and task-oriented to multidimensional. People who once did as they were instructed now make choices and decisions on their own instead. Assembly-line work disappears. Functional departments lose their reasons for being. Managers stop acting like supervisors and behave more like coaches. Workers focus more on the customers' needs and less on their bosses'. Attitudes and values change in response to new incentives. Practically every aspect of the organization is transformed, often beyond recognition."

The innovative organizations discussed in the previous section illustrate this model. In most instances, the key player making the innovation happen is the front-line worker: the administrative officer adjudicating parking tickets in Chicago, the social worker keeping in touch with a caseload by voice mail in Seattle, members of a unit management team in the Correctional Services of Canada, the mechanics in the Tactical Air Command, the lending officer at the Ontario Development Corporation, the case manager at the Alberta Workers' Compensation Board, the neighbourhood health worker in Baltimore, the applications officer at the Swedish National Student Aid Board, and the community development officer in the City of Cleveland.

Their work environment has changed in a number of ways. They have now been given supportive information technology. Their jobs have become more challenging and meaningful as they assume responsibility for coherent processes, rather than for limited functions. They coordinate the efforts of people in different organizations to deliver a service to their clients. They have more discretion and autonomy than previously.

These workers show how new, flexible, service-oriented public sector organizations are being built on the front lines. However, for this to happen, some conditions must be fulfilled. One is a more decentralized organizational structure, as we have seen in a number of cases. Another is supportive information technology. A third, closely related to the second, is management education. If front-line workers are to use new information technology effectively, they need to learn how. Realizing this, the Gore Report (1993:79-80) recommends a major investment in technology training. As front-line jobs become more challenging along other dimensions besides technology, many other kinds of training, such as management skills and quality management, will also become necessary (Gore 1993:77-8 and 90-1). The experience of the California Franchise Tax Board, consistent with many critiques of the public school system, suggests that the new work force lacks the necessary skills of literacy and numeracy to function effectively in today's more demanding front-line jobs. This underlines the need for government organizations to invest more in educating their workers. However, government organizations have traditionally lagged behind their private sector counterparts in training, as measured, for example, by the percentage of total expenditures allocated to training. This will have to change.

Another area where the government will be spending more money is on technology itself. The application of information technology has been slower in the public than in the private sector, in part because of the accounting system in the former. Public sector organizations are traditionally funded by annual budgets. Information technology is a major up-front investment; its productivity increases and resulting cost-savings will become evident in subsequent years. Unless the results are so dramatic that the payback period is less than a year, financially constrained government agencies may be unable to afford information technology.[3] One way of dealing with this problem is through the creation of internal equivalents to the private sector's capital markets. For example, the Gore Report (Gore 1993:110-11), emulating the experience of the City of Philadelphia, recommends the creation of departmental innovation funds, which are designed to fund cost-saving innovations and investments in technology. Of course, another way to deal with this problem is to change the public sector's accounting system to an accrual, rather than a cash, basis.

This section has emphasized that front-line staff will become the winners in the new public sector. Will there be losers? Secretarial work (reception, typing, filing) will virtually disappear, as voice mail replaces receptionists, front-line workers learn to do their own typing at their work stations, and records are kept electronically. Clearly, there will be major cost-savings here to fund the acquisition of modern telephone systems, computers, software, and the cost of training.

A second threatened group will be middle managers. Their role as information conduits is being superseded by information technology. As front-line workers gain more autonomy, they will need less supervision; they will need coaching, but that requires fewer people than with supervision. In the past, the optimal span of control was thought to be seven; in new organizations it is twenty-five or more. As a threatened group, it is likely that middle managers will tend to resist these changes. One would like to think that middle managers could be brought on board by retraining and by enlisting them to work as coaches for front-line workers. The problem with their being coaches is that they are unlikely to be comfortable with either new technologies or new management styles. If so, the only remaining alternative is to offer incentives to early retirement; like training, this will impose short-term costs on the public sector. Governments could facilitate this by establishing central early-retirement funds, similar to the innovation funds mentioned above, that individual departments can draw on.

This changed organizational structure will have implications for the pay structure. As front-line workers' jobs become more challenging and productive, we can expect their constant dollar salaries to increase. As hierarchies are flattened, salary differentials between managers and front-line staff may be reduced, as is consistent with academic institutions, where middle managers such as department chairs and deans usually receive only a small temporary bonus. If the output of front-line workers can be measured, rewards could be based on performance; for example, by means of the variable compensation schemes found in the private sector. Thus, the most productive front-line workers would be paid more than their managers, as is the case in the private sector, where a vice president of sales would be paid less than the best salesperson or a vice president of foreign exchange operations would be paid less than the best contracts trader.

During the 1960s and 1970s the public sector created many policy and planning units, staffed with people of much higher educational attainments than front-line workers. The young M.P.A.s and PH.D.s in these positions were often on the fast track to senior positions. These smart young staffers, lacking experience in service delivery, were often criticized by front-line workers for developing theoretically attractive but organizationally impractical new programs. If today's public sector organizations begin to take seriously their rhetoric about empowering front-line workers, it is clear that front-line workers will be playing a much larger role in policy development than previously and that, conversely, the policy and planning units will be playing a much more supportive role. This redefinition of the relationship between policy and planning units is another case of the breakdown of the bureaucratic paradigm that separated thinking from doing, assigning the former to the leadership and its staff and the latter to the line operations.

A classic example of this redefinition of the relationship between staff and line occurred at the New York City Bureau of Motor Equipment (New York City Bureau of Motor Equipment 1992; Contino and Lorusso 1982). It won one of the ten 1992 Ford Foundation-Kennedy School of Government innovation awards for the creation of an internal research network that dramatically improved the performance of that city's vehicle maintenance operation and worked with manufacturers to improve the design of the vehicles. A key step in this innovation was assigning mechanics, the front-line workers, to the research and development unit that had previously been staffed exclusively by more highly educated engineers. This innovation was launched in 1979 and refined in the ensuing years, so it certainly passes the sustainability test.

New public sector organizational structures will also have implications for the role played by public sector unions. It is no surprise that unions came into existence in the world of the machine bureaucracy: when jobs were being designed along dehumanizing Taylorist principles, workers joined unions to maximize their compensation from employers who were, in effect, renting their bodies. To some extent, unions have responded suspiciously to attempts to re-engineer production. As a consequence, employers establishing the most advanced production systems (for example, Japanese auto makers opening new factories in North America) have attempted to avoid unionization.

In the cases discussed in the previous section there are two examples about innovations encountering union opposition. When the County of Los Angeles proposed its telecommuting program, the union opposed it because they felt telecommuting ought to be an employee benefit, that employees with the most seniority should be given the first chance to telecommute, and that the county should provide the equipment. After negotiation, the county and the union agreed that telecommuting workers would still receive all normal benefits, including workers' compensation coverage, and that the county would inform the union of all changes in the program. However, participation was not determined by seniority. In addition, a survey that showed great employee willingness to provide their own equipment led the union to back down on its position that the county provide the equipment (County of Los Angeles Telecommuting Program 1993). The City of Chicago Parking Enforcement Program also faced union opposition because the program resulted in the elimination of some clerical jobs. However, the city was firm in its resolve to implement the program and agreed to help displaced employees find other assignments (City of Chicago Parking Enforcement Program 1991).

Unions that attempt to resist these trends may be fighting a losing battle, for several reasons. In instances where innovations, such as telecommuting, improve working conditions, workers will favour them and management will go, or threaten to go, directly to the workers for support. In instances where innovations increase productivity and lead to a reduction in employment, management will go directly to the overtaxed voters to override union opposition. Finally, governments are unlikely to face union opposition to attempts to reduce the ranks of middle management because managers are not unionized.

A final implication of these new organizational structures concerns the aggregate level of public sector employment. Undoubtedly, it will be smaller. For example, the Gore Report (Gore 1993:13-14) foresees the elimination of 252,000 positions, bringing the federal public service in the United States down to below two million jobs for the first time since 1966. Public service employment in Canada, at both federal and provincial levels, is moving in the same direction. As a result of the application of new technology and the implementation of new systems of organization, we will have a more productive public service, doing a great deal more work with fewer people. These fewer jobs will be more stimulating jobs than in the past.

However, like the private sector, which is also restructuring, downsizing, and re-engineering, the public sector will be contributing to the social problem of structural unemployment. That the private sector contributes to structural unemployment is no surprise, given that organizational survival depends on profitability. Nevertheless many people, particularly those holding the Keynesian view, see the public sector as the employer of last resort. The view developed in this chapter is quite the opposite. The forces of technology, international competition, and a changing work force are leading both the public and private sectors in the same direction – automation, restructuring, and re-engineering. Individual government departments and agencies should not be required to solve the structural unemployment problem through deliberate inefficiency.

Given the debt load faced by many governments, it is doubtful that fiscal policy, at either the national or subnational level, can do much to increase aggregate employment. Thus, the most sustainable role for the public sector may be to produce a skilled, imaginative, and inventive work force. Even that modest role will provide a substantial challenge to the public sector's capacity to deliver training and educational programs. If such programs are effective, the resulting work force should be able to find work by attracting mobile capital. If public sector organizations are innovative in their application of technology and design of jobs and organizational structures, public sector careers will appeal to that same work force and attract many of the best and the brightest. And that would be a much more compelling vision for the public sector than using outdated technology and management practices to be the employer of last resort.

NOTES

1 The comments of the editors and other authors of this volume, as well as the participants in a seminar of assistant deputy ministers to whom a previous draft of this paper was presented, are gratefully acknowledged. Nevertheless, I assume full responsibility for the views presented here.
2 Brian Marson of c.c.m.d tells the story of the traditional public manager who, when told that his organization's customers were becoming angry at having to wait an average of 30 minutes for service, suggested that his staff simply remove the clock behind the counter.
3 In some instances, such as replacing receptionists with voice mail, the pay-back period is probably less than a year. It is interesting to note that, by now, over 80% of the Fortune 500 largest American corporations have voice-mail systems.

BIBLIOGRAPHY

Alberta Workers' Compensation Board. 1993. Application to the IPAC innovative management award.

Automated Child Support Enforcement Program. 1993. Semifinalist application to the innovations in state and local government awards program.

Baltimore Project. 1993. Semifinalist application to the innovations in state and local government awards program.

Barzelay, Michael, and B.J. Armajani. 1992. *Breaking through Bureaucracy: A New Vision for Managing in Government*. Berkeley: University of California Press.

Barzelay, Michael, and Jillian Dickert. 1993. The California Franchise Tax Board: strategies for a changing workforce. John F. Kennedy School of Government, case C16-93-1202.4.

Borins, Sandford. 1991. The encouragement and study of improved public management: the Institute of Public Administration of Canada innovative management award. *International Review of Administrative Sciences* 57:179-94.

_____ 1993a. Toward a theory of public sector turnarounds. Paper presented at the annual conference of the International Association of Schools and Institutes of Administration, July, in Toluca, Mexico.

_____ 1993b. Public management innovation awards in the u.s. and Canada. Paper presented at the Seminar on Concepts and Methods of Quality Awards in the Public Sector, October, in Speyer, Germany.

Children and Mothers Parenting Project. 1993. Semifinalist application to the state and local government awards program.

City of Chicago Parking Enforcement Program. 1991. Semifinalist application to the state and local government awards program.

Community Voice Mail. 1993. Semifinalist application to the state and local government awards program.

Computer Learning Centers. 1993. Semifinalist application to the state and local government awards program.

Contino, Ronald, and Robert Lorusso. 1982. The theory Z turnaround of a public agency. *Public Administration Review* (January/February):66-72.

County of Los Angeles Telecommuting Program. 1993. Semifinalist application to the state and local government awards program.

Creech, Bill. 1994. *The Five Pillars of TQM*. New York: Dutton.

Davenport, Thomas, and Nitin Nohria. 1994. Case management and the integration of labor. *Sloan Management Review* 35:11-23.

Finegan, Jay. 1987. Four-star management. *INC* (January/February):42-51.

Gore, Albert J. 1993. *Creating a Government that Works Better and Costs Less: Report of the National Performance Review.* New York: Times Books.

Government Action on Urban Land. 1993. Semifinalist application to the state and local government awards program.

Hammer, Michael, and James Champy. 1993. *Re-engineering the Corporation.* New York: HarperCollins.

Heskett, James. 1987. Lessons in the service sector. *Harvard Business Review* (March/April):118-26.

InfoCalifornia. 1993. Semifinalist application to the state and local government awards program.

Jenkins, Glenn. 1992. Economic reform and institutional innovation. *International Bureau of Fiscal Documentation Bulletin:*588-96.

Kelman, Steve. 1992. Managing student aid in Sweden. John F. Kennedy School of Government, case C16-93-1161.3.

Mintzberg, Henry. 1979. *The Structuring of Organizations.* Englewood Cliffs, NJ: Prentice-Hall.

Morgan, Gareth. 1986. *Images of Organization.* Beverly Hills, CA: Sage.

New York City Bureau of Motor Equipment. 1992. Semifinalist application to the state and local government awards program.

Patton, Phil. 1993. Disk-Drive Democrats. *The New York Times* (28 November):v, 7.

Public Electronic Network. 1993. Semifinalist application to the state and local government awards program.

Simon, Harvey. 1993. InfoCalifornia: where do electronic government tellers belong? John F. Kennedy School of Government, case C16-93-1204.0.

Supply and Services Canada. 1993. Application to the IPAC innovative management award.

Vantour, Jim. 1991. Ed. *Our Story: Organization Renewal in Federal Corrections.* Ottawa: Canadian Centre for Management Development.

Vendor Information Program. 1993. Semifinalist application to the state and local government awards program.

Weber, Max. 1959. *From Max Weber: Essays in Sociology.* Ed. H.H. Gerth and C.W. Mills. New York: Oxford University Press.

The Public Service, the Changing State, and Governance

B. GUY PETERS

Dwight Waldo (1968) once wrote that public administration has had so many identity crises that in comparison the life of the average adolescent appeared idyllic. Professor Waldo was discussing public administration as an academic discipline, but the contemporary practice of public administration displays much of the same uncertainty. The questions of practice concern the structure of government, management of those structures, and the proper role of public administration in governance. Many of the old certainties about government and the role of the public service are now either totally altered or subject to severe questioning. At least four of the old chestnuts that have guided our thinking about the public service and its role in the process of governance clearly are simply no longer as canonical as they once were.[1] The first of these principles is the assumption of an apolitical civil service, and associated with that the politics/administration dichotomy and the concept of the "neutral competence" (Kaufman 1956) within the civil service. It is increasingly clear that civil servants do have significant, if not necessarily dominant, policy roles in most contemporary governments (Peters 1992) and that governance is probably better because they do.

The problem then is how to structure government in ways that recognize the reality, and even the desirability, of the enhanced policy roles for civil servants while at the same time preserving the requirements of democratic accountability. This is a difficult balance for the designers of government institutions to achieve, especially given the historical legacy of thinking about the neutrality of the civil service in Anglo-American democracies and public demands for enhanced accountability (Gruber 1987; Day and Klein 1987). Furthermore, political leaders have come to recognize the growing role of civil servants in formulating policy, and in response they have often acted to try to minimize that role (Ingraham 1987; Aberbach and Rockman 1988). The struggle over the competence to make policy, therefore, is now more obvious to those working within government, as well as to citizens on the outside. The politicization of the role of the civil service, if not the members of the civil service themselves, may make the delicate balance of policy competencies mentioned above all the more difficult to achieve.

The second significant change in government relevant to this discussion is the decline of the assumption of hierarchical and rule-based management within the public service, and the authority of civil servants to implement and enforce regulations outside the public service. The neat Weberian model of management does not apply within public organizations to the extent that it once did, and in its place we encounter a variety of alternative sources of organizational power and authority. As one example, the market may be an increasingly significant standard against which to compare the structure and performance of government organizations (Lan and Rosenbloom 1992; Hood 1990; Boston 1991). While the inherent differences between the public and private sectors are crucial to understanding governance (Allison 1980), even governments on the political left have implemented a number of market-based reforms in their structures and procedures.[2]

An alternative to the market model, as well as to traditional models of bureaucracy, is the "dialectic" or participatory organization. This model has been discussed by scholars for a number of years, but government organizations are being placed under increasing pressure to accommodate the interests of lower-level employees, as well as clients, in their decision-making processes (Barzelay 1992). This change in management is at once a manipulative mechanism for increasing efficiency and a genuine moral commitment to participation (Thomas 1993). Contemporary public organizations may also be expected to negotiate societal compliance with their decisions and compliance with contracts for service delivery, rather than directly implement programs through law and other authoritative means. The spread of network conceptualizations in the social sciences has been paralleled by increased network practices in governance (Scharpf 1991; Kenis and Schneider 1991). Finally, civil servants increasingly may be expected to make their own decisions about what constitutes the public interest, and they must at times make determinations that are diametrically opposed to the stated policies and desires of their nominal political masters.[3] All of the above changes make the role of civil service managers even more difficult than it has been, and they also make the role of civil servants within governments all the more ambiguous.

The third change in the assumptions about governance and the public bureaucracy concerns the permanence and stability of the organizations within government. Joining a public organization is sometimes seen as being the same as joining a Japanese corporation once was – as a lifetime's employment. The permanence of public organizations is frequently overestimated (Peters and Hogwood 1988) but it has been an important partial truth about government. Increasingly this pattern of permanent organization is being attacked. The increased recognition of the dysfunctions of permanence, as well as the recognition that many of the most significant social and economic problems currently exist in the interstices of existing organizations, has led to some discussion of alternative forms of government organization. The character of the alternative organizational structures remains somewhat inchoate at present, but the discussion has begun. In particular, ideas about task forces, "czars," interdepartmental committees, and similar structures have generated options for thinking about a more flexible pattern of governance.[4]

In addition to impermanent government organizations, the personnel commitments of government also have come to be considered less permanent. Government organizations increasingly expand and contract to meet the variable demand for work, for example, in tax offices. While this style of personnel management has the potential to save governments money, it produces a number of empirical and normative questions for managers and policy makers. This change may produce even more difficulties for citizens: they may have to cope with public employees who lack the commitment to service and the other public values that, in most instances, have characterized the civil service.

The last of the "chestnuts" is that the civil service should be acquiescent and respond almost entirely to the policy directives given to them by their nominal political masters. This goes beyond the question of political neutrality mentioned above. Many of the problems associated with government, and especially with the public bureaucracy, are a function of the controls imposed by political leaders seeking greater control and accountability (Walters 1992). Government organizations are generally among the most stringently regulated organizations in any society (Wilson 1989). Therefore, if the skills and entrepreneurship of public employees could be employed more freely, then government is likely to be able to perform more efficiently and effectively (Osborne and Gaebler 1992).

Rather than looking back to these vestiges of the past, this chapter will attempt to be prospective and to examine several alternative paths of development for the public service. We will develop these several alternative models of the state that appear to be emerging, and we will then look at the implications of these state models for the civil service. Except for the "market model," these alternatives have not been articulated in any comprehensive fashion, and we will have to extract these, almost as ideal types, from academic and practical discussions of governing. Further, there is some similarity of analyses and prescriptions across some of these models, although the meanings attached to them may be quite different (Roth 1987). They all have the effect, however, of "hollowing" out the state and making it, and particularly the public service, a less significant actor in society (Peters, forthcoming). This discussion will concentrate on these developments in governance within the United States, but it will also make some comparative allusions. What is perhaps most interesting in the comparative analysis is the extent to which the alternative visions have appeared more strongly and clearly in official documents than they have in scholarly writings in many countries.[5] Although focused on alternatives, we will also argue that one possible model is a vigorous restatement of the status quo ante and its less manifestly political and policy-making role for the civil service. For many civil servants, and probably for even more politicians, the "old time religion" may still be the best way to run a government.

Few governments in the Western world have remained untouched by the wave of reform that has swept through the public sector over the past several decades. The reforms that have been undertaken in most political systems may have been unprecedented, but they have also tended to be rather piecemeal and unsystematic (Savoie and Peters, forthcoming). This absence of clear visions and integrated strategies may explain, in part, why the results of the reforms have tended to disappoint so many of their advocates (Caiden 1990). What we will attempt to do in this chapter, therefore, is to explicate several more integrated visions of possible futures for the state bureaucracy. The nature of each image will, in turn, influence the manner in which governance might be practised under such a regime. If the implications of these alternative visions are more fully explored and understood, and contrasted with the conventional wisdom about governance, then there is some possibility, albeit no guarantee, of more effective planned change in government.

Our concern here with alternative visions does not mean that any of these schemes is superior to the traditional model of the civil service in governance. I tend to think that is not the case, but I do think that continuing reform in government is likely, and if that reform is to occur it is more likely to be effective if it is systematic and integrated. We should also, however, remain cognizant of the internal contradictions of some of these approaches. It may be that like Simon's discussion (1947) of the "proverbs of administration," thinking about the complexities of the public service, even when guided by a relatively strong set of theoretical assumptions, tends toward situational rather than systematic remedies.

As we look at these several alternatives to the traditional system of governance we will be looking at the implications and prescriptions of each "vision" for several aspects of governing. The first of these concerns structure: how should the public sector be organized? The second issue is personnel: how should the members of the public sector be recruited, motivated, and managed? Third is the policy process: what should the role of the career public service be in the policy process and, more generally, how should government seek to influence the private sector? Finally, these visions of governance each contains a conception of the public interest and an overall conceptualization of what constitutes "good government."

Market Model

The most familiar, and seemingly the most popular among politicians, of the alternatives to the traditional model of administration is the market model. The development of this model has several intellectual roots. The first is the analysis of the failings of conventional bureaucracies made by scholars such as Niskanen (1971), Tullock (1965), Moe (1984; 1989), Ostrom (1986) and a host of other devotees of public choice (Bendor 1990). They argued that because of the self-interest of the members of the organizations, especially the "bureau chiefs" at the apex, public bureaucracies tended to expand at an unjustifiable rate and to charge their sponsors (read legislatures) too much for the services produced. The permanence of bureaucrats and their monopoly of information were considered to put them at a competitive advantage when dealing with the legislature. The root of any failings in the public sector, as seen from this perspective, is the self-interest of bureaucrats.[6]

The second intellectual root of the market approach to governance in the public sector is generic management and its ally the "new public management" (Pollitt 1990; Massey 1993). This corpus of analysis functions under the assumption that management is management no matter where it takes place and that instruments used to organize and motivate personnel are as applicable in the public sector as they are in the private. Thus, rather than deploring the absence of a sense of the public interest, as the public choice literature often appears to do, this approach to the public sector assumes the lack of any meaningful difference between the two sectors and then builds a series of management recommendations on that similarity.

At a relatively high intellectual plane the recommendations of this variant of managerial thinking can be based upon the ubiquity of principal-agent relationships (Perrow 1986) and the applicability of transaction cost analysis (Williamson 1975; Calista 1989) in organizations, whether they are public or private. At a lower level of academic development, generic management is often the accepted doctrine of outsiders who want to export their favourite management techniques – MBO, TQM, etc. – to the public sector.7 At both levels of conceptualization the approach has been criticized by insiders (scholars and practitioners), who consider management in the public sector to be a distinctive form of activity.

Structure. The market approach assumes that one of the principal problems with the traditional structure of the public sector is a reliance on large, monopolistic departments that receive little direction from their environment. The size and complexity of government organizations, combined with their delivery of unpriced goods and services, is seen (especially by students of public choice) to be the root of a good deal of the (perceived) inefficiency and ineffectiveness of government. These structural difficulties are accentuated by the emphasis on formal rules and authority as the guides for action within traditional public organizations, rather than a dependence on either market signals (Rose 1989) or the entrepreneurial spirit of individuals to guide decisions.

The prescriptions arising from this diagnosis of the source of problems in public organizations are rather obvious. One of the central elements of reform is the decentralization of policy and implementation decisions. This decentralization can be done through the splitting up of large departments into smaller "agencies," through assigning functions to lower levels of government, or through using private or quasi-private organizations to deliver public services. This advice is particularly applicable when the good or service in question is marketable. In the most extreme versions of this approach, government would create multiple, competitive organizations to supply the same goods and services, with the expectation that the same competitive mechanisms presumed to work in the private sector would also work for the public sector.

The advice to divide large departments into smaller segments is less applicable to the United States than it has been to government in other developed democracies. We have not had to go through the exercise of creating a large number of agencies and corporate bodies as in the United Kingdom, New Zealand, and the Netherlands

(Davies and Willman 1991; Boston 1991; Kickert, forthcoming). The cabinet departments in the United States have traditionally granted substantial autonomy to their component agencies, and those organizations have been able to act somewhat autonomously. Of course, the admonitions of market proponents about the relationship of these agencies to market forces have not been followed very often, so that they were autonomous more in a political sense than in the sense of operating as quasi firms supplying goods and services in the marketplace. For the United States, the structural recommendations have been more in the direction of creating private and quasi-private organizations that will provide the services once provided by government. Full privatization has been more significant at the state and local level, but contracting and other instruments for introducing market forces have been significant at the federal level.

This approach has some structural recommendations at the microlevel within organizations, as well as for the macrolevel of entire departments. The emphasis on entrepreneurial activity and individual responsibility (see below) tends to press for relatively flat organizations with little of the layering that traditional public organizations tended to consider essential for control and consistency in decisions. Advocates of the approach tend to presume that the leader of the organization, as well as the "bottom line" resulting from the organization's dealings with the external environment will be more effective than a hierarchy would be in producing appropriate decisions. This observation points to the importance of relatively integrated as opposed to piecemeal reforms. Structural changes, without the associated changes in management, are unlikely to produce the benefits presumed by the theoretical presuppositions.

Management. The managerial implications of the market model also should be rather obvious. If workers in the public sector are considered to be very much the same as workers in the private sector, then the same managerial techniques should apply. This would mean that some of the cherished traditions of personnel management within government would have to be modified. These changes are already underway in a number of personnel areas, most obviously in the reward of public officials for their participation in government. In the public personnel system, individuals in the same grade of the civil service have traditionally been paid the same amount. This system is being replaced with a merit principle that says that people should be paid more closely to what they could earn in the market, and that better performance should be rewarded with better pay, regardless of any difference that may emerge between workers.

The emphasis on differential rewards for differential performance is especially important at the top management level of the small, relatively autonomous agencies created as a part of this approach. In several of the rewards schemes already implemented, managers are hired under contracts that contain specific performance standards. If the agency manager and his or her organization achieve those standards, the manager is eligible for full pay and perhaps bonuses. If the organization does not reach these goals then the manager may lose pay or be fired. In this model of the public sector, the manager is an entrepreneur responsible for what happens in the agency and is rewarded accordingly. Lower echelons within these organizations may be rewarded under similar contractual arrangements based on performance standards. The managerialist reward system in the United States, implemented as a part of the Civil Service Reform Act, is similar to those described above and depends upon bonuses at those echelons with some possibility of being dismissed. Merit pay programs also have been implemented at lower echelons. One of the greatest difficulties with these programs in the United States has been the failure of the political leadership to fund the bonuses and other incentives contained in the plans.

These reward schemes depend upon the capacity of government to measure the performance of its employees and their organizations. Any number of studies have demonstrated the severe difficulties encountered in attempting to perform this seemingly simple managerial task (Metcalfe and Richards 1990; Boston 1992). This is especially true if performance is to be measured at the output or impact level, rather than merely at the activity level. This measurement problem means, then, that either performance contracts and effective managerialism will be limited to the relatively few agencies or other parts of government providing marketable or otherwise measurable services, or it must depend upon a number of specious measures of performance. In either case the capacity to implement this aspect of the market vision of the public sector appears at least a little suspect.

We should also point out that these managerialist trends are not neutral in their effects on the perceived role of the public service. Although it is still difficult, measuring performance is substantially easier for the managerial and service delivery functions of the civil service than it is for the policy advice functions. As a result of this difficulty, adoption of managerialist performance evaluations and pay schemes will tend to have some bias in the direction of a more managerial and less policy role for civil servants. This may be true both because of changes in the signals coming from evaluators above and decisions on the part of the evaluated, who realize that they can maximize their own rewards by playing the managerial game.

Policy making. The third aspect of the market vision of the state we will examine is the conceptualization of the manner in which public policy should be made. In particular, we are concerned with the appropriate role of the career public service in making policy. A fundamental contradiction appears to reside at the heart of the role that this vision assigns to the bureaucracy. On the one hand, the market approach advocates the decentralization of bureaucratic functions and the creation of multiple, "entrepreneurial" agencies that would be expected to make autonomous decisions. These decisions presumably would be based either upon signals received from the market or on the judgment of the entrepreneurial leadership of the organization. Breaking the bonds of bureaucracy is meant to liberate decision making and produce more risk-taking and innovative activity.

On the other hand, the practitioners who have advocated this approach have expected compliance by these quasi-autonomous organizations with the policy and ideological directives coming from above. One of the consistent observations about the Reagan, Thatcher, and Mulroney governments and other similar regimes is that they have attempted to impose their own views on the civil service. Bureaucrats were seen as too committed to the growth of their own organizations, as well as being, perhaps, too committed to serving their narrow clientele rather than "the public interest." Attempts at politicization are by no means new, but they have been more overt over the past decade. Politicization has been seen by defenders of the traditional view as the erosion of one of the most important features of merit systems and the civil service. In some ways, however, this is merely a reaffirmation of the traditional view that civil servants should be on tap but not on top and that the political leaders were responsible for policy. Whether it is a part of the traditional conceptualization or not, there is some inconsistency and bureaucrats are having a set of perhaps unreasonable demands being placed upon them.

Even if that apparent inconsistency could be resolved, there would be some additional problems for policy making arising out of the application of this approach. One of the most important of these is the problem of coordination and control. The rather radical decentralization of policy making to more autonomous organizations provides relatively little opportunity for either senior bureaucrats or politicians to coordinate policy. One of the critiques of the traditional approach to governance has been that de facto the independence of the bureaucracy thwarted consistency across policies and often produced destructive competition (Allard 1990). The market approach appears to exalt that competition and potential inconsistency – so long as the actions conform to the political ideals of those political leaders. It is perhaps too much to believe that the leaders of autonomous agencies would be content to be managers of these organizations and would not become concerned with policy.

Finally, at a more conceptual level there is the problem of the role of the citizen. The market model tends to conceptualize the recipients of government programs, and the public more generally, as *consumers*. This is at once empowering and demeaning for the public. As a beneficial change, this conception provides the citizen with the same expectation of services that he or she has from a private sector firm.[8] Changes such as the Citizen's Charter in Britain and PS 2000 in Canada have many of these elements of consumerism in them (Lovell 1992). On the other hand, the citizen is now little more than a consumer, and his or her role as the holder of rights and a legal status vis-à-vis the state appears somewhat diminished. Government may be more than a matter of buying and selling, and probably should be more. If it is reduced to that level, then the citizen is a less significant figure in political theory than he or she is usually thought to be.

The Public Interest. The final component of the market vision of governance is how it defines the public interest. Although it is not clearly articulated as such, this vision does contain such a conceptualization. In the first place, government can be judged on the basis of how cheaply it can deliver public services. To achieve that goal government may have to undertake its activities in rather unconventional ways, for example, through creating multiple competing service providers. In the long run, however, the public – in their role as taxpayers – will be better served by services provided in this manner.

The second component of the market conceptualization of the public interest is that citizens should be considered to be consumers as well as taxpayers. Therefore, the public interest can be served by allowing citizens to exercise their free choices in a market for services. This can be accomplished both by breaking up the monopolies that traditionally have provided most public services and by providing to citizens the means of exercising freer choices. The options for citizens exercising their consumer choices can be expanded by providing vouchers for services such as education and perhaps housing (Chubb and Moe 1990). Those options might also be increased by expanding the information available to citizens about the service options available.

Summary. As noted, the market vision has been the most popular alternative view of the state and government. It tends to consider that public sector agencies face the same managerial- and service-delivery tasks as do organizations in the private sector, and that they are amenable to the same techniques for performing those tasks. It assumes that if the rule-based authority structure usually associated with bureaucracy is removed or de-emphasized, then there can be a flowering of the creative and administrative talent of individuals working within the public sector. Usually associated with the political right, some devotees of this approach consider that its successful implementation would result in a more effective and efficient public sector, whether delivering defence or social services.

The Participatory State

The second alternative view of the state we will discuss is almost the antithesis of the market approach in terms of the political ideologies of most of its advocates, but in some instances the analysis and recommendations appear remarkably similar. We have called this approach the "participatory state," but it has been discussed with a number of different names. An alternative characterization might be the "empowerment state," in which groups (presumably) excluded under more hierarchical models are permitted greater organizational involvement (Kernaghan 1992). Like the market approach, this approach considers the hierarchical, rule-based organizations usually encountered in the public sector to be a severe impediment to effective management and governance. However, rather than concentrating attention on the upper echelons of leadership in organizations who are the proto-entrepreneurs within government, this approach concentrates on the lower echelons or workers, as well as on the clients of the organizations.

The fundamental assumption in this approach is that there is a great deal of energy and talent being underutilized at the lower echelons of hierarchies, and that the workers and clients closest to the actual production of goods and services in the public sector have the greatest amount of information about the programs. It is assumed that if those ideas and talents are harnessed government will work better. The general prescription, therefore, is for greater participation and involvement on the part of those groups within government who are commonly excluded from decision making. Somewhat predictably, the advocates of this approach tend to come more from the political left, although some supporters from the right, interested in empowerment and self-management by clients, also advocate versions of this approach.[9]

The intellectual roots of the participatory state are also somewhat diverse. On the one hand there is a body of literature that argues that involvement and participation is the best way to motivate individual employees, even if it is somewhat manipulative. Another strand of literature argues that the lower echelons of public organizations are central to the effective functioning of those organizations and as a simple reality the role of "street level bureaucrats" needs to be recognized. At a higher intellectual level there are various strands of literature on "discursive democracy" and the like that argue for enhanced participation by clients and workers in the identification and clarification of problems within organizations.

Structure. The structural implications of this approach are somewhat less clear than are those for the public choice approach. For this approach process appears more important than the structures within which the processes take place. At one level, the formal patterns of organization may be irrelevant if there are other opportunities for the workers and clients to participate in decisions. There are, however, structural reforms that may make their participation easier, and therefore this approach is not entirely silent on the issue of the design of public organizations. In considering both participation and decision making we need to note the extent to which enhanced participation by one group – either lower-echelon employees or clients – may minimize the impact of the other.

The most obvious implication for structure is that, very much like the public choice approach, public organizations would be much "flatter" and have fewer tiers between the top and bottom of an organization. If indeed the lower echelons are perceived as having a great deal to offer in decision making and are highly motivated to provide good services, then hierarchical levels of control are merely impediments to good performance in an organization. The alternative implication, however, is that if clients and lower-echelon employees are to be given substantial involvement in making decisions there may be a need for greater control from above to ensure that public laws and financial restraints are adhered to faithfully.

One of the other structural implications of the participatory approach to governing is that there may need to be a variety of structures to channel participation. This is especially true for participation by clients, but it may also be true for lower-level employees who have not been as involved in decision making as is envisioned in this approach. As governments have come to implement programs of participation for both clients and workers, a variety of councils, advisory groups, and the like have come into being. It is interesting that much of this definition of the rights of participation, albeit defined as citizenship rights, in practice forms the rights of consumers. Again, this approach is brought closer to the market approach than might be expected from the political ideologies of its typical adherents.

Management. The participatory approach to governance contains somewhat more obvious implications for management within the public sector than it has for structure. The basic premise is that government organizations will function better if the lower levels of the organizations, and perhaps their clients, are included more directly in managerial decisions. At one level, this involvement might be considered to be manipulative, with top management exchanging a little bit of participation for greater productivity and loyalty from workers. While early "human relations" management had some of this manipulative character, the more contemporary advocates of participation have been more ideological and believe in the human as well as organizational importance of participation. Even then, however, there can be something of a manipulative element in thinking that overall societal governance can be enhanced through permitting and encouraging greater social "discourse" in the process of making decisions.

Perhaps the most important feature of the participative approach is its attempt to involve societal interests in governance more explicitly. We should remember, however, that these managerial ideologies are by no means the first theoretical justifications of enhanced participation. The neocorporatist and corporate pluralist literature represents another very strong strand of thinking about how to gain the advantages of the knowledge held by social groups and also their quiescence (Olsen 1986). The difference may be that this level of legitimate involvement of social interests is now becoming popular in countries with an Anglo-American political cultural legacy as well as in countries with a more Continental legacy. Thus, while the market model above may denigrate the role of the citizen, the participatory model appears to enhance the role of the citizen and to attempt to induce democratic participation in means other than voting.

Policy making. The implications of the participatory vision of governance for policy making are for a "bottom up" versus "top down" version of the policy process.[10] That is, this vision does not assume that governments can govern best by making decisions in a centralized fashion and then implementing them through laws and relatively rigid hierarchies. Rather, the vision is one of decentralized decision making. This is true both in the sense of the lower echelons of organizations having a substantial, if not determinant, impact on policy decisions and in the sense of the organizations themselves having a great deal of control over the decisions that determine their own fates. There is also the assumption that decisions made in this manner will be objectively better, given the presumed higher levels of information possessed by these lower levels of the organization. In this emphasis on decentralization the participative approach shares a good deal with the theorists, if not always the practitioners, of the public choice approach.

Given this concern with the involvement of lower-echelon workers, the participative approach is almost silent on the involvement of top-echelon bureaucrats – those usually referred to as at the "decision-making" level – in policy selections. One possible implication would be that political leaders, having somewhat greater involvement with the public, might be more suitable conduits for participatory input into decisions. On the other hand, if communications within organizations is even moderately efficient, the lower echelons should be able to send up messages to the top that would have an influence on policy. In either case, the design question really is how can those usually excluded from decisions have an impact on those decisions, and there is no simple answer.

The other perspective that the participatory model may have on policy making is the realistic statement that the lower echelons of the bureaucracy do have a major impact on policy in almost any political system (Lipsky 1980; Adler and Asquith 1981). Most decisions that governments make are not made by their political leadership, or even by the upper echelons of the civil service. Rather they are made by the lower echelons – the street-level bureaucrats – who have to make numerous decisions about particular cases every day. Not only are those decisions crucial for the actual determination of citizens' claims against the state for services, they are also crucial for popular perceptions of government. For most people, government is the policeman, or the tax collector, or the safety inspector, and the interactions between the citizen and the representative of the state may shape the public's ideas about what government does and what it thinks about its citizens. Thus, a participatory emphasis in governance may make government more popular with clients, if not necessarily more efficient in delivering services.

The Public Interest. The participatory state assumes that the public interest can be served by allowing employees and citizens the maximum involvement possible in decisions. This involvement can occur in at least three ways. First, for employees it can occur through their enhanced capacity to make independent decisions and to have influence over the policy directions taken by their organizations. This concept of governance is sometimes considered to confer power on "street-level" bureaucrats and to make policy making a "bottom up" as opposed to "top down" process (Peters, forthcoming). This is assumed to make the decisions of government objectively better, given that they will reflect the knowledge of the portions of the organization most closely in touch with the environment.

The second meaning of participation in this context is a political one. This version of the participatory state would have its decisions made through a "dialogical" process permitting citizens to exert a substantial influence over policy (Linder and Peters, forthcoming). Thus, the public interest will emerge through the right of citizens to say what they want and to bargain directly with other citizens with different views of appropriate public policy. This view would stand in rather sharp contrast to the "decisional" approach more common in traditional representative and bureaucratic government.

The final meaning for the public interest within the participatory state is one that is dependent upon citizens themselves being involved in making some choices about policy. In this way the participatory state is similar to the market state, given that both would prescribe allowing citizens to make more consumer choices and would give them more direct control over the programs. The manner in which these consumer choices would be exercised in the participatory state would be more political. Rather than voting in the market place with dollars, citizens would vote through some sort of political process. This participation might be in referenda on policy (in the style of Ross Perot) or it may be in local structures, as is found with parental involvement on school management committees in Chicago. The fundamental point is that better decisions (procedurally if not necessarily substantively) are made through participation rather than through technocracy.

Summary. The participatory model is not as well articulated as is the public choice model. Still, it is possible to extract some of the implications of this "vision" for the role of the civil service in governing society, as well as for the nature of governance itself. This vision of governance is ideologically very different from that of public choice, and it also differs in its assumptions about human behaviour within organizations. Even with those differences, the prescriptions for design in the two approaches are not all that dissimilar. For example, the principal prescription is for decentralization and some transfer of power to the lower echelons of organizations, as well as to the clients of the organizations. Further, this model recognizes the role of the bureaucracy in making public policy just as does the public choice approach, although the participatory model considers this involvement more positively than does the first alternative we presented.

Although the prescriptions of the participatory approach for governance are not dissimilar to those of public choice, the meaning attached to those designs for governance are markedly different. In the participatory model, decentralization is intended primarily to channel control to a different set of bureaucrats, or to the clients, rather than being used as a means of creating competition among service providers so that a market can work. This could be thought to be the very type of capture that the public choice model seeks to avert (Macey 1992). Likewise, the involvement of those lower-level bureaucrats in decision making is considered positively, but with the alternative seen to be domination by the upper-level bureaucrats rather than by political leaders. In this model both of those elites are considered equally antithetical to the interests of clients, rather than as competitors between themselves for power.

Flexible Government

The third alternative to the traditional model of governmental organization will be discussed as the "flexible government" model. As noted above, joining a government organization often has been conceptualized as accepting lifetime employment, assuming that the individual wants to remain in government. Likewise, forming an organization is usually thought to be creating a permanent entity, no matter how transient the reasons for the structure may appear (Kaufman 1976). This permanence frequently is overstated, but it tends to guide thinking about the formation and management of the public sector.

The dysfunctions inherent in permanence, evident in the attitudes of individuals to employment and in the ethos of organizations, are well known and governments have begun to address them. This is probably the least clearly articulated of the four approaches to administration, but these ideas and practices do appear to be emerging in a number of governments. Permanence has come to be considered as the source of the excessive conservatism of policies, and as the source of commitment to an organization more than to the policies being administered by the organization: organizations embody political interests.[11] Individuals who work for an organization may be more concerned with keeping their job and keeping the organization healthy in budgetary terms than in doing anything in particular. Further, a commitment to permanence tends to institutionalize prevailing conceptions of policy, and even to conceal the real policy problems. In all, despite some obvious attractions, permanent government structures can present significant problems for effective and efficient governance.

In addition to the recognition of the dysfunctions of permanence, the changing nature of the problems of governance and the labour market have tended to produce movement away from permanence. First, an increasing number of the significant problems that government confronts fall between the stools of the existing organizations. For example, although there is a Drug Enforcement Agency, a large number of other agencies – the Coast Guard, Department of Defense, The Customs Bureau, the FBI, inter alia – also are involved in "The War on Drugs." This widened involvement of agencies in policies has already created a fourth or fifth or nth branch of government that attempts to coordinate and control the existing organizations and policies. We would argue that the "policy space" and the organizational space for governments is already well populated (Hogwood and Peters 1983) and any new initiatives are likely to confront existing actors.

The other pressure creating impermanence in government organizations is the fundamental transformation of the labour market in most industrialized societies, with much less full-time and permanent employment and an increasing level of part-time and temporary employment. Government has already begun to adjust to these broader economic changes and has found more part-time employment to be a way of saving money and enhancing organizational flexibility. Thus, even when there is a permanent organization per se, the members of that organization may themselves be transients. This is certainly a shift from the tradition of government employment and has important managerial and policy implications discussed below.

Structure. The fundamental advice that this approach offers is for the creation of alternative structural arrangements within government. Rather than relying exclusively on the traditional forms of departments, agencies, and bureaus that perceive themselves to have a virtually permanent claim on a particular policy space, this approach would seek some flexibility and the frequent termination of existing organizations.[12] Such action would be taken to prevent the ossification that can afflict permanent organizations. Further, it might be expected to allow government to respond more rapidly to changing social and economic conditions. There might, for example, be less resistance to creating organizations intended to respond to novel circumstances if there were some assurance that these organizations would be terminated when their task was completed. Further, the ability to create and then destroy organizations might appeal to fiscal conservatives and critics like Niskanen, who argue that permanence and bureaucratic monopolies create excessive costs along with policy rigidities. In fact, in many ways, the organizational universe emergent from this approach would be not dissimilar to the "agencies" being created by advocates of the market approach, with the added factor that these organizations would be subject to rapid change.

As well as being structurally impermanent, these organizations might not be populated to a large degree by full-time employees, who (at least in the United States) spend most or all of their careers within the same organization. This change in career patterns is already occurring in government. For example, the proportion of total work hours put in by temporary federal employees has been gradually creeping up since the 1960s, and appears likely to continue to increase. The predictions of almost all studies of the labour

market is that the trend toward temporary employment will continue in almost all segments of the economy. This trend may be ap-
plauded by fiscal conservatives who want to save money in the
public sector, but it potentially does damage to other conservative
values about the accountability of the civil service and its stability
as a source of advice and values in an otherwise rapidly changing
government.

Management. The manifest managerial implications of the temporary
state are rather clear, while the latent implications are perhaps more
interesting and more important. At the manifest level this approach
stresses the ability of managers to adjust their work force requirements to match demands. As noted, this can be used as a means of
saving a good deal of money for government, as well as mitigating
some of the public perceptions of waste and empire-building by government organizations. Further, this approach may permit governments to respond more quickly and effectively to crises or rapidly
increased demands for service, although the potential upside benefits
tend to be discussed less than the cost-cutting benefits.

The latent implications of this approach are some diminution in
the commitment of employees to their employers and with that a
potential threat to the values and ethos of the public service. It now
may appear somewhat idealistic to discuss the commitment of civil
servants to their organizations and to the principle of public service.
On the other hand, there is some evidence that civil servants have
been motivated by these values and that many of them would like
to continue to be so motivated. Making more public sector jobs temporary and part-time will almost certainly diminish the commitment that employees feel to their jobs and with that also will tend
to minimize their motivations for excellent performance on the job.
This approach is, therefore, to some extent the antithesis of the participatory state, given that temporary employees would be unlikely
to be interested in any real involvement with the organization. Further, the temporary status may make all the civil service values of
probity, accountability, and responsibility all the more difficult to enforce. In short, we could argue that a good deal may be sacrificed to
gain some reductions in expenditures.

Policy making. As noted above, this is the least developed of the approaches to the role of the public service in governance. In particular, the "temporary state" approach to questions of governance has little to say directly about the role of the public service in making public policy. We can, however, attempt to explore the logical implications of this approach to governing for an active policy role for the civil service. These implications appear to be potentially contradictory, with some pointing toward an enhanced role for the civil service and others seeming to reaffirm the older wisdom of a political dominance of the elected classes over policy, with civil servants being in a subordinate position.

On the one hand, by placing so much emphasis on the fragility of organizations in government, the traditional sources of organizational power in a common culture and commitment to the existing policies would be diminished. The old bureaucratic structures had both the advantage and disadvantage of stable personnel and, with them, stable policies. On the one hand the permanent personnel provided a great deal of direction to policy and provided an experiential knowledge base for the construction of any new policy initiatives. On the other hand, this stability has been a barrier to innovations extending beyond the conventional wisdom about what is "feasible" in the policy area (Majone 1989, 69-94). This absence of a mortmain from the past may permit political leaders to have a stronger role in altering policies than they might otherwise have had. A group of radical reformers, such as the Thatcherites or Reaganauts, would be pleased to have less of an organizational inheritance to counteract.

All the pressures from this approach do not, however, go toward making the life of political leaders easier. By removing the anchor of large, stable organizations beneath them, the elite of the civil service may be able to develop their own policy ideas more autonomously. To some extent the conception of the Senior Executive Service in the United States was that of a free-floating resource that could be used in a variety of managerial and policy advice situations. Without large, permanent organizations to encumber them in the exercise of their own conceptions of good policy these senior officials may in fact be able to be creative forces in policy development.

The Public Interest. As this is the least clearly articulated of the four alternative models of governance, it also has the least clearly articulated concept of the public interest. One obvious component of the idea of the public interest in this model is that lower costs for government are beneficial. If having more temporary employees will reduce costs, then it can be argued that the public as a whole will benefit, even if particular clients of government services are potentially disadvantaged by less knowledgeable and committed public sector employees.

A second implicit concept of the public interest is that the public will be better off with a more innovative and less ossified government. One standard complaint about government is that the organizations within government that represent interests outside the public sector fight for their turf and preserve themselves whether or not there is any real justification for their continued existence. This is a somewhat exaggerated version of the reality (Peters and Hogwood 1988) of the permanence of government organizations, but there is still some truth in it. If change could be made as much a part of life in government as is permanence, then there would be some chance of greater creativity and, perhaps again, some opportunities for saving the public money.

Deregulated Government

The final option for changing government is to unleash the potential power and creativity of government by "deregulating government" (Wilson 1989; Bryner 1987). This is almost the complete antithesis of the politics of the 1980s, which sought to reduce the activity of government and severely control those actions that remained. The politicians of the 1980s appeared to have a special dislike and distrust of the public bureaucracy and sought to curtail its powers over policy. The assumption of deregulating government is that if some of the constraints on action are eliminated, government could perform its current functions more efficiently, and it might be able also to undertake new and creative activities to improve the collective welfare of society.

Structure. The structural implications of this model are rather sparse. Although its advocates do not say so directly, it would appear that structures are much less important than are the procedures used to control public organizations and the people within them. It may also be that in its concern about the ability of governments to act effectively, traditional hierarchical management is less of an anathema than in other "modern" conceptions of organizations. The premise that bureaucratic structures are almost inherently undesirable is now almost the conventional wisdom, but this model argues that they are indeed acceptable, and even desirable, in certain situations.

Another possible structural implication of this model is that the control agencies that political leaders have developed at the centre of government are less desirable than those leaders have assumed. The reduction of centralized control would permit the individual organizations to develop and implement more of their own values than would be true when central agencies are in control (Campbell and Szablowski 1979). The further implications, therefore, are not too dissimilar from those coming from the market model. If bureaucratic organizations are not all bad, then the active, entrepreneurial agencies implied by the market model, for example, Next Steps in Britain, might be even better. The fundamental point is to get government to use its skills and energy to achieve goals.

Management. The managerial implications of this model could go in two opposite directions, in large part because management does not appear to be one of its central concerns. On the one hand, as noted above, this approach to governance seems to argue that traditional forms of structure and management may not be as bad as some contemporary critics would argue. This being the case, this model would tend to find hierarchical management acceptable and even desirable. That style of management would permit policy entrepreneurs, who presumably would be positions at the top of the hierarchies, to generate action throughout the organization. This would, in turn, depend to some degree on a common organizational culture within the organization supporting the policy direction being advocated from above.

The alternative managerial implication would be for something very similar to that advocated in the participatory state model above. If the creative powers of government are indeed to be unleashed, then it may be done best by involving all levels of the organizations. Thus, if government wants to be effective and creative it will need the commitment of all of its available resources, most importantly its employees. Like the participatory model, this approach is in contrast to the "flexible state" model, which does not assign any real importance to the involvement of employees of government.

Policy making. The implications for policy making are somewhat clearer than are the other implications of this model. The traditional view of policy making in government was that it was the prerogative of political leaders. The "deregulating government" model would appear to assign a somewhat stronger role to the bureaucracy in making policy. The logic is that these organizations tend to be major repositories of ideas and expertise and hence should be allowed to make more decisions. To the extent that this also implies that the lower echelons of the organization, because of their expertise and close contacts with the environment, should have somewhat more influence, then this model has implications similar to those of the participatory state model discussed above.

This characterization of the deregulating government model should not be taken to mean that policy-making powers should be abrogated by political institutions in favour of the public bureaucracy. Rather, it should be taken to mean that policy making is likely to be better on substantive grounds – if not in terms of democratic theory – if there is a more active role for the bureaucracy. The policy stances adopted by this more-involved bureaucracy are likely to be more interventionist than those that have been characteristic of the more conservative governments of the past decade. Thus, in this case the choice of a model of governance will clearly have some implications for substantive policy choices.

The Public Interest. The deregulatory model of governance assumes that the interest of the public can be served through a more activist, and a seemingly less accountable, government. The characterization concerning accountability is perhaps unfortunate, given that there is more of a difference about the form of accountability than about the need for that all-important feature in any democratic government. In most of the attempts to control government through the use of structural and procedural devices there has been the contradictory assumption that without the use of such devices the public bureauc-racy will either behave abusively, or will do next to nothing. The deregulatory model, on the other hand, assumes that the civil serv-ice is composed largely of dedicated and talented individuals who want to do as good a job as possible in serving the public. This is in many ways simply a restatement of the familiar Friedrich/Finer debate over accountability.

As well as making assumptions about the role of civil servants in governance, this model also makes a rather clear statement about the role of government in society. Again, that would be a role that is quite different from the one assigned to government by most politicians during the 1980s. The assumption is that the pub-lic interest would be better served by a more active and interven-tionist public sector, and that collective action is part of the solution and not part of the problem for contemporary societies. This is not a knee-jerk reaction in favour of "big government" but rather appears to be a recognition that many of the most important problems facing society can only be solved collectively, and that this in turn implies a major role for the public bureaucracy.

CONCLUSION: CAN WE GO HOME AGAIN?

We have now looked at several alternative movements away from the traditional model of administration in the public sector. Some of these models are already being implemented, while others are only in the nascent stages (if that far along in their development). In each case, the implicit or explicit comparison is made with the traditional model of administration, with clear separation of roles between administra-tion and politics, a hierarchical management style and structure, largely permanent organizations, and career civil servants.

The obvious question is whether, even if those in government wanted to, they could ever return to the comfortable system that has now passed. To some degree the emphasis on management, the emphasis on political reliability of the civil service, the empha-sis on the empowerment of staff and clients, and the emphasis on flexibility all press toward an alteration of the tacit bargain that has existed among the participants in governance. Both sides can gain some advantages from these changes, although by far the most advantages appear to run in the direction of politicians and, secondarily, to the previously disadvantaged tiers within organizations. Similarly, the principal disadvantages appear to accrue to the senior levels of the civil service. Politically, then, returning to the status quo ante may be impossible.

If there is to be a return to the bureaucratic Garden of Eden, then there will need to be a strong restatement of the desirability of such a move. Given that the public service is not the most popular element of government in almost every polity, there is probably not a natural constituency for such a move. Therefore, there will have to be political activity to produce the movement. This can be justified in part through the traditional values of neutrality and competence in the civil service. There will also be a need to stress values, such as public service, rather than positioning government merely as the provider of services, like any other "business." The waning of market ideology in a number of other Western countries, may initiate public discourse on ideas of public service in a way not possible recently.[13]

The governance role of public administration is perhaps the most significant aspect of any reassertion of the role of the public service. Again, we must contrast the role of the civil service as expressed through the "ideology" of the traditional model of governance versus the reality of their role in the model as it evolved in practice. The existence of a powerful and entrenched civil service created in essence the conditions for a strong policy role for that bureaucracy in governance. Although the market model in particular would appear to give somewhat enhanced power to the civil service, any redistribution of power would be in their managerial role rather than as policy makers and advisers. Indeed, the practice of the market model has been to attempt to centralize power in the political leadership and to limit the autonomy of the presumably entrepreneurial actors created by the reforms.

The traditional model of the public service and its role in government is, however, more than merely a rationalization enabling civil servants to make policy. It is also a statement of basic values about matters such as accountability and responsibility on which the alternatives, and the market model in particular, have little to say. The concept of a permanent and professional civil service providing policy advice as well as management is seen by the advocates of the traditional model as almost a sine qua non for good government. It is seen as embodying the means of providing citizens (and their politicians) with the means of receiving both the best advice and the best service. While to critics the permanence of the bureaucracy is a severe problem, to its advocates it is the source of stability and reliability. It is also seen as the best means of insuring that government can be held accountable for its actions.

We have been, to this point, discussing these four models as distinct alternatives for organizing the entire public sector. Another way to consider this set of options is to think of the possible and desirable matches between particular governmental tasks and the alternative forms of organizing (Wilson 1989). It may well be that for the provision of certain marketable services the market model is adequate and desirable, while that same model would be totally inappropriate for many social services, education being one commonly discussed exception. Likewise, the participatory model would be well suited for urban planning or for environmental issues, but it would produce difficulties for many criminal justice programs. The temporary model probably would suit complex issues such as drug control as well as transient concerns such as disaster relief. While attempts at full-blown contingency theories for public administration appear to have generated relatively little benefit, we should still think about ways of making the punishment fit the crime.

Again, the purpose of this chapter is not so much to force choices among the alternative visions of governance but rather to make the choices available to governments more evident. To the extent that these models have been implemented in the real world (particularly the market model) they have been put forward for ideological reasons as much as from any thorough consideration of their relative merits. Each of the alternatives does have its merits, but each may also impose some costs on society and on the actors in government. Any choice of paradigms for government and administration is unlikely to be Pareto optimal, but we should be clear about what we receive and what we sacrifice when we make these judgments about governance.

NOTES

1 For a discussion of the (no longer?) "conventional wisdom" see Walsh and Stewart (1992).

2 Indeed, the most radical use of the variety of market-based reforms available to government was implemented by the Labour government of New Zealand.

3 This autonomous role is not unfamiliar in the u.s. but is extremely unusual and threatening in Westminster systems. The Ponting affair in the u.k. and the al-Mashat case in Canada are examples of the importance of this change in the norms of governing in Westminster governments (Chapman 1993; Sutherland 1992).

4 This pattern is already used rather widely in several European systems. See, for example, Fournier (1987) and his discussion of coordination within French government.

5 Obvious examples are statements of the public choice approach in New Zealand and of the participatory model in Canada.

6 This characteristic of bureaucrats does not differentiate them from other individuals. The problem is the assumption that members of the public service will necessarily act in the public interest.

7 They usually want to export these techniques at a profit.

8 Those of us who deal regularly with airlines and Blue Cross-Blue Shield may consider being treated like the customer of a private concern to be a threat.

9 Jack Kemp as Secretary of Housing and Urban Development in the u.s. is one prime example.

10 This language is usually reserved for the implementation process but can also be applied to the process more generally. See Peters 1994.

11 Interestingly, some of the public choice literature has been seeking means of designing organizations that will be conservative and will preserve the same policies over time (McCubbins, Noll, and Weingast 1989).

12 State and local governments have already made more moves in this direction with "sunset laws" and other devices that force relatively frequent consideration of the existence of their organizations.

13 The Major government is substantially less ideological than the Thatcher government before it, the Tories were defeated in a landslide in Canada, the right-leaning Schluter government has lost office in Denmark, etc.

BIBLIOGRAPHY

Aberbach, J.D., and B.A. Rockman. 1988. Mandates or mandarins? Control and discretion in the modern administrative state. *Public Administration Review* 48:607-12.

Adler, M., and S. Asquith. 1981. *Discretion and Power.* London: Heinemann.

Allard, C.K. 1990. *Command, Control and the Common Defense.* New Haven: Yale University Press.

Allison, G. T. 1986. Public and private management: are they fundamentally alike in all unimportant respects? In *Current Issues in Public Administration,* 3d ed., ed. F.S. Lane. New York: St. Martin's.

Barzelay, M., and B.J. Armajani. 1992. *Breaking Through Bureaucracy: A New Vision for Managing Government.* Berkeley: University of California Press.

Bendor, J. 1990. Formal models of bureaucracy: a review. In *Public Administration: The State of the Discipline,* ed. N. Lynn and A. Wildavsky. Chatham, NJ: Chatham House.

Boston, J. 1991. The theoretical underpinnings of public sector restructuring in New Zealand. In *Reshaping the State: New Zealand's Bureaucratic Revolution,* ed. J. Boston, J. Martin, J. Pallot, and P. Walsh. Auckland: Oxford University Press.

_____ 1992. Assessing the performance of departmental chief executives: perspectives from New Zealand. *Public Administration* 70:405-28.

Bryner, G.C. 1987. *Bureaucratic Discretion.* New York: Pergamon.

Caiden, G. 1990. *Administrative Reform Comes of Age.* Berlin: Aldine de Gruyter.

Calista, D.J. 1989. A transaction-cost analysis of implementation. In *Implementation Theory,* ed. D. Palumbo and Calista. Lexington, MA: Lexington Books.

Campbell, C., and G. Szablowski. 1979. *The Superbureaucrats: Structure and Behaviour in Central Agencies.* Toronto: Macmillan of Canada.

Chapman, R. A. 1993. Reasons of state and the public interest: a British variant of the problem of dirty hands. In *Ethics in Public Service,* ed. Chapman. Edinburgh: University of Edinburgh Press.

Chubb, J.E., and T. Moe. 1990. *Politics, Markets and America's Schools.* Washington, DC: The Brookings Institution.

Davies, A., and J. Willman. 1992. *What Next: Agencies, Departments and the Civil Service.* London: Institute for Public Policy Research.

Day, P., and R. Klein. 1987. *Accountabilities.* London: Tavistock.

Fournier, J. 1987. *Le travail gouvernemental.* Paris: Presses Universitaires Françaises.

Gruber, J. 1987. *Controlling Bureaucracies: Dilemmas in Democratic Governance.* Berkeley: University of California Press.

Hogwood, B.W., and B.G. Peters. 1983. *Policy Dynamics.* Brighton: Harvester.

Hood, C. 1990. De-Sir Humphrefying the Westminster model of bureaucracy. *Governance* 3:205-14.

Ingraham, P. W. 1987. Building bridges or burning them? The president, the appointees and the bureaucracy. *Public Administration Review* 47:487-95.

Kaufman, H. 1956. Emerging doctrines of public administration. *American Political Science Review* 50:1059-73.

_____ 1976. *Are Government Organizations Immortal?* Washington, DC: The Brookings Institution.

Kenis, P., and V. Schneider. 1991. Policy networks and policy analysis: scrutinizing a new analytical toolbox. In *Policy Networks: Empirical Evidence and Theoretical Considerations,* ed. B. Marin and R. Mayntz. Boulder, CO: Westview.

Kernaghan, K. 1992. Empowerment and public administration: revolutionary advance or passing fancy? *Canadian Public Administration* 35:194-214.

Kickert, W.J.M. Forthcoming. Administrative reform in the Dutch civil service: organization and management in the past ten years. In *Comparative Civil Service Systems,* ed. J.L. Perry and H. Bekke. Bloomington: Indiana State University Press.

Lan, Z., and D. H. Rosenbloom. 1992. Public administration in transition? *Public Administration Review* 52:535-7.

Linder, S.H., and B.G. Peters. 1995. A design perspective on the structure of public organizations. In *The Structure of Public Institutions,* ed. David Weimer. Dordrecht: Kluwer.

Lipsky, M. 1980. *Street-level Bureaucracy.* New York: Russell Sage Foundation.

Lovell, R. 1992. The Citizen's Charter: The cultural challenge. *Public Administration* 70:395-404.

Macey, J.R. 1992. Organizational design and political control of regulatory agencies. *Journal of Law, Economics and Organization* 8:93-110.

Majone, G. 1989. *Evidence, Argument and Persuasion in the Policy Process.* New Haven: Yale University Press.

Massey, A. 1993. *Managing the Public Sector.* Aldershot: Edward Elgar.

McCubbins, M. D., R.G. Noll, and B.R. Weingast. 1989. Structure and process, politics and policy: administrative arrangements and the political control of agencies. *Virginia Law Review* 75:431-82.

Metcalfe, L., and S. Richards. 1990. *Improving Public Management*. 2d ed. London: Sage Publications.

Moe, T. 1984. The new economics of organizations. *American Journal of Political Science* 28:739-77.

_____ 1989. The politics of bureaucratic structure. In *Can the Government Govern?*, ed. J.E. Chubb and P.E. Peterson. Washington, DC: The Brookings Institution.

Niskanen, W. 1971. *Bureaucracy and Representative Government*. Chicago: Aldine/Atherton.

Olsen, J.P. 1986. *Organized Democracy*. Oslo: Universitetsforlaget.

Osborne, D., and T. Gaebler. 1992. *Reinventing Government*. Reading, MA: Addison-Wesley.

Ostrom, E. 1986. An agenda for the study of institutions. *Public Choice* 48:3-25.

Perrow, C. 1986. Economic theories of organization. *Theory and Society* 15:11-45.

Peters, B.G. 1992. Public policy and public bureaucracy. In *History and Context in Comparative Public Policy*, ed. D. Ashford. Pittsburgh: University of Pittsburgh Press.

_____ 1994. Top-down and bottom-up visions of the policy process. *Politische Vierteiljahrschrift* 37:289-322.

Peters, B.G. 1994. Managing the hollow state. *International Journal of Public Administration* 6:246-59.

Peters, B.G., and B.W. Hogwood. 1988. Births, deaths and marriages: organizational change in the U.S. federal bureaucracy. *American Journal of Public Administration* 18:119-33.

Peters, B.G., and D.J. Savoie. 1994. Civil service reform: misdiagnosing the patient? *Public Administration Review* 54:418-25.

Pollitt, C. 1990. *Managerialism and the Public Service*. Oxford: Basil Blackwell.

Rose, R. 1989. Charges as contested signals. *Journal of Public Policy* 9:261-86.

Roth, P.A. 1987. *Meaning and Method in the Social Sciences*. Ithaca, NY: Cornell University Press.

Scharpf, F. 1991. Die handlungsfahigkeit des staates am ende des zwanzigsten jahrhunderts. *Politische Vierteiljahrschrift* 4:621-34.

Simon, H. 1947. *Administrative Behavior*. New York: The Free Press.

Sutherland, S.L. 1992. The al-Mashat affair: administrative accountability in parliamentary institutions. *Canadian Public Administration* 34:573-603.

Thomas, J.C. 1993. Public involvement and government effectiveness. *Administration and Society* 24:444-69.

Tullock, G. 1965. *The Politics of Bureaucracy*. Washington, DC: Public Affairs Press.

Waldo, D. 1968. Scope of the theory of public administration. *Annals of the American Academy of Political and Social Sciences* 8:1-26.

Walsh, K., and J. Stewart. 1992. Change in the management of public services. *Public Administration* 70:499-518.

Walters, J. 1992. Reinventing government: managing the politics of change. *Governance* 6.

Williamson, O. E. 1975. *Markets and Hierarchies*. New York: Free Press.

Wilson, J. Q. 1989. *Bureaucracy*. New York: Free Press.

PART FIVE

CONCLUSION

Looking Ahead

DONALD J. SAVOIE

Aaron Wildavsky, several years ago, remarked that "the most senior bureaucracy now is only for the brave" (Savoie 1994). The chapters in this book point to some of the difficult challenges politicians and public servants must now confront and the demanding environment in which they work. They also suggest that the most senior bureaucracy will remain only for the brave for some time to come. The purpose of this concluding chapter is to give the last word to practitioners.

We know that bureaucrat-bashing has been in fashion for some time. As already noted, Herbert Kaufman concluded in the early 1980s that "antibureaucratic sentiment has taken hold like an epidemic." Bureaucracy has come to be seen as a barrier against, rather than a vehicle for, progressive change. Even people who had supported the ideas and social welfare programs of leaders such as Franklin Roosevelt, Clement Attlee, Harold Gaitskell, T.C. Douglas, and Adlai Stevenson were now taking dead aim at bureaucracy and calling for changes to the apparatus of government. Administrators are, of course, well aware of these developments. Perhaps because they were aware that their profession was under attack, the officials who participated in this study took a strong interest in the papers being prepared, were always willing to offer comments and suggestions for improvement, and were eager to offer new ideas to study or explore.

The challenges confronting governance and senior public servants do not by any means lie only with organizing and managerial skills. Without denying for a moment that there is still room for improvements on this front, the challenges are indeed much more complex. Societal problems are now even more "wicked" than they were when Harmon and Meyer first employed the word in 1986 to describe the challenges confronting the United States (Wamsley 1990). National governments everywhere are trying to cope as best they can with crippling annual deficits and ever-increasing debt. Few national governments know for certain any longer what is needed to maintain or promote a vigorous national economy in an increasingly competitive world. At the same time, vastly improved means of communications, notably television news reporting, are putting enormous pressure on government to make decisions quickly for fear of appearing indecisive and not in control.

Before suggesting new areas for research, it is important to ask whether the reforms of the past twelve years or so, some of which are outlined in this book, have been able to stick, and if so, have they changed the key challenges for government? In other words, are we still talking about the same challenges we talked about ten years ago, or are we looking at a new set of challenges? There is no denying that we have seen improvements in the management of government operations in recent years. Sandford Borins's chapter makes the case by presenting concrete examples of innovations in management in government. There is also evidence that managerialism has left its mark in more ways than one on the public services of the United Kingdom, New Zealand, and Australia.

Elsewhere, however, the verdict is less certain. Vice President Gore released his National Performance Review (NPR) with a great deal of fanfare in September 1993 (Gore 1993). The report was highly critical of the status quo and made the call to reinvent the federal government. A good number of the prescriptions outlined in his report are remarkably similar to a number of proposals made ten years earlier by the Grace Commission or several years ago in Reagan's Management Improvement Program: Reform 1988.

In Canada, a newly elected government in Ottawa quickly talked about the need to fix the "plumbing" inside government. John English, the Parliamentary Secretary to the Minister responsible for Public Service Renewal, speaking on behalf of his minister, outlined the guiding principles for public service renewal, which included: "The most important (principle) is the concept of building towards a public service that is increasingly *client-centred* in its performance, culture, and attitudes . . . This approach stresses more delegation of authority, more flexibility, more incentives to encourage initiative, greater attention to the training and development of staff, particularly in areas where there will be a direct payoff in terms of improved service to citizens, recognition of outstanding performance, celebration of successes both personal and institutional" (English 1994). The irony is that the above is precisely what a number of initiatives introduced two, three, and several years earlier sought to accomplish.[1] If the current political rhetoric is at all accurate, then the previous initiatives failed.

The above begs the question as to why political leaders are reporting the failure of past reform measures. Even in the case of the Thatcher reforms, it has been suggested that her Next Steps initiative was launched because her earlier reform measures were not living up to expectations and she needed something new to breathe life into her attempts to reshape the British civil service (Savoie 1994). In other words, despite the previous efforts, leading politicians are still today calling for "a client-centred approach [that will] condemn needless paperwork and mindless bureaucracy" (English 1994).

All of the above stresses a need for more research in this area. The most promising place to begin is probably looking at the requirements of political institutions and public law. The very things that we want from government – equality, fairness, and due process – are precisely the factors that produce some of the bureaucratic dysfunctions that politicians and many observers still complain about. There is a price to pay for ensuring that our case before government is considered fairly, equally, and deliberately. Some of the administrative controls are, no doubt, stultifying for civil servants and frustrating for the public. However, these controls still apply despite the waves of reforms, probably because they have proved to be beneficial.

We have also probably overlooked the importance of accountability in government operations in recent years. Ronald C. Moe's argument that the Gore report tends to look to "Congress as Managerial Nuisance" is to the point and it applies to other jurisdictions. He goes on to make the case that, fully implemented, the Gore report would result in "a government much less accountable to the citizens for its performance" (Moe 1994).

There have also been concerns expressed over accountability in government decision making in countries such as Britain, where management reforms have been in vogue for the past fifteen years or so. Some observers argue that accountability is being attenuated. *The Economist* ran a lead article on this subject and went on to argue that "the first necessity is to buttress the nonpartisan, incorruptible character of the civil service itself."[2]

Phil Cooper's chapter in this book points to a number of forces shaping accountability in the contemporary environment. His chapter met with a great deal of interest on the part of many practitioners in Canada. A good number of them were able to relate the findings of the chapter to their day-to-day work, and they urged new research efforts be launched to gain a better understanding of the requirements of accountability in modern-day governance. One practitioner summed up the views of his colleagues when he observed that "accountability is the missing hole in the doughnut, and unless we can make progress on this front other reform measures are always likely to fall short of expectations."

The above also speaks to the importance of involving practitioners in future research efforts. As pointed out earlier, this book was born out of strong collaboration between practitioners and students of governance. We held two meetings between the authors of the various chapters and leading practitioners with the Canadian public service. In addition, the great majority of the authors presented a draft of the papers to about fifteen senior level officials from central agencies and line departments. The sessions were at times lively and always stimulating. Both sides benefited from the exchanges.

There are, of course, a variety of models to involve practitioners in carrying out research on governance. The approach we employed worked well, but we recognize that it may not always work for different circumstances and research projects. The point, however, is that, whenever possible, practitioners should be invited to take an active interest in future research efforts.

As explained earlier, over the past eighteen months, while working on this single project, we have met in both formal and informal settings with about sixty senior Canadian public servants. In accepting to articulate the last word, practitioners looked to the future and sought to identify the key challenges for governance and for senior public servants.

There is a great deal of concern even among practitioners about the ability of the public service to generate objective policy advice. John Halligan's chapter identifies a number of issues that are preoccupying Canadian practitioners. Halligan writes about public servants being "handmaiden" or "adviser" to politicians and reports on the two competing models of "hierarchy" and "market." As he notes, an over-reliance on hierarchy tends to produce a monopoly, while too great a reliance on market can give rise to control and management problems. This discussion only begs the question: What is the appropriate mix, if a mix is the way ahead? Some practitioners would go even further and call for a fundamental rethinking of how policy advice is prepared and presented to politicians.

Some practitioners also insist that the old bargain between politicians and public servants has broken down. The old bargain saw "mutual self-respect" between politicians and public servants and an understanding that "neutral policy competence" was superior to policy advice with a partisan bias. Politicians now appear to prefer "responsive competence" on the policy front, but many of the old structures and processes still exist. Peter Aucoin deals with these issues in his chapter and practitioners expressed a strong desire for more research on this front.

Indeed, a good number of them are of the view that the main challenge ahead now is one of policy, not management. What we ought to be doing today is rethinking what it is we expect from government and what it is that government ought to be doing, rather than attempting to re-engineer government machinery by turning to the latest management fashion or fad.

They asked such fundamental questions as: How should we do policy in future? Is there a market for objective policy advice emanating from a permanent public service? How do we consult with people in a meaningful way? How can we best speak truth to politicians on policy? How can we restructure the policy advisory function so that the advice can more easily cut across government departments?

Practitioners also expressed concerns over the push to import private sector management techniques to their operations without first asking whether they fit public sector circumstances. They are not alone. Christopher Pollitt persuasively argues in his chapter in this book that "currently fashionable techniques still contain a high faith-to-fact ratio and that the faith itself could usefully be confronted with some persistent doubts." After reviewing for this book the application of Total Quality Management techniques to the public sector, Patricia Ingraham concluded that "discussion of utility for public organizations has proceeded with little attention to its broader impact on governance. It is increasingly obvious, however, that no public management reform is or can be simply technical or managerial."

There is little doubt that supporters of a more entrepreneurial type of government believe firmly that private sector management is much superior to public administration and that government and the private sector "are similar in their essentials and respond similarly to management and processes."[3] There is also little doubt that these views, which are widely shared by political leaders, observers, and some management gurus have shaken the confidence public servants have in their institution. Bureaucrat-bashing has also taken its toll. When a leading politician suggests that his government wishes to take dead aim at "mindless bureaucracy," he is in effect arguing that "bureaucrats" are both the root cause of the problem and that they support "mindless bureaucracy."

Long-serving public servants know intuitively that there are fundamental differences between private sector management and public administration. It has everything to do with the role of politicians, the requirements of accountability, and basic values. They know, for example, that boards of directors and top management of large businesses do not as a rule engage in "bashing" their employees. If they did, they would lose consumer confidence and would soon be out of business. Luc Rouban summed it up well when he wrote that a total disappearance of civil service values would be dangerous. "When civil servants," he explains, "act and become regarded as private wage earners, there is greater room for politicization."

There is plenty of evidence to suggest that morale has plummeted in the public services of many countries in recent years. This is not to suggest that practitioners, at least the ones we worked with, are simply circling the wagons and adopting a strictly defensive posture. We certainly did not pick up a profound desire to protect the status quo. Indeed, a number of practitioners expressed a strong desire for more research on the impact of importing private sector management techniques to government operations. They would like to see if a line could be drawn, beyond which activities would be sure to spell trouble for accountability and compromise basic public service values. Some practitioners suggest that a number of private sector management practices in the personnel management field probably hold promise for government operations.

A good number of practitioners stressed the importance of the chapter written by Jon Pierre and called for new work in this area. They insisted that the past several years have unleashed new forces that are redefining how citizens relate to government services and that we need to determine where these forces are now heading and how far they are likely to go.

Practitioners were also quite willing to point to some of the shortcomings of their own operations when suggesting new research efforts. Some reported that senior civil servants still do not manage human resources well. One argued, for example,that when "it comes to downsizing we still can do no better than shoot the second, or seventh person." Another reported that it is exceedingly difficult to assess in an objective fashion the performance of public servants, including senior officials. Many of the assessments carried out thus far have been highly subjective, and it is not uncommon to find six senior officials singing the praises of one of their colleagues but then just as easily find six others who would report serious shortcomings. All of this suggests that practitioners would take a strong interest in new research on managing human resources in a government setting and on identifying ways to assess their own performance in an objective fashion.

The practitioners, however, did not limit their suggestions to themes found in this book. In fact, adding up all the suggestions for new research themes points to an extremely ambitious agenda. They spoke of a crisis of representation in society, with no one certain any longer about how interests should be articulated. The citizen-client dichotomy points to potential problems with a strong shift to the client paradigm leading to a possible rationalization of inequalities in society. The point here is that citizenship suggests a system of mutual obligations and entitlements between the individual and the state, while the concept of "the client" draws its inspiration from economic theory and the market. But that only tells part of the story. From where practitioners sit, they see that Parliament and politicians are also coming under strong criticism. They, too, see the old bargain between politicians and citizens as broken or hurting, with no new bargain yet emerging. A crisis of representation holds obvious implications for their work and more generally for governance.

They also spoke of the possible need for a new look at government structure. The role of central agencies, the need for stronger horizontal coordination, and the importance of ensuring close consultation and participation on the part of citizens and public servants speak to the need for scholars to attach as much importance to the study of institutions and structures as they do to process and management reforms.

Lastly, they called for a review of the role of the state in society. They report that we are now discovering that some of the measures introduced twenty or thirty years ago were assumed to be strongly beneficial to society, but that we are now sensing a negative impact. Some such measures include transfer payments to individuals for one reason or another, which have served to make some individuals at least strongly dependent on continued government assistance. But that, too, only tells part of the story. At the macro level, we are seeing an increasing number of observers saying that we can no longer afford to pay for the government we now have. The only way to address the issue properly is to take a fundamental look at what governments do and what they can do best.

This then is how practitioners view, in broad terms, a new research agenda for public administration. To be sure, it is ambitious and it is unlikely that one, two, or a handful of scholars working individually or together could possibly carry out all of the research identified above. Still, the challenge ahead for governance is great and, as we noted earlier, at least for the foreseeable future "the most senior bureaucracy will remain only for the brave."

NOTES

1 Some of these measures introduced by the Mulroney government included: Increased Ministerial Authority and Accountability, Special Operating Agencies, Shared Management Agenda, the make or buy concept, delayering, and the high-profile Public Service 2000 initiative. See Savoie, *Thatcher, Reagan, Mulroney,* chaps. 4-8.
2 See "A Very British Civil Service," *The Economist,* 19 March, 1994, p. 4.
3 For an excellent discussion of this point see Moe, "The Reinventing Government Exercise: Misinterpreting the Problem, Misjudging the Consequences," pp. 125-36.

BIBLIOGRAPHY

English, John. 1994. Renewal in a changing context. Notes for an address, 28 April, Privy Council Office, Ottawa.

Gore, Albert J. 1993. From red tape to results: creating a government that works better and costs less. Report of the National Performance Review. Washington, DC: Government Printing Office.

Kaufman, Herbert. 1981. Fear of bureaucracy: a raging pandemic. *Public Administration Review* 59, 1:1.

Moe, Ronald C. 1994. The reinventing government exercise: misinterpreting the problem, misjudging the consequences. Public Administration Review 54, 2 March/April:131.

Savoie, Donald J. 1994. *Thatcher, Reagan, Mulroney: In Search of a New Bureaucracy.* Pittsburgh: University of Pittsburgh Press.

Wamsley, Gary L., et al. 1990. *Refounding Public Administration.* London: Sage Publications.

The Contributors

Peter Aucoin
McCullough Professor in Political Science
Department of Political Science
Dalhousie University
Halifax, Nova Scotia

Sandford F. Borins
Chair
Division of Management and Economics
University of Toronto
Scarborough, Ontario

Phillip J. Cooper
Chair
Department of Public Administration
University of Kansas
Lawrence, Kansas

John Halligan
Director
Centre for Research in Public Sector Management
University of Canberra
Canberra, Australia

Patricia W. Ingraham
Department of Public Administration
The Maxwell School
Syracuse University
Syracuse, New York

B. Guy Peters
Maurice Falk Professor of American Government and Chair
Department of Political Science
University of Pittsburgh
Pittsburgh, Pennsylvania

Jon Pierre
Department of Political Science
University of Gothenburg
Gothenburg, Sweden

Christopher Pollitt
Dean
Faculty of Social Sciences
Brunel University
Uxbridge
Middlesex, England

Luc Rouban
Fondation nationale des sciences politiques
Centre de recherches administratives
Paris, France

Donald J. Savoie
Clément-Cormier Chair in Economic Development
The Canadian Institute for Research on Regional Development
Université de Moncton
Moncton, New Brunswick